OCS Study
MMS 2004-041

Economic Impact in the U.S.
of Deepwater Projects:
A Survey of Five Projects

I0438994

U.S. Department of the Interior
Minerals Management Service
Gulf of Mexico OCS Region

OCS Study
MMS 2004-041

Economic Impact in the U.S. of Deepwater Projects: A Survey of Five Projects

Authors

John J. Stiff
Joachim Singelmann

Prepared under MMS Contract
1435-01-99-CT-31019
by
ABS Group, Inc.
16855 Northchase Drive
Houston, Texas 77060

Published by

U.S. Department of the Interior
Minerals Management Service
Gulf of Mexico OCS Region

New Orleans
May 2004

DISCLAIMER

This report was prepared under contract between the Minerals Management Service (MMS) and ABS Group, Inc. This report has been reviewed by the MMS and approved for publication. Approval does not signify that the contents necessarily reflect the views and policies of the Service, nor does mention of trade names or commercial products constitute endorsement or recommendation for use. It is, however, exempt from review and compliance with MMS editorial standards.

REPORT AVAILABILITY

Extra copies of the report may be obtained from the Public Information Office (Mail Stop 5034) at the following address:

U.S. Department of the Interior
Minerals Management Service
Gulf of Mexico OCS Region
Attention: Public Information Office (MS 5034)
1201 Elmwood Park Boulevard
New Orleans, Louisiana 70123-2394

Telephone Number: (504) 736-2519 or
1-800-200-GULF

CITATION

Suggested citation:

Stiff, J. and J. Singelmann. 2004. Economic impact in the U.S. of deepwater projects: A survey of five projects. U.S. Dept. of the Interior, Minerals Management Service, Gulf of Mexico OCS Region, New Orleans, LA. OCS Study MMS 2004-041. 184 pp.

TABLE OF CONTENTS

FIGURES

TABLES

1. SUMMARY AND OVERVIEW

1.1. PROJECT OVERVIEW

The aim of the project was to study five specific deepwater Gulf of Mexico developments and show how their fabrication, installation, and operation has had an economic impact around the United States and, to a lesser extent, the world. The five developments studied cover a number of different methods for developing deepwater reserves in the Gulf of Mexico. The projects are summarized in the two tables below. Table 1 gives the type and general costs. These are not entirely consistent as discussed in the notes, but the major deviation concerns Pompano that does not include many additional costs associated with the project. Table 2 gives a very broad layout of where the major components were fabricated or assembled. Figure 1 shows the locations of the different projects on a map of the Gulf of Mexico.

Table 1

Projects Studied

Project Name	Operator	Structure Type	Water Depth	Cost (see notes)
Ursa	Shell	Tension Leg Platform (TLP)	3,800 feet	$950 million[1]
Sir Douglas Morpeth	British Borneo (now Agip)	Mini-TLP	1,690 feet	$159 million[2]
Neptune	Oryx (now Kerr-McGee)	Spar	1,930 feet	$130 million[3]
Baldpate	Amerada Hess	Compliant Tower	1,650 feet	$215 million[4]
Pompano	BP Amoco (now BP)	Conventional Jacket	1,294 feet	$100 million[5]

Notes on costs:

[1] This cost includes the hull, tendons, deck, facilities, risers, pipelines, and installation. It is based on Shell published total project cost of $1.45 billion, of which 65% is for the facilities and 35%, or $500 million, is for the development drilling and completion.

[2] Includes TLP, subsea, pipelines, and project costs, but does not include development drilling.

[3] Includes hull, mooring, topsides, installation, risers, and project costs. Development drilling and completion were an additional $42 million.

[4] Includes the tower, facilities, pipeline, and project costs. Development drilling and completion were an additional $117 million.

[5] Includes the fabrication costs ONLY; does not include installation, pipelines, or any drilling costs.

Table 2

Areas of Major Fabrication or Assembly

Project	Type	Deck	Hull/Jacket	Tendons/Mooring
Ursa	TLP	Louisiana	Italy	Japan
Sir Douglas Morpeth	Mini-TLP	Louisiana	Louisiana	Japan
Neptune	Spar	Louisiana	Finland	Pennsylvania/Spain
Baldpate	Compliant Tower	Texas	Texas/Louisiana	N/A
Pompano	Conventional Jacket	Louisiana	Texas	N/A

Figure 2 shows the approximate breakdown between the cost of the installed structure, and the cost to drill development production wells. There are many factors that affect the cost of development drilling, and while water depth is important, it is not necessarily the most important factor. As an example, Shell had serious problems drilling the development wells for Ursa, and had to abandon the first wells. The Morpeth wells were also far more expensive than expected.

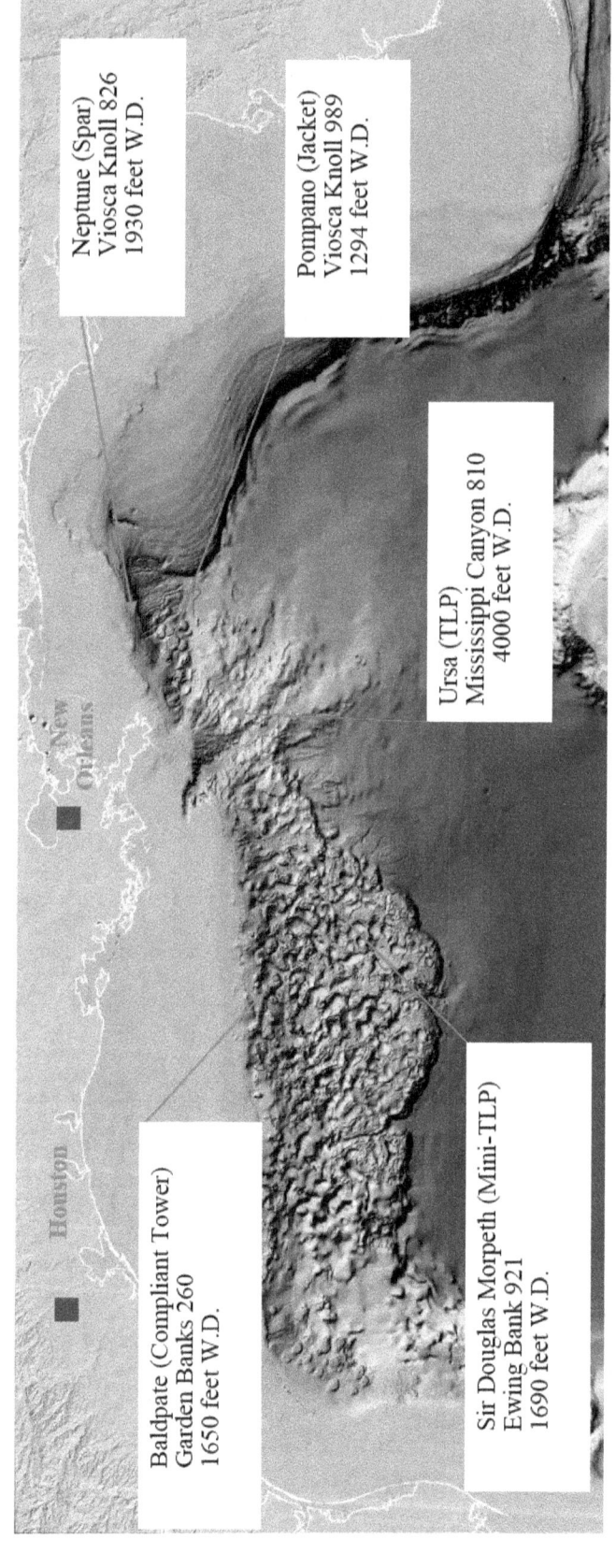

Neptune (Spar)
Viosca Knoll 826
1930 feet W.D.

Pompano (Jacket)
Viosca Knoll 989
1294 feet W.D.

Ursa (TLP)
Mississippi Canyon 810
4000 feet W.D.

New Orleans

Houston

Baldpate (Compliant Tower)
Garden Banks 260
1650 feet W.D.

Sir Douglas Morpeth (Mini-TLP)
Ewing Bank 921
1690 feet W.D.

Figure 1.   Gulf of Mexico Seafloor Relief Map Showing Locations of Platforms in Study (Courtesy of Geoscience Earth & Marine Services, Inc. (GEMS)).

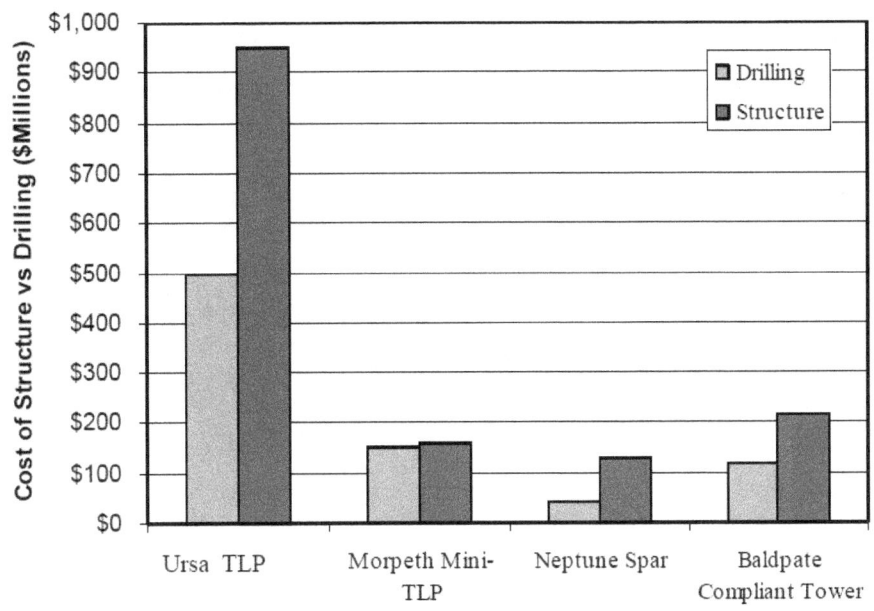

Figure 2.   Distribution Between Cost of Development Drilling and Structure.

1.2. REPORT STRUCTURE

The purpose of this report is to present the information gathered during the course of the project, as requested by the Minerals Management Service (MMS) as part of the contract. The report is split into five major parts. These include:

1. Summary and Overview: This section of the report briefly discusses the deepwater projects that were studied, an overview of each project, a brief discussion of the findings, and a possible way forward that could be taken by a new study to gather the information that was wanted.

2. Summary of Information Gathered: This section presents the information that was possible to gather on the different deepwater projects concerning where the structures were fabricated, the major sub-contractors, and any other additional information discovered during the course of the study.

3. Economic Analysis: The section presents the results of an analysis of information obtained from one fabrication yard. The analysis was performed by Dr. Joachim Singelmann of Louisiana State University in Baton Rouge. Only one suitable data set was given to the project team during the course of the study. Other data were found, but not in sufficient detail to warrant analysis.

4. Chronology of Field Development: The section goes through the process of developing a deepwater prospect from pre-lease acquisition to abandonment. This had been requested by the MMS team at the start of the project. It is known that some of this information is available in other MMS published documents, but the intent was to present the information in a slightly different form.

5. Shallow Water vs. Deepwater: The section discusses some of the major differences between developing a deepwater and shallow water field, as required by the contract.

1.3. COMPONENTS OF DEEPWATER FACILITY

Some very general discussions can be made concerning the information contained in Table 2. The major components are discussed at a high level in the following subsections to help give an overview of how each deepwater facility was developed.

1.3.1. Decks

The deck of an offshore installation is the main part above water that supports all the living quarters, process equipment, power generation, etc. While there will normally be a significant amount of structure, the main cost will normally be in the installed equipment (Figure 3 shows a deck installed on a jacket. This is not a deep water structure, but shows the major components of accommodation and equipment. Some decks will have drilling capability, although this does not have a derrick.). The decks for all the structures were fabricated within the Gulf Coast region. Decks are generally fabricated at a location from which they can easily be loaded onto a barge for transportation to the installation site. The Gulf Coast region has extensive experience fabricating decks for offshore installations, and can do so efficiently. In addition, transportation costs and risk make overseas fabrication significantly less attractive. This is illustrated by the example of the Nemba deck that was being transported from the fabrication yard in the Far East to the installation site in West Africa. The ship capsized after hitting an unmarked obstruction in the Sunda Strait, Indonesia. Both the deck and ship were total losses, and the field development was seriously delayed at significant cost to Chevron, the operator.

Figure 3.   Deck Installed on a Jacket.

The vast majority of the components used to assemble these decks are supplied by local vendors, including most of the process equipment. One of the major exceptions is solar turbines that supply the power generation equipment on many of the deepwater projects. They are based in California where the gas turbines are fabricated[1]. There are other non-Gulf Coast vendors, but they tend to total a relatively small percentage of the overall deck fabrication cost. This is generally true for all decks, regardless of structure type, or even water depth. What is less clear is where the vendors get their supplies, and this is possibly an area for future study.

---

[1] As discussed later, even this can be confusing since Shell has Solar based in Texas on their vendor list for Ursa, their contract being with the local office.

1.3.2. Jackets

A jacket is the main support structure for most types of conventional shallow water offshore platforms, and some deepwater platforms, up to approximately 1,300 feet water depth. It is called a jacket because it encloses and supports the conductors that carry the piping through which the hydrocarbons are produced. Because they have to act as a support structure for the deck, taking the loads all the way to the seabed, as the water depth increases, the size of the jacket increases enormously.

There are two structures on the list that are essentially jacket-based, Pompano (a conventional jacket structure; see Figure 4) and Baldpate (a compliant tower; see Figure 5). Both of these structures employed similar construction methods. As with decks, jackets need to be fabricated close to the sea so that they can be loaded onto a barge and towed to location. The Gulf Coast has many years experience fabricating jackets for the Gulf of Mexico and West Africa. The yards and labor force can efficiently fabricate jackets without incurring the additional risk and cost of trans-oceanic towing[2].

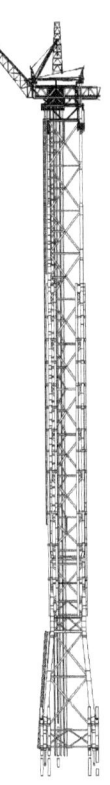

Figure 4. Pompano Platform on Location (Artist impression courtesy of J. Ray McDermott, Inc.).

Figure 5. Baldpate Compliant Tower (Courtesy of Amerada Hess).

With years of experience, jacket construction is relatively straightforward and involves a large labor force to roll the steel, cut and prepare the tubulars, and weld them in place. The major costs besides the local labor force are the fabrication materials including steel members, sacrificial anodes (to protect the jacket from corrosion), and welding rods.

---

[2] Most of the large California jackets installed in Santa Barbara Channel were built in Japan. One of those suffered significant damage during transportation. The others involved very expensive analysis and modification to ensure no damage. Other jackets not going to California have been total losses after falling off the barge in heavy seas.

1.3.3. TLP and Spar Hulls

A tension leg platform (TLP) is a floating structure that is held to the seabed by vertical tendons that are kept in high tension by the buoyancy of the TLP hull (Figure 6 shows the Shell Ursa TLP, and Figure 7 shows the Sir Douglas Morpeth mini-TLP on location). A spar is a large vertical cylinder (although variations now exist) that floats in the sea, and is moored to the seabed by relatively conventional mooring lines and anchors (Figure 8 shows the Neptune spar on location). The TLP and spar hulls can be likened to conventional steel plate construction common to many shipyards. However the unique cylindrical shape of a conventional spar necessitates setting up a series of special "jigs," to aid in construction and assembly, which requires a relatively large capital expenditure. A yard so equipped has an automatic advantage over its competitors. When Spars International was established as a joint venture between McDermott and Aker, it was agreed that any spar contracts would have a hull built in Aker Rauma, Finland, and the deck built by McDermott. This put Aker Rauma in a strong competitive position. Future spars, especially those with modifications to the original spar concept[3], will be built on the Gulf Coast. Indeed, since the start of this project, Kerr McGee has contracted to have a cell spar built for the Red Hawk field development by CSO Aker in their yard near Corpus Christi. As with conventional jacket construction, such projects would primarily involve local Gulf Coast labor.

Figure 6.   Shell Ursa TLP (Courtesy of Shell Exploration
and Production Co.).

The Shell TLP hulls have been built at Belleli Offshore Oil and Gas in Italy. There is no reason that TLP hulls could not be built around the Gulf Coast, except that there are not many shipyards that can competitively undertake that sort of plate construction on a large scale, particularly given some of the Italian government incentives. However, the mini-TLP's (Morpeth in this study, but also Allegheny, Prince, and others) installed in the Gulf of Mexico have been built on the Gulf Coast, though there have also been some contracted for construction in Korea. Typically the expense and risk of open ocean transportation makes the Korea fabricators less appealing, but the lower construction costs in Korea are challenging this view. At this time domestic shipyards are still at an advantage over their foreign competition for mini-TLP's. It is also of note that these mini-TLP's would probably not have been installed without the previous Gulf of Mexico experience with full-size TLP's (e.g., Ursa, Mars, etc.). In effect, the foreign content spawned domestic work around the Gulf Coast.

---

[3] There has been some research into the use of noncylindrical spars, including truss braced versions. There is a truss spar being fabricated at this time in Finland, although there is no reason that this could not have been economically fabricated on the Gulf Coast. The Finland connection is through Spars International, the contractor. There has also been discussion concerning the fabrication of rectangular spars. These would not need the expensive jigs, and could be easily fabricated on the Gulf Coast.

Figure 7. Sir Douglas Morpeth Mini-TLP (Courtesy of Atlantia Offshore Ltd.).

Figure 8. Neptune Spar Operating on Location (Courtesy of Kerr-McGee Oil and Gas Corp.).

1.3.4. TLP Tendons

Sumitomo Corporation, out of Japan, has supplied nearly all the tendons used on TLP's. The pipe is shipped to Aker Gulf Marine yard in Texas where the tendons are assembled, and end connections fitted. It is not that other steel mills cannot supply the material, but Sumitomo have gained significant credibility over the years, which is extremely important, particularly if the oil company is trying to finance the venture. Banks prefer proven technology for their loans (see section on Financing). The top and bottom tendon connectors were supplied by ABB Vetco Gray (Houston, Texas) and the tendon connectors were supplied by Oil States Industries out of Aberdeen, United Kingdom. Like Sumitomo, both of these companies have a proven track record, which gives them the edge in their respective fields.

1.3.5. Spar Moorings

The Neptune spar moorings are made up of both wire rope and chain. The chain was supplied by Vicinay in Spain. Figure 9 shows 6-inch diameter chain being manufactured and inspected for defects at the Vicinay fabrication facility in Spain. There are three main offshore chain manufacturers, and none is domestic (the other two are Scana Ramnas in Finland and Hamanaka in Japan). The cost of the chain was approximately $3.5 million, or just under 3 percent of the spar costs. The wire rope was supplied by Williamsport Wire Rope, out of Williamsport, Pennsylvania, for approximately $2 million, including the cost of sheathing it at Wellstream in Panama City, Florida.

Figure 9. Studless Chain (Courtesy of Vicinay International Chain Co.).

1.4. PROJECT OVERVIEW – DISCUSSION OF FINDINGS

There is no doubt that much of what goes into the deepwater development in the Gulf of Mexico comes from all over the United States, but the present level of study has not uncovered this. The problem is that most of the fabrication is centered on the Gulf Coast, and most of the equipment vendors are local to the fabrication. It is not until one gets to at least the next level down that one is likely to uncover the diverse sources of the supply.

As an example, Shell supplied a list of their Ursa vendors to the study team. This list contained approximately 1,000 company names coming from all over the U.S. Of those, probably less than 10 percent represent individual expenditures of over 1 percent of the TLP cost (approximately $1 million). The other 90 percent of vendors represent small to very small expenditures (the lowest being under $10). While the list is not in error, it can be misleading. As an example it states that Sumitomo Corporation of America, in Illinois, supplied the pipe for the tendons. While this is no doubt where it was ordered, and to whom the money was paid, the actual pipe came from Japan, not Illinois. Another example has the turbines ordered from Solar Turbines Inc. in Texas. In fact the turbines would have been fabricated in California, although these were some of the few components that came from outside the Gulf Coast area.

Under the original scope of work, ABS Consulting agreed to trace back to major vendors. This, however, has not shown the level of diversification sought from the study. It has shown that the majority of the work is centered on the Gulf Coast, with only a very limited number of major vendors situated outside that area. While the study has not been successful in obtaining detailed information on the project vendors, it has certainly discovered that the vast majority of the major vendors and sub-contractors are from around the Gulf Coast. It is only at the next level down, or even deeper than that, that the diversification comes to light. As an example, Hydralift was one of the Ursa vendors. The size of their contract was approximately $10 million, and they supplied the tensioner system for the risers. What they supplied was assembled in Houston, but their suppliers included cylinders that came from Chicago (cost a

8

few million dollars), and specialist composite accumulators that came from Nebraska. Of their ~$10 million contract, maybe as much as $6 million was for hardware that came from areas other than the Gulf Coast.

Compounding the problem has been the reluctance with which certain companies have supplied data: information has been slow, and at times very difficult to obtain. The number of telephone calls needed to obtain any meaningful data has been excessive in the vast majority of cases. There have been some notable exceptions, which is the main reason for the progress on the Morpeth project: the major players in the development of that project have been extremely helpful, but that cooperation did not necessarily filter down to the next level of companies. Unfortunately, British Borneo has now been taken over by Agip, and most of the staff have had to find alternative employment.

Shell has been extremely cooperative with information on vendors, but have been reticent in supplying any cost data. It is corporate policy not to disclose the value of contracts that make up the development. This has made it difficult to meaningfully assess their fabrication vendor list, and impossible to determine labor usage at the various facilities. Alternatively, they have supplied excellent data on their operating expenditures and project management labor usages. These data have been helpful in putting deepwater facility operations into perspective, but they cannot be analyzed with respect to labor markets because the number of persons employed in any given aspect is so small. Indeed, this could be a problem associated with gathering data on suppliers to the subcontractors: each supplier will have a relatively small percentage of their output assigned to any specific project, so at the lower levels, the impact of deepwater development on any given company is reduced. It should not be inferred that the overall impact is low, but as one investigates further down the supply hierarchy, the impact is reduced.

Difficulty in gathering data was not necessarily because the companies were trying to be uncooperative: there has been a major change in the way oil companies work over the last decade, and they do not currently have the personnel to supply the requested information. Their personnel are extremely busy, particularly at this time of increased development. There was a willingness in some companies to help the study, but no time to put in the level of effort required. It is only the major oil companies that have a strong public relations department that can field questions about a particular development. Most of the independent oil companies would have to rely on the project personnel to supply the needed information, and while these people may be willing to "talk over lunch," they have full time jobs managing the next development.

The lack of cooperation at the next level down, the vendors of equipment to be installed on the decks, and the process equipment suppliers, was probably more due to a lack of understanding as to the advantage in assisting the project. They supply a certain type of separator, for example. It makes no difference to them if it is on a deepwater or shallow water platform. Hence, they do not see any advantage in showing diversification of input to deepwater facilities. In addition, they are in a highly competitive market and see no advantage in using their time to supply the requested information, and are possibly somewhat concerned that the data may help their competition: why risk supplying data when there is no advantage, even if the risk is small?

1.5. POSSIBLE WAY FORWARD FOR FUTURE STUDIES

The extant study has had limited success in unearthing the desired level of national involvement in deepwater developments. This is for two main reasons: the main contractors are all located around the Gulf Coast, and because of a general unwillingness to dedicate resources to gather information. Also it is clear that while there are differences between the different development methods, they are largely ones of magnitude rather than content. Consequently, it may be possible for a future study to take a deepwater project that is under development and trace the content one stage further back – to find out where the vendors get their supplies.

Gulf Island Fabricators, who were the major fabricator for the Morpeth hull and deck, gave the study team a list of their suppliers of steel and paint. Over 40 percent of their expenditure on basically steel and paint was in Louisiana. How many steel mills are there in Louisiana? Clearly they are buying from suppliers rather than from the mills themselves. This will be, in part, because of the way the project was structured. They did not have the opportunity to purchase the steel in one block. Some of this steel will have come from overseas, some from within the U.S., but this could not be determined through the present study.

If one were to research an ongoing project, it may be possible to trace the equipment suppliers back more easily than is possible on an old project, but this will not be a simple task. When equipment is ordered, there are situations in which the supplier does not know to which project the equipment is going. They simply know that a specific customer has ordered a specific "widget" based on a specific purchase order, and it must be supplied to a specific specification. They cannot necessarily tie that to any particular project. In addition, the oil companies are using single contracts that cover almost the entire project. Hence they will generally have less information about the details of the constituent components that are ordered by their engineering, procurement, installations, and construction (EPIC) contractors. Hence, an extra level is added that must be penetrated in order to determine the true source of the equipment. In addition, the power of the oil company to pressure the contractor is diminished as one moves away from the main contractor.

When an installation is classed by ABS, surveyors will attend to ensure that all the major components are manufactured to the required classification society rules. Consequently, they will attend all over the U.S. and the world inspecting equipment. These data could be used to determine where the pieces of equipment which make up an installation come from, but even this would not be simple. The ABS contract will normally be with the vendor of each piece of equipment. Hence, to release that information, they would need to get the permission of each vendor. In addition, there would be no information on the value of each component, and certainly no information on the percentage of a company's capacity used in each item. There are a number of ways that parts of the required information could be obtained, but the systems are not set up to gather additional information. It would probably not be possible to get the individual surveyors to try to get additional information because of the number of different surveyors involved, and because of the added expense – who would pay for it, and how would it be tracked? In addition, unless the process equipment is specifically being classed, there could be large holes in the data collected.

It is not entirely clear what is the best way forward. In part it depends on the priority for the different types of information. If the source of supplies is wanted, then that could probably be determined from classification society records, with permission from each vendor, but even this would need to be done on an ongoing construction project: it could not realistically be done retroactively.

Information on the price breakdown on a specific project could probably be gathered from the oil company via their AFEs (Approved for Construction Expenses). But this again would need to be agreed to up front, before project start-up, and getting cooperation from all parties could still be problematic.

The greatest difficulty comes in getting all the information tied together: the source of the steel: the value of the steel: the effect of that steel production on local labor. The AFE records will say who was paid a specific sum of money, but not where they subsequently spent it. Hence, the tracking back will be, at best, difficult. The class survey records will give the location of the supplies (although these may be limited if the topside is not classed) but will have no information on value. The individual sub-contractors may have a high percentage of their business with the offshore industry, but any specific project may have a minor impact on their labor usage, and an even smaller effect on a local market. The components of the information may well be discoverable by one method or another. It may even be possible to get all the information, but it will be very difficult to get all the information tied together in a way that it can be analyzed. A map similar to the one produced by Shell (see Figure 14) could be produced through use of class records. Analyses of labor may be possible by using AFE data, and through company assistance, but that would be much more difficult.

It should be possible to complete a project similar to this on a project that is identified prior to its commencement, but realistic goals will need to be set, and the types of data wanted realistically identified.

2. SUMMARY OF INFORMATION GATHERED

This section sets out the basic data that was gathered during the course of the project. Unfortunately, in few cases was it possible to get sufficient information on all the projects to undertake a meaningful comparison: where there is good data on one project, there is poor data on another. The three projects undertaken by the independent oil companies (Neptune by Oryx[4], Baldpate by Amerada Hess, and Sir Douglas Morpeth by British Borneo) were each the subject of special sessions of technical papers at the Offshore Technology Conference (OTC) in 1997, 1999, and 1999, respectively. These papers were a very good starting point for gathering the needed information, and gave a high level breakdown of the project costs. There were no technical sessions for Ursa or Pompano as neither represented particularly new technology at the time (there had already been sessions on a full-size TLP in the Gulf of Mexico, and a deepwater jacket at earlier OTC's), but Shell had an excellent web site that gave a good overview of the Ursa project, including the overall cost of the project. Unfortunately, very little information was available about BP's Pompano project, either on the web, or through published sources.

Having surveyed the public sources, the next step was to gather information directly from the oil companies, and their contractors. To help in getting consistent information, a guide was developed that would help set out the types of information needed, and to document other possible sources. This guide allowed the gathering of a broad range of information on costs, from overall project, exploration, project management, and fabrication, through to final operations. It was well understood that not all companies would be able to supply all the requested information, but it had been hoped there would be more consistency than was achieved.

The following subsections set out an overview of the information obtained from each of the oil companies, or other sources, on each of the projects. Analysis of the data is not realistically possible because of the lack of consistency in quantity and quality of the data, but the results are presented in graphical form. As these are generally isolated pieces of information, one cannot draw conclusions as to, for example, the difference in project management costs between a project by a major oil company, and one by an independent. Notwithstanding this, there is a significant amount of data that could be used for other projects in the future.

The purpose of the study was not just to gather data on the costs of the projects, but to tie that into socioeconomic effects of the projects on the local communities. This issue is addressed in the section on Economic analysis, but as with much of the other data, no firm conclusions could be drawn.

It may be constructive to initially give a visual presentation of the costs of the studied offshore projects in comparison with some other objects (or in one case, a sport's contract). The shallow water minimal platform is at the lower end of the cost of an offshore structure, but there are certainly some that cost significantly less than $1 million, even as a new installation. However, when one then includes the cost of drilling the wells, then the price will normally increase significantly. Clearly the costs are approximate, but give an indication of the level of expenditure in different classes of industry. It is amusing to note that Alex Rodriguez's 10-year contract is approximately the same as the cost of a new modern baseball stadium (see Figure 10).

---

[4] The names given are those of the companies that installed the facilities. Ownership has changed in some cases since installation.

Figure 10. Cost of Offshore Platforms Compared to Other Structures and Contracts.

2.1. URSA PROJECT

2.1.1. Shell Supplied Data on Ursa - Fabrication

Shell has a corporate view that they do not supply detailed information as to the cost breakdown of their projects. They have a web site for the Ursa project that sets out the basic information they are prepared to share with the public. This gave the overall cost of the project (at $1.45 billion) and described a split of approximately 65 percent to facilities ($950 million), and 35 percent to development drilling and completion[5] ($500 million). Figure 11 gives a diagrammatic estimate of the distribution of costs over the phases of the Ursa project. This diagram is based on corporate experience with similar projects, and has not been supplied by Shell, but the general distribution is likely to be reasonable.

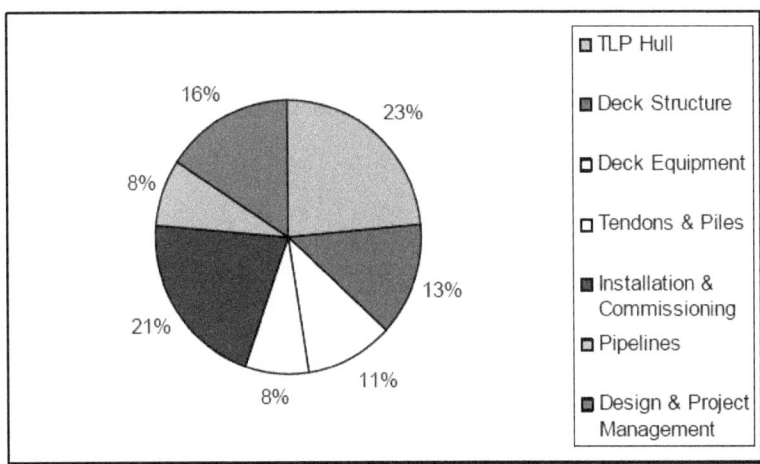

Figure 11. Approximate Distribution of Costs for Ursa TLP (100% is $950 million).

Shell was extremely helpful in supplying other related information and costs for the project, if little data was supplied for the fabrication and installation. Each of the phases discussed in this section is covered in greater detail in the relevant section of Chronology of Field Development later in this report, but normally without costs.

The Ursa field was first discovered in 1991 by wells drilled by the drillship *Discoverer Seven Seas* (see Figure 12). This is a dynamically positioned drillship that was built in 1976 in Japan. For many years the *Discoverer Seven Seas* held the water depth record for drilling in the deepest water, and after an upgrade in 1996, is still operating as a drilling unit. The rig is operated by Transocean based in Houston, although in 1991 the owners were Sonat, also based in Houston[6]. The whole issue of employment in the offshore industry is complicated by the phases in which a field is developed. As an example, most mobile drilling units employed in drilling exploratory wells are built overseas, but the operating companies, and many of the operating personnel are American. In addition, much of the equipment on an exploratory rig, although installed in a foreign yard, has been exported from the U.S. for that purpose. Hence, the domestic and foreign content of even the initial drilling is complex and difficult to trace.

---

[5] It was almost impossible to get any direct information on the cost of exploratory drilling of the lease. The oil companies do not track this as part of the development cost. One must assume exploratory drilling is an overhead that is given a corporate budget, but not tracked through project development. It is possible to make some estimates of the cost based on the type of mobile drilling unit used, day rates at the time, and estimated consumable costs.

[6] This is another example of consolidation within the offshore oil industry. Sonat became Transocean, then acquired some other drilling contractors, changed its name, and then reverted to the name Transocean.

Figure 12. *Discoverer Seven Seas* (Courtesy of Transocean).

Prior to deciding on using a TLP to develop Ursa, Shell assessed a number of other development options, including a spar, compliant tower, and a conventionally moored semisubmersible option. These studies continued for approximately 9 months and employed approximately 12 technical staff. Based on normal consulting rates, this effort would be worth approximately $2 million although it is likely some additional work was undertaken by independent outside consultants.

Once it was decided to use a full-size TLP for development, engineering design companies were contracted to undertake much of the design. Shell maintained a strong influence over the design, and employed a considerable number of direct personnel in the design effort. However, the detail topside design (deck and processing) was undertaken by an alliance between Waldemar S. Linder and W. H. Nelson (called DCA), and the hull structural details were developed by Han Padron (part of ABB), a company with many years experience with design of TLPs. The DCA had approximately 40 full time employees working on the project based in New Orleans. Han Padron had approximately 15 engineers and 15 drafting personnel based in Houston.

This phase would also have involved model testing. In this a scale model of the chosen structure is built and placed in a wave basin so that its performance in a seastate can be assessed. This work was undertaken at Texas A&M university in College Station, Texas. The cost of the model testing was $155,000, excluding the cost of the model, and employed three engineers and four technicians for 4 weeks. Typically a model will take 6 weeks to produce and will employ one engineer and two fabricators. Undertaking the model testing at a university helps the university support its facilities, and gives students a better understanding of genuine industrial projects. Texas A&M also did the model testing for the Neptune Spar and Morpeth mini-TLP. The costs for these were comparable to those for Ursa, but in each of the other cases, the University built the models.

Project management is an extremely important part of any major project. The oil company needs to ensure that the contractors are doing what they are supposed to, on time, and on budget. Even on a fixed price contract one needs to keep careful monitoring of the budget as if the job goes too far over budget, and the contractor goes bankrupt, there is little recourse for reimbursement. In addition, there will be changes required to the contract, design, detailing, etc. and these need to be monitored. Shell had 40 engineering technical leads in direct project management. These individuals would have each been responsible for a specific area of the platform (e.g., hull, deck structure, drilling equipment, risers, processing, power generation, and operational aspects such as installation, etc). Their job is to ensure that, apart from the schedule and budget issues, there are no incompatibilities at the interface between modules and components, that the design is progressing as expected, and that what is being produced is functionally as expected.

In addition to the direct project managers, there were approximately 130 personnel employed in interface operations. These individuals would be more involved in the details of ensuring the components

14

are fabricated as designed. Independent of these, there would be, for example, a large number of welding inspectors, but it would be the job of the interface personnel to ensure that everything required to be inspected is inspected, that testing is in compliance with the specification, etc. Figure 13 gives the distribution of personnel by both discipline, and their location.

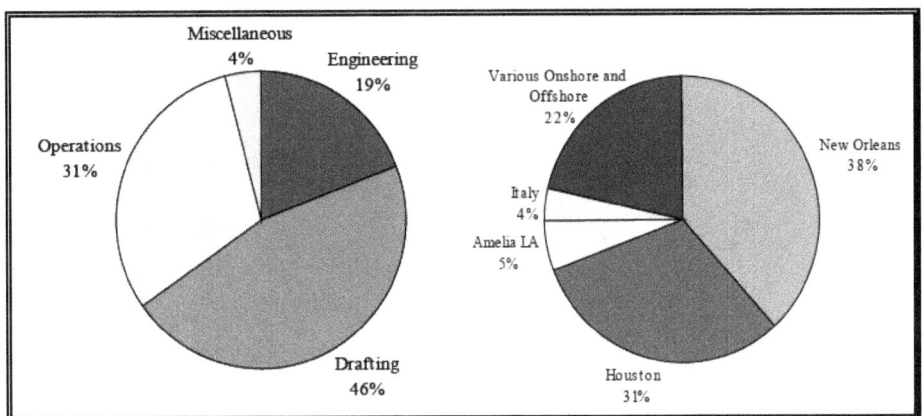

Figure 13. Ursa Project Management: Distribution of 130 Interface Personnel Between Disciplines and Locations.

The seven personnel based in Amelia, Louisiana, will have been working in McDermott yard on the deck and process equipment installation. Those in Italy will have been in Belleli shipyard working on the TLP hull. There were 28 personnel who were at various locations, both onshore and offshore. These would, in part, have been attending fabrication shops around the U.S. and the world ensuing that all the individual components that are part of the overall TLP are manufactured to specification, and suitably tested prior to installation. It is the locations of these 28 personnel that give an indication of the distribution of component fabrication, but even their locations would not be sufficient to show the full extent of the distribution of fabrication.

Shell supplied a chart showing where they had expended costs on the Ursa project around the U.S. (see Figure 14). The number given in the state represents the number of vendors from that state supplying the Ursa project. This diagram gives some good information, but unfortunately, it is only part of the picture, and can be somewhat misleading. The difficulty is that the magnitude of the expenditure is not given. The largest single contract on the Ursa project, the hull fabrication, is estimated to be somewhat over $200 million, and was expended in Italy. The next largest was to J. Ray McDermott Inc, the deck fabricator, based in Amelia, Louisiana. This contract would probably have been a little under $150 million, and is one of the 536 costs shown in Figure 14 to have been expended in Louisiana. At the other end of the spectrum, the smallest expenditure of the approximately 1,000 costs covered on the chart was also one of the 536 costs in Louisiana, and was for under $10. There is no indication within the chart as to the weighting of expenditure between the states.

Another problem with the diagram is that it gives only where the costs were paid. This does not necessarily coincide with where the components were fabricated, or where the labor used in the fabrication was situated. As an example, the back-up to the chart gives the tendons as being paid for in Illinois. In fact the tendons were produced in Japan. Similar problems were found when assessing supplied data on the Morpeth project. The only realistic way to circumvent these problems would be to undertake this type of study on a project in progress at the time of the study. This way the real source of expenditure, and labor input to that expenditure, could be determined and documented, as discussed at the end of this section.

15

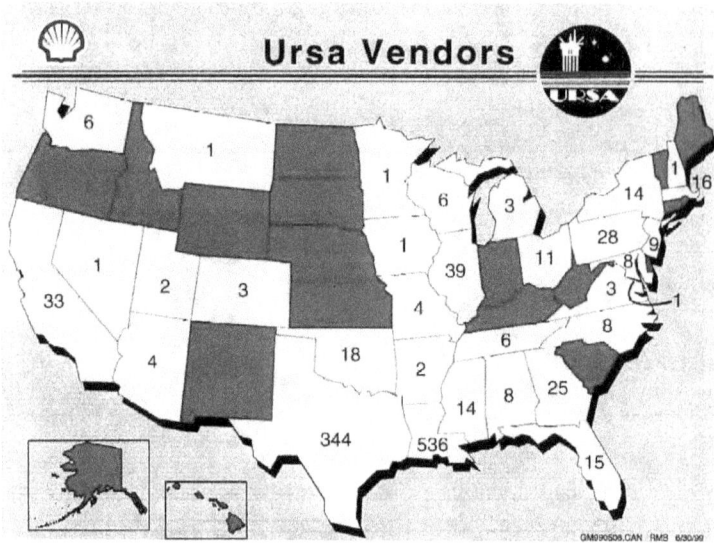

Figure 14. Number and Location of Vendors on Ursa Project by State
(Courtesy of Shell Exploration and Production Co).

McDermott supplied a limited amount of information on the Ursa project, but they did say they employed an average of approximately 450 personnel on the deck construction in the Amelia yard, near Morgan City, Louisiana. Their maximum number of personnel employed on the project was 700. They also stated that the project came in under budget, and they received some additional monies in the form of bonuses.

Commissioning is a major exercise on any production facility. The normal plan is to commission as much equipment as possible onshore, prior to installation of the facility offshore. This significantly decreases costs, and problems are more easily solved onshore, but it is difficult to do all the commissioning before all the components are together in their final place. Hence offshore commissioning is still a major exercise. Independent of vendor personnel, who look after the equipment that they supply, there were consultants, 2 Shell engineers overseeing the operation, and approximately 40 Shell operations personnel. It is not clear if it was the case with Ursa, but on many platforms, the greatest number of personnel that will ever be onboard a platform is during commissioning, and often additional temporary accommodation is supplied for their housing.

2.1.2. Shell Supplied Data on Ursa - Operations

Shell supplied a considerable quantity of data on the operating costs, and personnel levels for Ursa. When Ursa was originally put on location, only 3 of the planned 24 possible wells had been pre-drilled. The general plan for a deepwater installation is to pre-drill a limited number of wells so that production can be started as soon as possible after installation. This ensures that there is some income from the platform soon after installation. However, it is expensive to pre-drill wells from an exploratory drilling unit, so the number of pre-drilled wells is limited. Once the platform is on location, and the pre-drilled wells are completed for production, the platform will be generating income. It is then that the rest of the wells are drilled. The reason it is cheaper to drill them from the platform rather than a mobile drilling unit is that you are not having to pay the market rate for a deepwater drillship or semi-submersible, in effect a complex support platform for the drilling equipment. The platform is already installed, and a relatively inexpensive drilling rig can be mounted on the TLP to drill the additional wells. Not all platforms are designed to allow a drilling rig (and all its associated equipment) to be installed on board because they are too small. This becomes a trade-off between the capital cost (CAPEX) of installing a bigger platform and the operating cost (OPEX) of paying for a mobile drilling unit to drill and maintain the wells. In the case of Ursa, because of the required size of the platform for the production equipment, and the time expected to drill the wells, it was clear that a platform mounted drilling rig would be the safest and most cost effective way to proceed. It is of note that the drilling rig is not owned by Shell, but leased from Helmerich & Payne, who also supply the drilling crew.

The accommodation unit on Ursa is sized for the number of personnel expected during the simultaneous operations of drilling and production, 156 persons. Drilling and production are 24 hour a day operations and there are two "tours" on the unit at any given time, each working for 12 hours. The crews are paid a monthly wage, but work only half a month offshore, although if working 12 hours per day, for 14 days out of 28, this is equivalent to a "normal" workday length of over 8 hours[7]. Figure 15 shows the range of basic pay for offshore personnel. It needs to be noted that some of these individuals can get additional income from working overtime, when needed, but others are exempt, and expected to work the hours needed to complete the tasks. The chart covers both the drilling and the production personnel, so not all are employed by Shell.

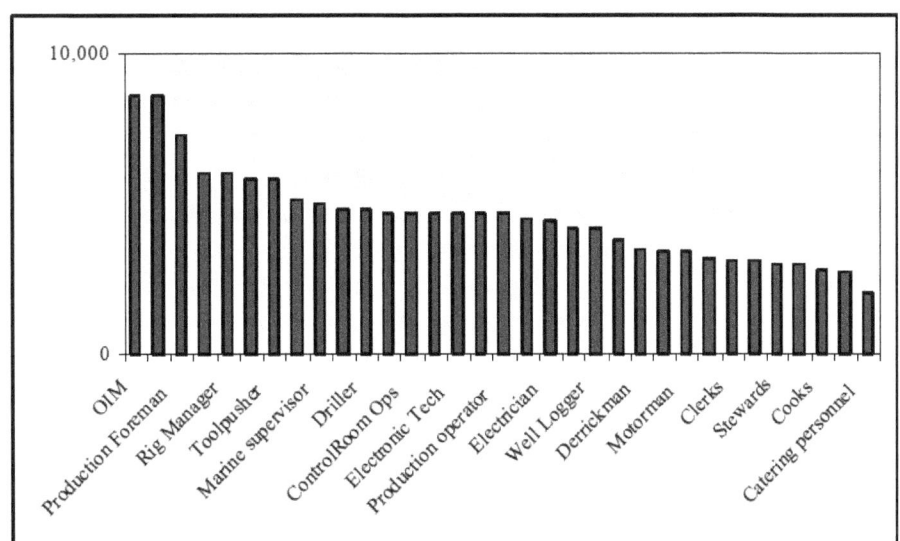

Figure 15. Approximate Monthly Pay for Offshore Personnel (US$ per calendar month).

In addition to the full time personnel offshore, there will be other service personnel who come out for a specific task. As an example, it is common to employ a casing crew whose job is purely to run the well casing (piping installed in the hole to prevent the sides collapsing, and drilling mud leaking out of the hole). They come out to the rig, complete their job, and return to shore. There will also be maintenance personnel, United States Coast Guard (USCG) inspectors, Minerals Management Service (MMS) inspectors, and many individual specialists out for a specific task.

In addition to the salaries of offshore personnel, there are many other expenses that need to be paid to keep the installation running, and the greatest of these when drilling operations are underway are consumables. The mud used in drilling is not just a mixture of clay and water, it is a specialized mix of constituent parts. Even the water has to be taken out to the rig as generally one needs to use fresh, not salt water. Occasionally oil based mud will be used. For this special types of oil are used that have the required properties, but are also nontoxic. Mud is an expensive commodity, and it all has to be transported out to the platform. Indeed, the transportation costs are significant, particularly during drilling. Because of the high usage of consumables, there will normally be approximately one boat a day visiting a platform during drilling, but this will be reduced to one or two a week during normal production operations.

Figure 16 shows the Edison Chouest C-Port in Fourchon, Louisiana. This is an all weather facility for loading the supply boats that keep the offshore platforms operational. Although not a specific part of

---

[7] Assume working 14 days on the rig, and 14 days at home. Time worked in a month is 14 days x 12 hours = 168 hours per 28 days. But a normal 28-day period has 20 working days, so equivalent workday length = 168/20 = 8.4 hours per day.

this study, it is of note that Edison Chouest Offshore operates over 100 boats in the Gulf of Mexico, and the vast majority of these will have been fabricated in their own yard. They have two yards, one called North American Shipbuilding which employs over 500 shipyard workers in Larose, Louisiana, and the other called North American Fabricator yard in Houma, Louisiana, that employs 300 shipyard workers.

Figure 16. C-Port Supply Boat Base in Fourchon, LA
(Courtesy of Edison Chouest Offshore).

Edison Chouest, with its head office in Galliano, Louisiana, has over 3,000 employees worldwide with the majority domestic, and 200-300 overseas. A significant number of their employees are foreign nationals on H2B visas, and they have difficulty getting local labor because of the low unemployment levels in southern Louisiana (we were informed that it was less than 3%). The recently completed Laney Chouest, the largest anchor handling towing supply (AHTS) vessel in the world, "... represents tens of thousands of man-hours..." involved in the design and fabrication in Louisiana. At the present time,[8] the yard is producing one 280 feet long offshore supply vessel (OSV) every four months.

Another significant expense is helicopter transportation, costing nearly $500,000 per year. For some of the near shore platforms it is reasonable to use crew boats to change out personnel, but at the greater distance to deepwater installations, the extra time makes it impractical.

Figure 17 shows the operating costs for the Ursa platform, both for drilling and production. The production costs are given at the top of the diagram above the line, and drilling is below the line. It can be seen that the drilling costs far outweigh the production costs. This is not just because of the increased consumable costs, but the contractor fees are significant, and these include all the direct drilling contractor labor costs. Figure 18 shows similar data to that in Figure 17, except that it is shown by the same categories in both drilling and production.

It can be seen that out of the total cost per day, the drilling consumables and rental costs account for nearly all of those expenses. The labor input to consumables is not known, but the drilling rental costs do not just support the cost of new construction for the drilling equipment (a platform rig will have a useful life of around 20 years) but also supports the office staff in the head office and the field office close to the shore base.

---

[8] Summer 2003

18

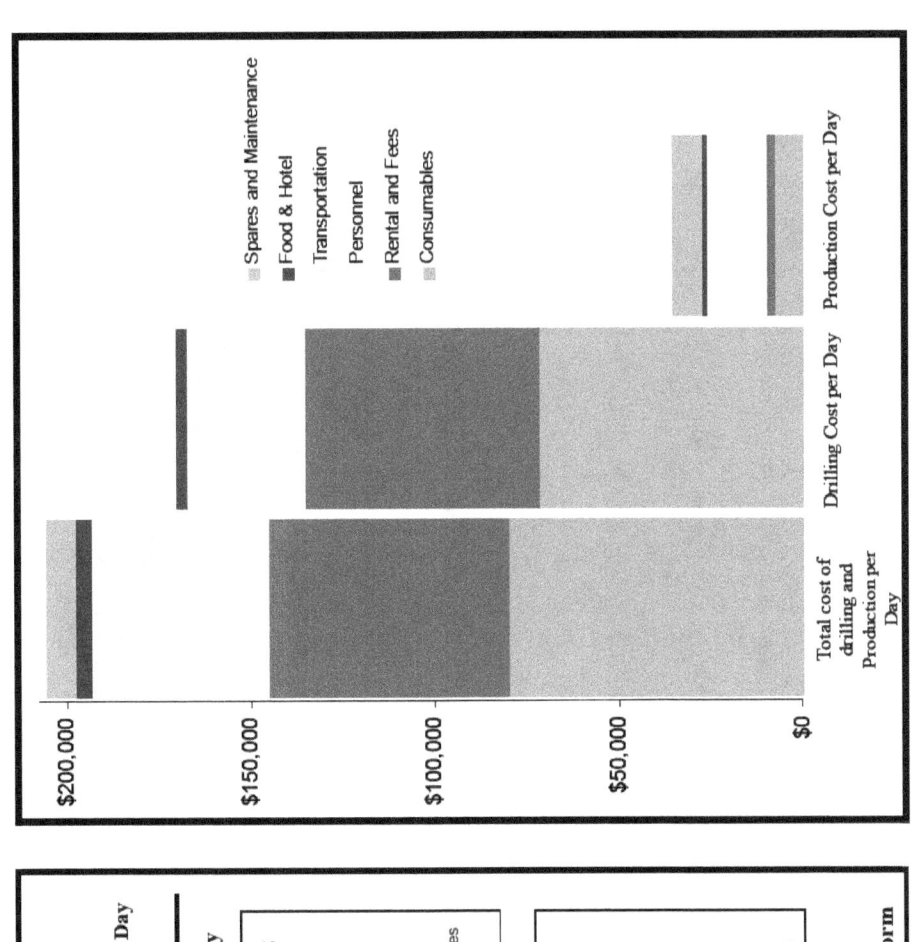

Figure 18. Ursa Production and Drilling Costs Per Day.

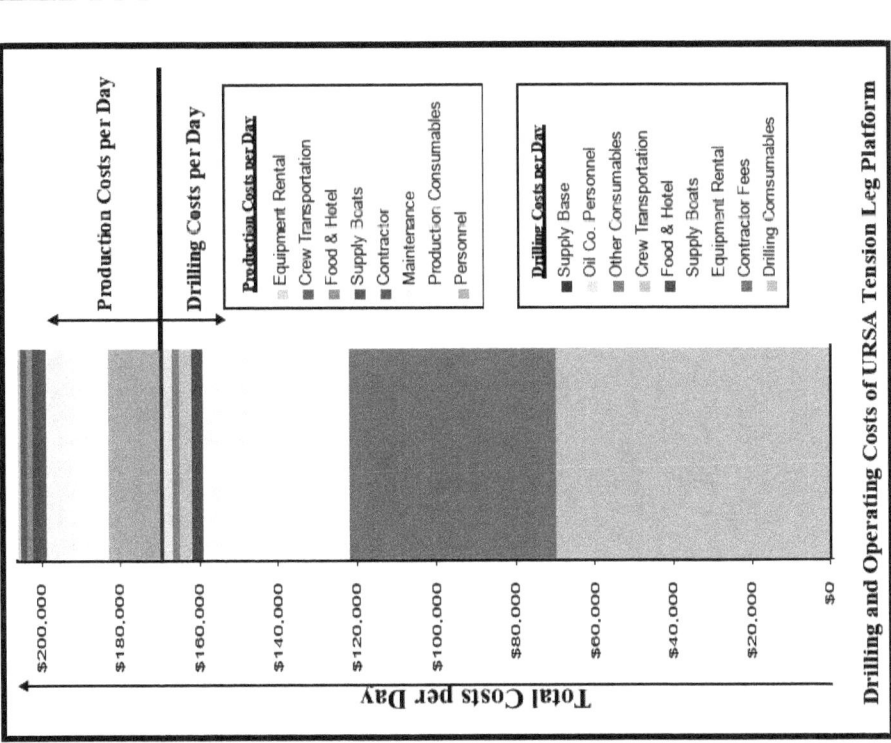

Figure 17. Drilling and Production Operating Costs of Ursa TLP.

2.2. BALDPATE

A limited amount of information was gathered on the Baldpate development. There was an OTC session on Baldpate, and a certain amount of costing information was presented, but Amerada Hess was reticent in giving additional cost information. Table 3 gives the basic costing information contained in the OTC paper on Baldpate, paper 10914 in 1999.

Table 3

Overall Costs of Baldpate (extracted from OTC paper 10914)

Capital Expenditure	Cost ($ Millions)
Tower	$137.6
Facilities	$64.0
Pipelines	$13.4
Subtotal Construction	$215.0
Development Drilling/Completion	$116.9
Total Project Capital Expenditure	$331.9

Some points that were given are that they spent between $2 and $3 million on assessing other possible development options. This is comparable to the amount spent by Shell on Ursa, although in the case of Amerada Hess, most of the work was undertaken by independent consultants.

Another point of interest is while no specific data were available on the cost of predevelopment seismic, interpretation, and exploration drilling, it was estimated they were between $100 and $200 million.

One area in which good data on the Baldpate project was available was from Paragon who did the topside engineering, equipment procurement, design, inspection, and much of the project management (see Figure 19).

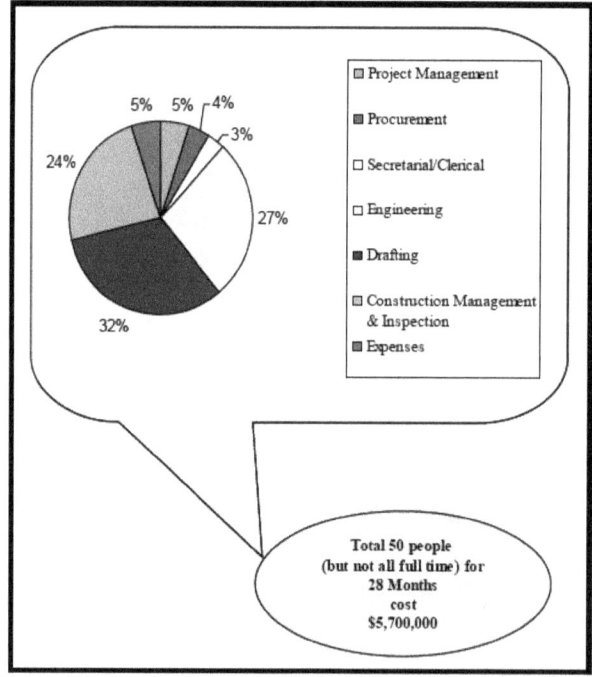

Figure 19. Baldpate Compliant Tower: Topside Engineering, Procurement, Inspection, Project/Construction Management.

2.3. POMPANO

Almost no information was available about Pompano, a jacket based structure installed in 1,294 feet water depth in 1994. The jacket and deck were both built by J. Ray McDermott on a lump sum cost basis, who also did the procurement, front end engineering design (FEED), detailed design, and marine installation. The deck was constructed in Amelia, Louisiana (near Morgan City), and towed out directly from there to site for installation. The jacket was assembled in Harbor Island facility near Aransas Pass, Texas. Some of the components for the jacket were fabricated in Amelia and then transported by barge to Harbor Island. The total weight of the jacket was 34,000 tons, and the deck weight was 4,600 tons[9].

J. Ray McDermott was cooperative in supplying photographs of the various installations with which they were involved, but did not supply significant additional information. Contacts were made within the organization, and there was a general willingness to cooperate, but there never appeared to be sufficient time to gather and supply the needed data. Some information was supplied on the overall project costs as charged by McDermott, but there was no breakdown of labor costs. It is interesting to note one individual at McDermott stated he had gathered some of the labor statistical data together in the past for MMS, but could not supply it now.

Very little information is known about the cost breakdown on Pompano, but there can be some very general estimations made concerning the labor costs and expenditures. A fabricated steel jacket costs approximately $2,000 per ton. The original plate steel will cost about $500 per ton. The two major stages the steel has to go through include rolling and seam welding it into pipe, then cutting and assembling the pipe into the jacket. The cost of the rolled and welded pipe increases the value of the plate steel from about $500 to $700 per ton. McDermott will roll most of their own pipe (it is assumed that this will have been carried out in Amelia, Louisiana) and then transport it to Harbor Island. There are some other incidental costs involved in jacket construction (welding rods, oxygen/acetylene, anodes, coatings/paint of the "splash zone") but the vast majority of the added value is from the input of labor. McDermott gave the cost of jacket fabrication as $66 million, which is very close to the estimated $2,000 per ton. Given a jacket of 34,000 tons, the cost will be comprised of $17 million for the steel, $7 million is the cost of rolling and welding it into pipe, and around $42 million will be for fabrication labor.

The deck cost was given as $35 million, but that will have included a significant quantity of third party equipment that will have been installed by McDermott in their Amelia yard. Although it did not affect the cost to BP, the deck fabrication costs went slightly over budget, but the jacket was on budget.

Personnel were found within BP who knew about the project, but either they did not have the time, or the authority to release information on the project. The only information available was obtained from a very limited number of published data sources. Part of the reason was that the project had long been completed at this project start up, so most of the relevant information had been previously filed. It is of note this is the project that probably had the least foreign content. The jacket was fabricated in south Texas, and the deck in Louisiana. While much of the steel may have come from foreign sources, all the fabrication was in the U.S., and probably most of the equipment was of U.S. origin.

2.4. NEPTUNE SPAR

The Neptune spar was originally fabricated for Oryx as the operator, but since installation, Oryx has become part of Kerr-McGee. It was the world's first spar to be used as the base for well production operations, and is located in Viosca Knoll Block 826 in a water depth of 1,930 feet. Prior to committing to a spar, Oryx considered a number of other development options, including a TLP, a compliant tower, a floating production system, and a floating production, storage, and offloading (FPSO) system. The main reasons for choosing a spar were that it would be equipped with dry surface trees that would allow easy access to work on the wells, and remove any build up of paraffin. Another consideration was that it would be possible to move the spar a limited distance should it prove necessary to access some different reservoirs that could not be reached by directional drilling.

At the time it was decided to develop the field with a spar, there was a patent held by Deep Oil Technology, Inc. (DOT) on spars, and DOT had formed a consortium for the use of spars to develop

---

[9] The weight supplied by McDermott is 5,200 short tons (each 2,000 lbs), equivalent to 4,600 long tons (each 2,240 lbs) for the deck, and 38,000 short tons for the jacket.

fields. Consortium members included DOT, J. Ray McDermott for topside fabrication, and overall installation, and Aker Rauma Offshore for design and fabrication of the hull and mooring system.

The spar has a diameter of 72 feet and a length of 705 feet. The weight of the hull was 12,900 tons, and the topside weight grew from an original design of 1,200 to 1,600 tons.

Table 4 gives a high level cost breakdown for the major components of the Neptune spar, as extracted from the OTC paper 8381, given in 1997.

Table 4

High-Level Cost Breakdown for Neptune Spar

Item	Cost $ Million
Spar Hull and Mooring	$53
Topside and Installation	$47
Production Risers	$14
Drilling and Completion	$42
Engineering, Project Management, Permitting, & Misc.	$16
Total	$172 Million

The hull was fabricated in Pori, Finland, at Aker Rauma yard. Aker was approached to supply additional information contained in the OTC papers, but was somewhat reluctant. They did, however, state that most of the steel within the hull would have been Finnish, with the iron ore probably coming from Sweden, and coal for processing coming from Poland. The price given for rolled steel was $750 per ton, but this would be increased considerably by the time it is fabricated into the hull. The main US input on the hull was from certain import duties, and for the mating of the two sections at Ingalls Shipyard in Pascagoula, Mississippi.

The hull was fabricated in 17 sections under cover, and then the sections were welded together to form two cylinders, one 390 feet long and the other 315 feet. The two sections were then put onto a dry transport semisubmersible ship and transported across the Atlantic to Pascagoula where they were discharged. The two sections were then floated into alignment, and welded together. Figure 20 shows a photograph of the Neptune spar after the two parts have been mated at Ingalls, and just as the tow is started out to the location. Once on location, it was upended, and the deck placed on top.

Figure 20. Neptune Spar After Mating and Under Tow to Location.

The Neptune topsides were fabricated by J. Ray McDermott in Amelia, Louisiana. The value of the fabrication contract was $28 million, which included equipment design and procurement. The contract

22

was lump sum, and went slightly over budget. The duration of the contract was approximately one year from September 1996 to September 1997 during which time McDermott used a total of 337,000 man-hours.

The mooring system for Neptune had two main suppliers: Vicinay for the chain, and Williamsport Wire Rope for the wire. Vicinay manufactured the chain in Bilbao, Spain. Their facility employs 237 people of which approximately 100 skilled workers would have worked on producing the chain for 2½ months. The facility can run two or three projects at any given time, and they have four machines for producing chain of less than 3-inch diameter, and four for producing chain of over 3 inches. The Neptune chain is 4.75-inch. (The diameter of a chain is the basic diameter of the steel bar stock from which it is made. A single link of 4.75" chain will be just under 30 inches long, 16 inches wide, and will weigh approximately 400 pounds.) The total cost for the chain was $3.5 million at a price of $1.85 per Kg.

The wire rope was manufactured in Williamsport, Pennsylvania, and was sheathed by Wellstream in Panama City, Florida. The total cost of the wire rope, including sheathing, was $2 million.

2.5. "SIR DOUGLAS MORPETH" DEVELOPMENT

2.5.1. Overview of Project

The "Sir Douglas Morpeth" (Morpeth) development is operated by British Borneo (since taken over by Agip) in Blocks 921, 964, and 965 of Ewing Banks area. The water depth at the location is 1,690 feet, and the installation of the Atlantia designed SeaStar mini-TLP was completed in the latter half of 1998. British Borneo acquired the field from Shell Offshore Inc. in 1995 and had a 100% working interest in the field. Shell maintains a financial interest.

The development of Morpeth followed a somewhat unusual course: normally a field is chosen for development, and then a development option is chosen to suit that field. The reverse was the case for Morpeth[10].

British Borneo started developing shallow water interests in the Gulf of Mexico in 1989. They quickly formed an informal partnership with Atlantia Offshore Ltd. who supplied them with a number of minimal shallow water platforms on a turnkey basis. These tended to be low value contracts, mostly under $1 million, but they led to a confidence between the parties. Figure 21 shows a Sea Pony, similar to the small platforms installed by Atlantia for British Borneo[11]. When in 1993 British Borneo decided to speed up their move into international oil and gas exploration, they decided to build on this relationship.

At the time, Atlantia was developing the SeaStar concept (see Figure 22), a mini-TLP that was to be ideally suited to marginal field development in deepwater. Through their previous working arrangements British Borneo saw the potential for a mini-TLP within their own deepwater plans, so entered a strategic alliance with Atlantia to gain early access to a SeaStar. In effect, British Borneo selected a development concept in parallel with the search for a field to develop.

The SeaStar mini-TLP has a single central column that supports the deck above the water. At the bottom of the column there are three pontoons that radiate out from the column. At the outer end of these pontoons there are two tendons that are attached to piles in the seabed directly below them. The pontoons give spread between the tendons, thereby ensuring the platform's stability.

The choice of the Morpeth field was in part driven by what was suitable for development by a mini-TLP. The requirements were that the field could be developed with subsea trees[12]. This meant there had to be low workover/intervention requirements, a field that could be developed with a small number of wells, and wells that had good flow assurance. Figure 23 shows the overall layout of the Morpeth field,

---

[10] Much of what follows by way of background comes from the Offshore Technology Conference paper 10854, 1999, "Morpeth Field Development Overview."

[11] Atlantia has recently been acquired by IHC and has sold off the shallow water platform business to Seahorse Platform Partners Ltd.

[12] Since the installation of Morpeth and Allegheny, Atlantia have developed a version of the SeaStar that can have dry trees up on the deck. This option was not available at the time.

Figure 21. Sea Pony Shallow Water Platform (Courtesy of Seahorse Platform Partners Ltd.).

Figure 22. Sir Douglas Morpeth Mini-TLP Installed (Courtesy of Atlantia Offshore Ltd.).

Figure 23. Morpeth Field Layout Showing Subsea Wellheads and Pipeline to Shallow Water Facility (Courtesy of Atlantia Offshore Ltd.).

with the subsea wellheads on the left side of the picture, with risers coming up to the platform, and export risers/pipelines going off to the shallow water facility 19 miles away in 366 feet water on the right of the diagram.

The project to install a platform at Morpeth was carried out under two main contracts: Atlantia to supply the mini-TLP, and J. Ray McDermott to install it[13]. The setup of the supply contract was somewhat unusual in that it was on a cost plus basis, with Atlantia being the main contractor. In effect, British Borneo gave Atlantia the responsibility of supplying a suitable structure on budget, and on time. It would not have been possible for Atlantia to undertake the project on a lump-sum basis the way they had done for the shallow water developments. Given the size of their organization (roughly 200 employees) they would not have been in a position to offer a turnkey contract on a platform costing nearly $100 million. None of their subcontractors would have had sufficient confidence in being paid unless British Borneo guaranteed payment. In addition, the design had not been completed by the time the contract was awarded.

The hull was built by Gulf Island Fabrication Inc. in Houma, Louisiana. They also built the deck structure, and assembled the various components supplied by other vendors. This was one of the largest contracts on the project. Gulf Island is an experienced yard that has been building jackets and decks for many years. They have tried, and are generally successful at keeping a stable workforce, and to this end train a large percentage of their own labor. This is supplemented, by additional labor taken on an as needed basis.

2.5.2. Information Gathered

Information has been supplied to the study team by British Borneo, Atlantia, Gulf Island, and a number of other contractors and subcontractors. Of assistance was a list of vendors supplied by Atlantia, although this contained only an indication as to the level of costs, not the actual costs themselves. It is through this list that most of the information has been obtained, however, the problem of where the various materials have come from, as discussed in the "Summary and Status", has not been overcome. Probably even more than the Ursa TLP, most of the direct labor and suppliers have been from around the Gulf Coast. Also as discussed in the Summary, it is likely that much of the equipment has origins outside the Gulf Coast area, but so far it has been outside the scope to follow that course. In addition, it is too late to get those sorts of details from the vendors: they will have changed their suppliers over the years, and will probably not remember whom they used.

---

[13] There were other contracts for the drilling, subsea systems, risers, pipelines, etc.

The project costs are given in an OTC paper from the special Morpeth session, OTC 10854. These are shown in Table 5. In addition to these costs was the cost of drilling the exploratory and development wells which were a total of $152 million. Figure 24 gives a high-level breakdown of the costs. The left side of the chart shows the total costs comprising the physical installation of the TLP at the top, and the drilling at the bottom. The costs for the TLP are graphically broken down to their major constituent parts. The drilling costs are broken into the three major costs, and an indication as to what is involved in each of those.

Table 5

Breakdown of Principal Costs for Morpeth (from OTC paper 10854)

Equipment/ Service	Cost ($MM)
TLP	
Foundation	$2.91
Tendon System	$15.10
Hull	$24.16
Deck	$6.98
Production Facilities	$24.59
Facilities Hook up	$12.08
Installation	$13.38
Subtotal	$99.20
Subsea	
Trees	$12.90
Controls	$3.49
Flowlines	$8.00
Installation	$3.15
Subtotal	$27.54
Pipelines	
Materials	$8.18
Installation	$12.41
Subtotal	$20.59
3rd Party Costs	
Subtotal	$11.67
Project Total	$159.00

Figure 25 gives a sample breakdown of the costs for constructing the physical TLP without any of the other associated facilities (e.g., pipelines, subsea equipment, etc.). It also shows the locations of some of the vendors that supplied goods or services to the facility. In some cases additional information is known about these vendors, and they are discussed in further detail later in this section, but in most cases, all that is known is what was supplied, and the location of the vendor.

British Borneo supplied some useful information about the project background, and some of the other costs, although, because of the way it was contracted to Atlantia, there were relatively few additional costs. It is interesting to compare the project management team size for the Morpeth development with that for Ursa. British Borneo had a maximum of 11 personnel on the team compared to 130 from Shell on Ursa, although this is not an entirely fair comparison as the Shell number includes more on-site personnel who would have been supplied by Atlantia in the case of Morpeth. The British Borneo project management budget was $750,000.

The operational aspects of Morpeth bear some comparison to those of Ursa. Morpeth, being a relatively small facility with limited production capacity of 35,000 barrels of oil per day (BOPD) and 38 million standard cubic feet of gas per day (MMSCFD), has living quarters for 18, with a normal crew size of 13. There are no facilities for drilling on Morpeth. Ursa, with production capacity of 150,000 BOPD and gas of 400 MMSCFD, has accommodation for 156 persons, and is normally full during drilling operations.

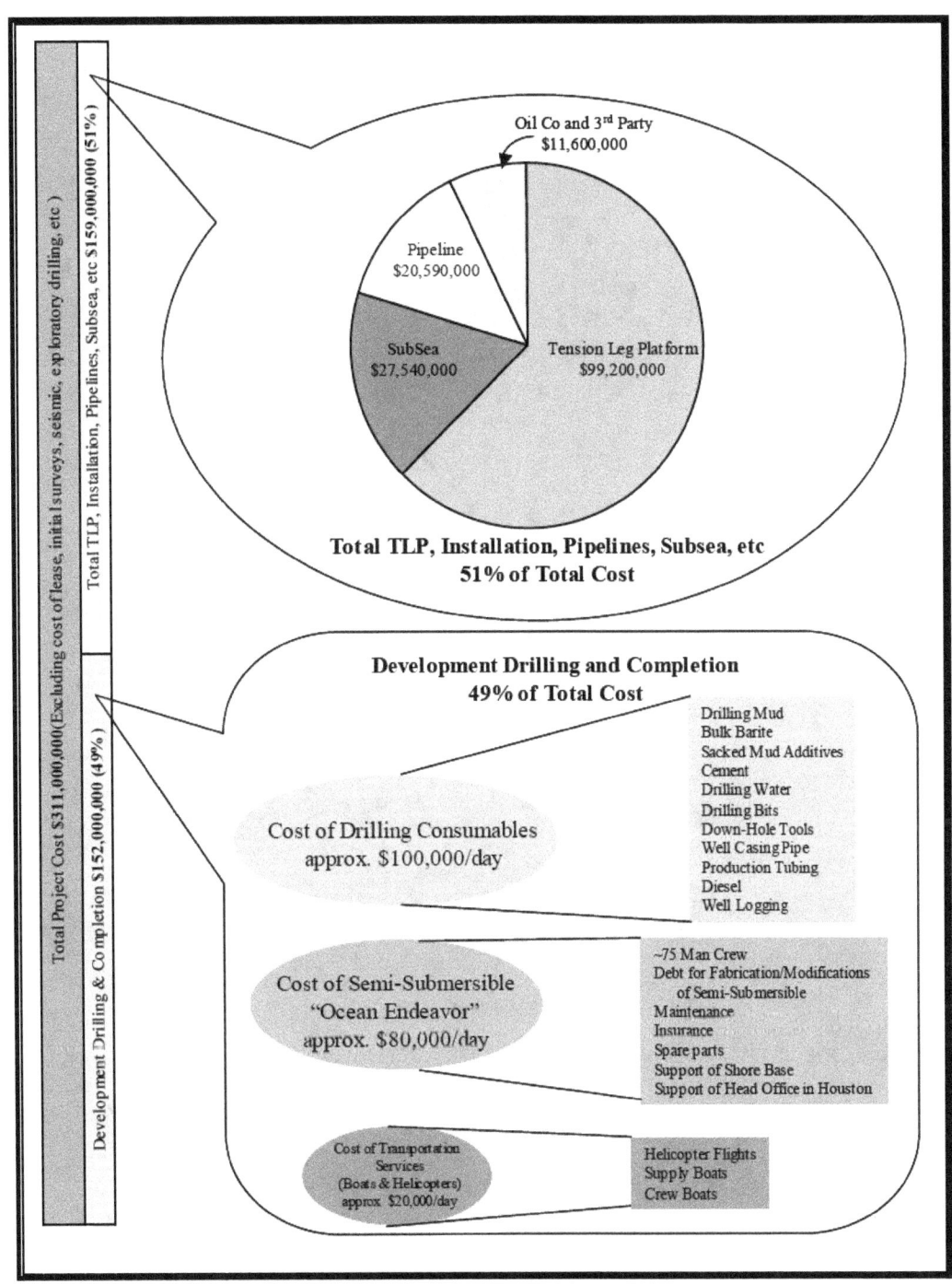

Figure 24. Sir Douglas Morpeth Mini-TLP: Cost Breakdown.

27

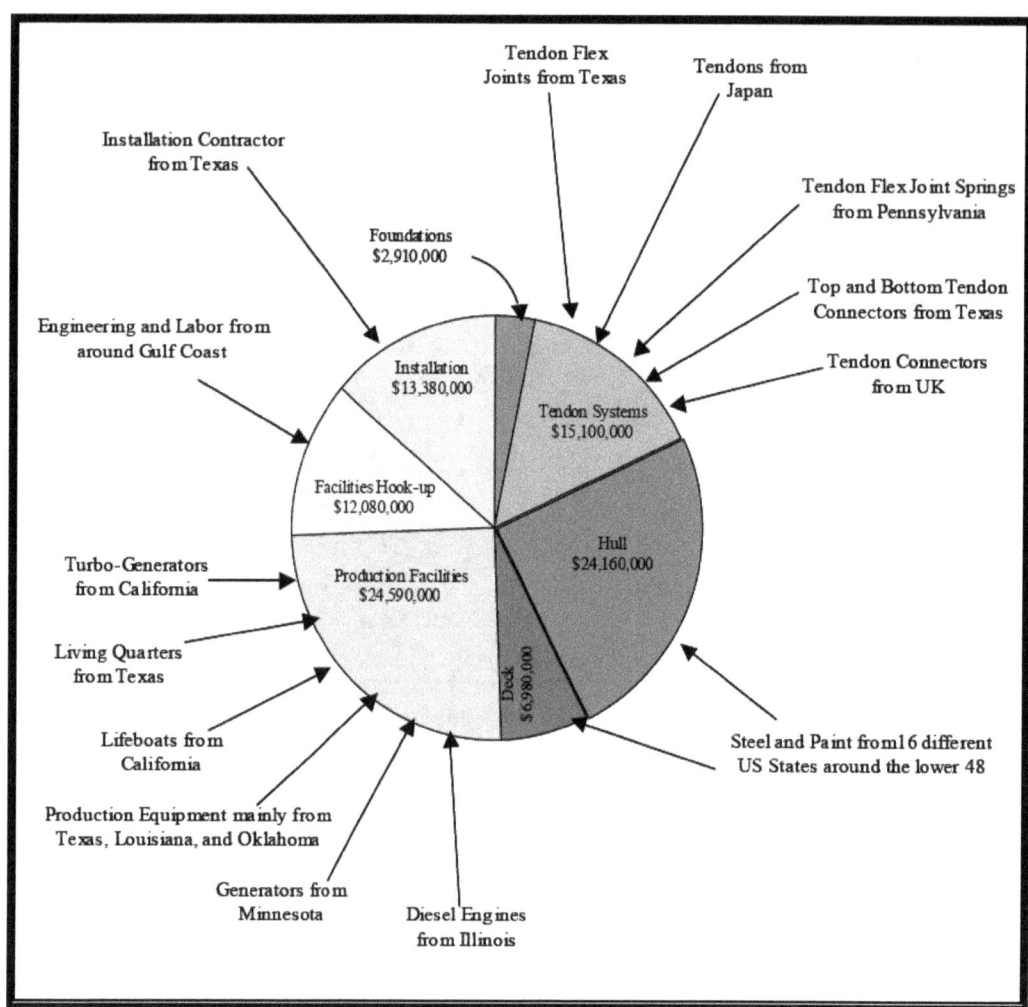

Figure 25. Breakdown of $99,200,000 Cost for Morpeth Platform with Sample Vendor Locations (Note: Costs do not include subsea and pipeline costs.).

The project was relatively fast track, so it is difficult to separate out the project planning costs, and those associated with considering alternative development options. The date of first oil was less than two years after completion of the appraisal well, and there was no separate tracking of early project management costs. However, as far as it can be determined, approximately $3.5 million was spent by British Borneo before the project was formally sanctioned.

The drilling cost for the development was split into two parts, the appraisal well and the development drilling. All the drilling was undertaken by the *Ocean Endeavor*, a semisubmersible owned by Diamond Offshore Inc. The unit was built in 1975 in Australia and has been based in the Gulf of Mexico since mid 1980s. It cost $35 million when built, and is capable of operating in water depths of up to 2,000 feet. It is operated by Diamond Offshore, which is based in Houston. Diamond has just over 30 semisubmersible units, approximately half operating in the U.S. Gulf, and half overseas. In addition they have 14 jack-ups, most of which are domestic. There are approximately 300 people employed in the Houston head office, with 3,000 domestically offshore. The overseas units will have a certain number of expatriate crew, but will also employ a significant number of local labor.

The day rate for the *Ocean Endeavor* ranged from $37,000 to $82,000 per day. Note that was a relatively low rate for a semisubmersible, but this is in part because of the age of the unit[14], and the relatively shallow water depth limit. Some of the constituent parts of the cost of drilling the wells is given in Figure 24, but it is of note the main costs associated with the rig day rate are normally debt repayment and labor. In the case of the *Ocean Endeavor* it is unlikely there is still any debt outstanding, but the maintenance costs may be increased, however, a large percentage of the day rate will be direct labor costs.

The appraisal well was flow tested to ensure the expected flow from the well, and this produced around $50,000 revenue, but this is insignificant by comparison to the cost of flow testing. It is the results of the flow testing that are important rather than the revenue generated.

It is interesting British Borneo estimates the cost of abandoning the structure and wells would be approximately $13.5 million. There is certainly a possibility the unit could be reused at another location, and the assumption is that the main components which would require replacement would be the tendons and piles.

2.5.3. Gulf Island Fabrication Inc. Data

Gulf Island Fabrication Inc., the company that fabricated the hull and assembled the deck, was extremely cooperative. They supplied the information that was the basis for the economic analysis undertaken by Joachim Singelmann (see next section of report). They also supplied information on the cost and source of their supplies to build the hull and deck structure. It needs to be borne in mind that the vast majority of the Gulf Island work involved steel construction and painting. Hence their main supplies would be steel, paint, and anodes. While the majority of those subcontracts are provided by companies located in Louisiana, there is no way of ascertaining the extent to which goods and services where produced at the site of those companies. It appears that for a substantial proportion of those subcontracts, funding was merely passed though that location for actual work performed elsewhere. It is clear, since there are no significant steel mills in Louisiana, most of the steel purchased in Louisiana must have been bought from suppliers who had imported it from either other states or other countries.

Keeping in mind the recorded expenditures may not represent any significant associated labor, simply a throughput of cash, most of the outside costs originated in two states, Texas and Louisiana. Together they account for 85 percent of all outside costs. This can clearly be seen by reference to Figure 26, which shows the expenditure by state. All other states are in the single digits, with Mississippi companies coming in as distant third, receiving 4.1 percent of all outside contracts. The information is shown by state on the U.S. map in Figure 27.

---

[14] It is normal to design a mobile offshore drilling unit to have a 25-year life. That does not mean they cannot successfully operate for longer, but maintenance will increasingly become a problem. On some units, technical obsolescence can also be important: the equipment is too old, and parts are not available to repair it.

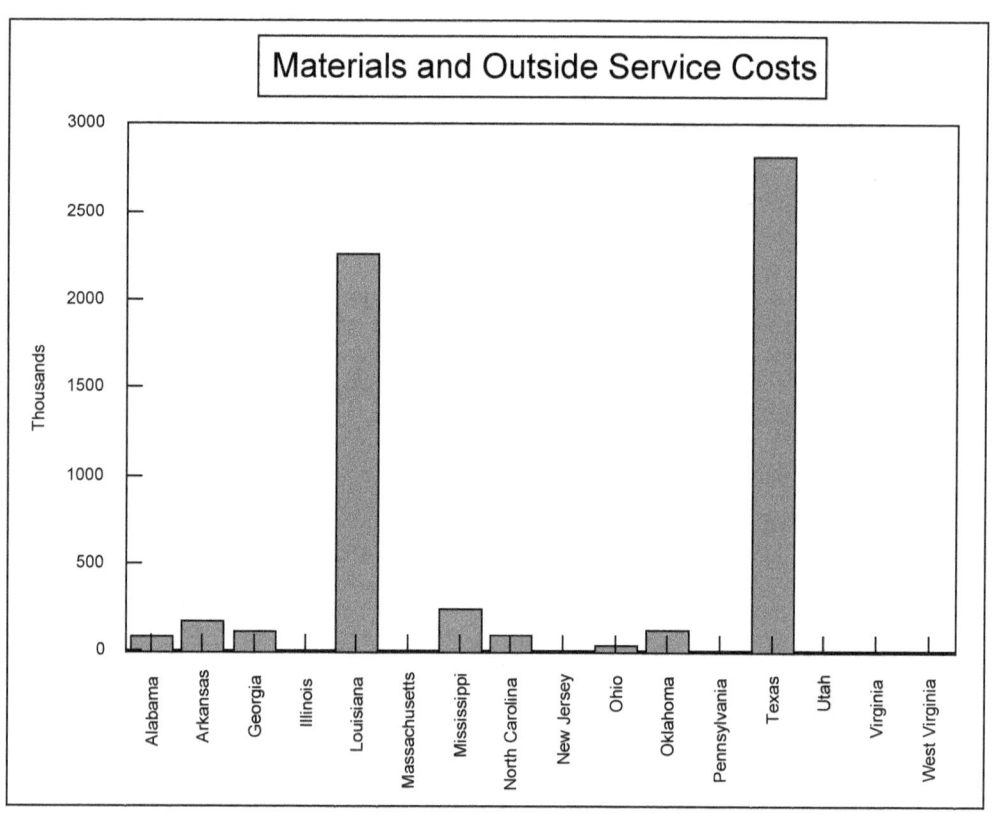

Figure 26.   Outside Expenditure by Gulf Island by State.

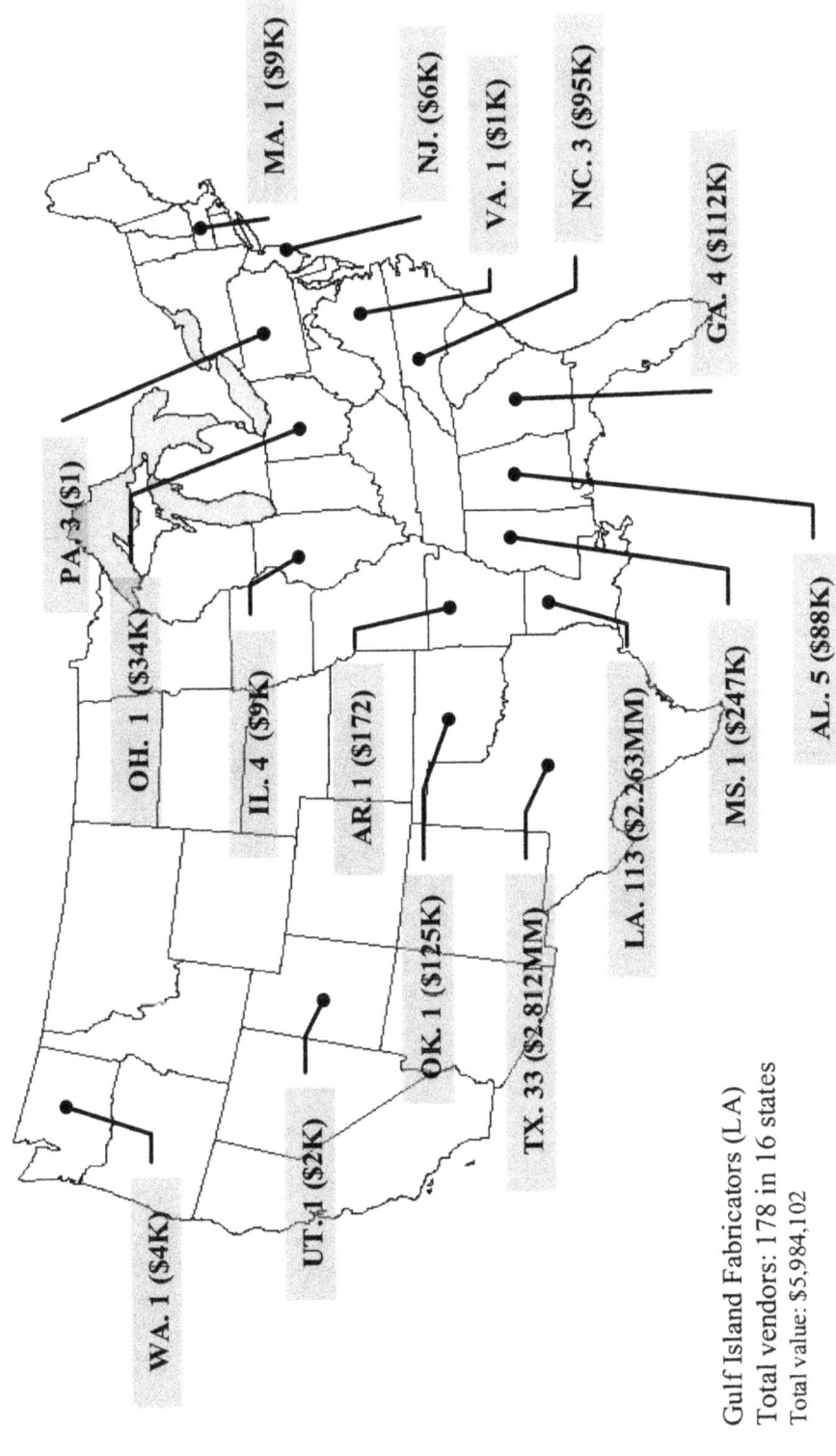

MA. 1 ($9K)

NJ. ($6K)

VA. 1 ($1K)

NC. 3 ($95K)

GA. 4 ($112K)

PA. 3 ($1)

OH. 1 ($34K)

IL. 4 ($9K)

AR. 1 ($172)

MS. 1 ($247K)

AL. 5 ($88K)

LA. 113 ($2.263MM)

OK. 1 ($125K)

TX. 33 ($2.812MM)

UT. 1 ($2K)

WA. 1 ($4K)

Gulf Island Fabricators (LA)
Total vendors: 178 in 16 states
Total value: $5,984,102

Figure 27a. Vendors to Gulf Island Fabrication for the Hull and Deck Structure Fabrication of Morpeth Mini-TLP (Primary supplies are steel, paint, and anodes.)

31

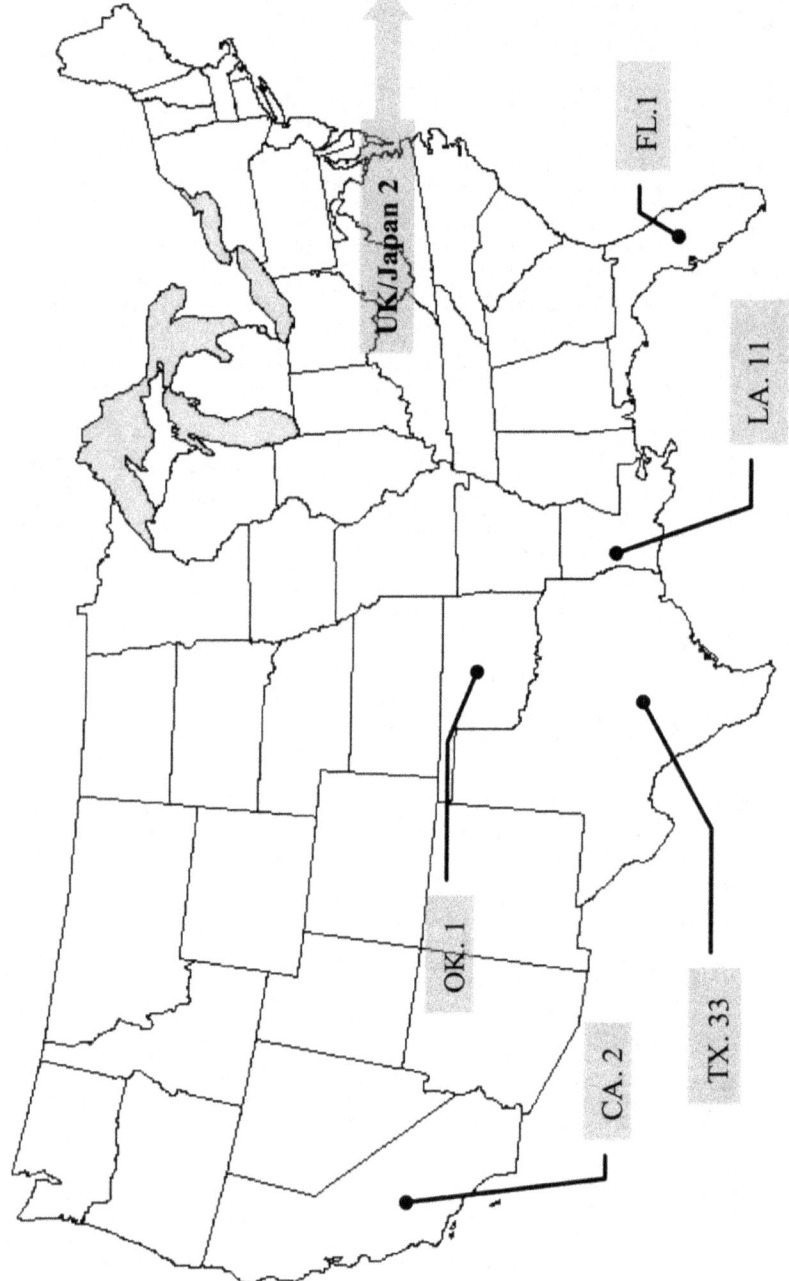

Figure 27b. Morpeth Mini-TLP Number of Primary Vendors by State.

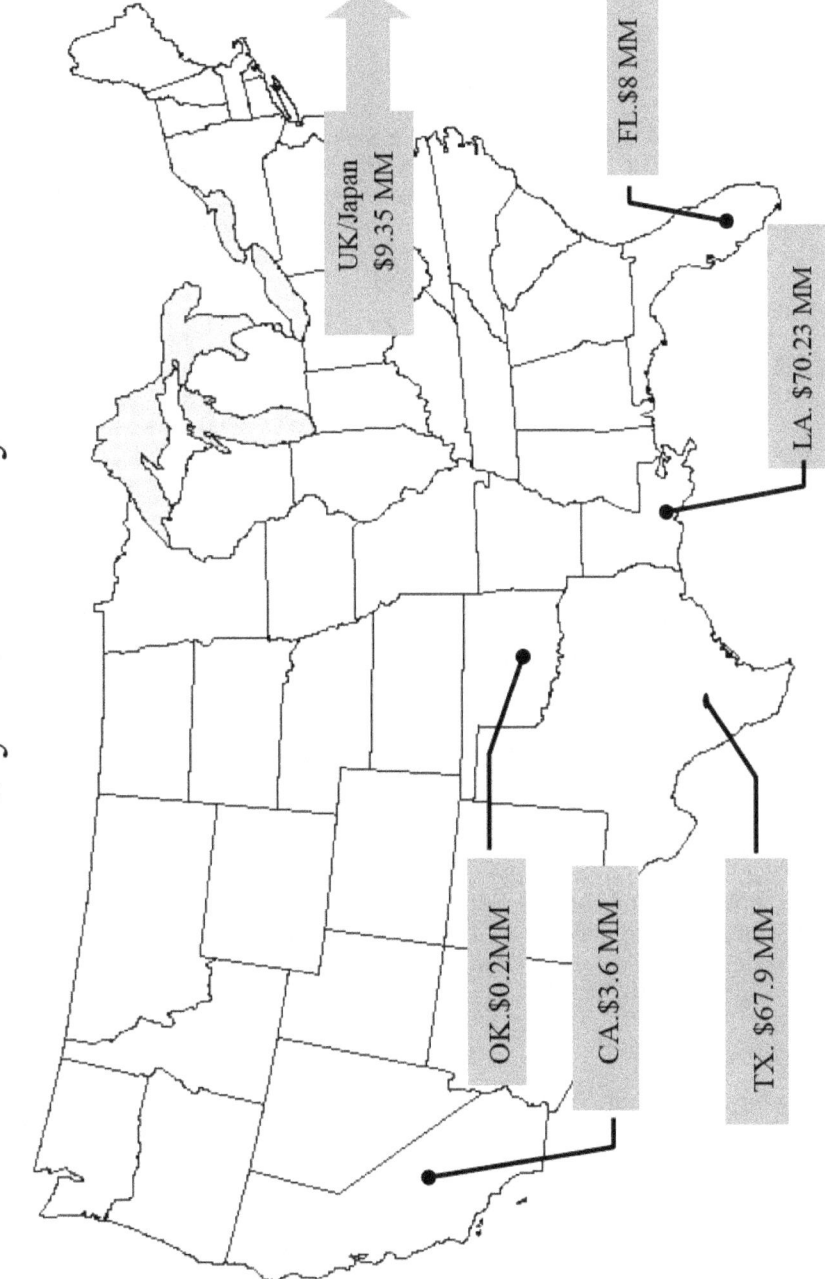

Morpeth Mini TLP Income for
Primary Vendors by State

UK/Japan $9.35 MM

FL. $8 MM

LA. $70.23 MM

OK. $0.2MM

CA. $3.6 MM

TX. $67.9 MM

Figure 27c.   Morpeth Mini-TLP Income for Primary Vendors by State.

2.5.4. Atlantia Supplied Information

Atlantia supplied a list of the main contractors and suppliers for the Morpeth TLP. Unfortunately not all the contact information was supplied, and some companies could not be contacted. In addition, there was no great rush to assistance from most of the companies approached. This was mainly due to a lack of time, but also there was no perceived benefit, and no desire to commit the needed time. Notwithstanding the difficulty in getting information, some companies were extremely cooperative. The following is not presented in any particular order, but gives an idea of the level of effort expended in supplying certain services or equipment.

2.5.4.1. Atlantia

Atlantia had some initial funding of $50,000 from the Small Business Administration (SBA) to help them undertake a scoping study on the SeaStar design of mini TLP. They later got an additional $500,000 grant to refine the design, and estimate they put in an additional $500,000 of their own money to help develop the design. All these costs were at a low hourly rate of $50 per hour, so the estimated level of effort to get a saleable design onto the market was $1 million representing 20,000 man-hours of engineering and drafting. When the contract was signed with British Borneo, Atlantia received the Tibbetts Award from the SBA.

When Atlantia started they had 25 persons committed to the project. This later increased to around 100 people by the end (and the subsequent start of Allegheny, another British Borneo mini TLP from Atlantia). The project management team started out as a single person, but grew to include a cost control staff of 2 to 3 full-time equivalent employees over a two-year period. In addition, there were 4 people in the contact & procurement department, 8-10 onsite inspectors, and 1 site construction manager/engineer based in Gulf Island's yard. It is an interesting comparison, but for a simple shallow water minimal platform, Atlantia would have had but one site inspection person.

2.5.4.2. Alan C. McClure and Assoc. Inc.

Alan C. McClure and Associates Inc. supplied shipyard drawings, and to a lesser extent, detail engineering on the project. McClure is a Houston based consultancy, and the value of their contract on Morpeth was $1.8 million over 14 months. There were up to 14 people working on the project, including a full-time project manager, with about 85% drafting and 15% engineering.

2.5.4.3. Survival Systems Int.

Survival Systems supplied the lifeboats used on both Morpeth and Ursa[15], and is based in Valley Center, California (zip code 92082) near Escondido. Morpeth has two 21-man boats, and Ursa has six 58-man boats. All the boats are built at the Valley Center facility where there is a 100,000 square feet factory employing 60 full-time employees. In addition, the company employs 25 people in New Orleans to do installation and maintenance on their boats. On average they produce three boats per month. Their supplies include the engines, glass fiber, etc., but most of the costs are down to labor. The Morpeth boats would have cost about $100,000 each, and the Ursa ones around $150,000 each.

2.5.4.4. Solar Turbines

The power generating system on Morpeth was supplied by solar turbines, based in San Diego, California. Not much information could be obtained, but the contract amount for Morpeth was approximately $3 million. Solar employs approximately 3,000 people at two separate facilities in California. Solar also supplied the turbines for Ursa.

2.5.4.5. Offshore Technology Research Center at Texas A&M

The Morpeth model testing was carried out in the model basin at Texas A&M, College Station (see discussion of model testing in section on Ursa, and in Field Development Chronology). The cost of the

---

[15] The lifeboats are sometimes referred to as Totally Enclosed Motor Propelled Survival Craft (TEMPSC).

tests was $230,000, including the cost of building the model. It took six weeks to build the model, and an additional 4 weeks to test it, employing two engineers and four technicians.

2.5.4.6. ABB Vetco

ABB Vetco designed and fabricated the tendon connectors. The value of the contract was not disclosed or known, but they said that up to 110 people would have been involved with the project. Steel supplies come from both domestic and foreign sources. Approximately 75 percent of the work would have been shop workers, and 25 percent office based. All work was in Houston.

2.5.4.7. Smithco

Smithco supplied the air coolers within the gas compression plant. The company is based in Tulsa, Oklahoma, where the work would have been carried out. The value of their contract was approximately $200,000, relatively low by comparison to their normal contract size of $500,000. The company has an annual revenue of $12 million and employs 200 people at two facilities (130 at one, 70 at the other). Under 40 percent of their work is for offshore applications, most of it being for onshore refineries. The shop personnel are paid between $8 and $15 per hour. They employ 8 degreed engineers, another 45 office personnel, and 145 shop staff. It takes around 5 weeks to produce a small unit, and 25 weeks to produce a large one.

2.5.4.8. American Bureau of Shipping

The American Bureau of Shipping (ABS) classed the TLP and acted as the Certified Verification Agent (CVA). The total cost of the work was $700,000 and involved approximately 7,000 man hours of engineering and survey effort. The split of work was one surveyor employed part-time in the fabrication yard (in Houma, Louisiana) over the duration of the project for a total of 700 hours, plus another 300 offshore for installation. There were 4,000 of office based engineering time employing up to 60 engineers in Houston, Texas. In addition to the standard engineering effort, there were another 1,000 hours spent on review of vendor equipment that is subject to class review. This includes items associated with power generation, fire fighting, safety equipment, electrical, emergency systems, etc. There were also surveys at the vendors' facilities that accounted for an additional 1,000 hours. These extra hours would have involved a large number of individuals for relatively short durations as the equipment and steel would have come from many different sources.

This breakdown of cost is comparable to the other projects on which ABS was involved. (Neptune spar was classed, and ABS was the CVA on Ursa. The costs for Neptune will have been slightly higher than for Morpeth. Those for Ursa somewhat lower.)

2.5.4.9. Global Maritime

Global Maritime had two separate functions on the Morpeth project: the first was as TLP consultants directly to British Borneo and the other as the marine warranty surveyor (MWS) for towage and installation. Their total fees were $400,000 of which $200,000 were for high level engineering consultancy involving a very limited number of personnel. The MWS work would have involved a mix of engineers and master mariners to ensure that good marine practices were adhered to during the transportation and installation. Although much of the work was in Louisiana, all the staff would have been based in Houston.

2.5.4.10. Wellstream

Wellstream, which is based in Panama City, Florida, supplied the flexible flowlines. Little additional information is known except that the cost of the flowlines was $8 million.

2.5.5. Morpeth Conclusions

Gathering information from the vendors to the project was extremely difficult and time consuming. It was not only difficult to determine the correct person to talk to, even if you knew which company and telephone number to call, but getting anyone to give the type of data needed was difficult. It was certainly impossible to get consistently good data that could be used for comparison even within a project. To get data that could be compared between projects was almost impossible. Many companies apart from those listed above were contacted, but in most cases it was not possible to get through to the relevant person, and rarely were calls returned. Indeed, it tended to be the smaller companies that were most cooperative, however these were the ones with the smallest expenditure, and hence the least impact on labor markets.

3. ECONOMIC ANALYSIS

ABS Consulting contracted Dr. Joachim Singelmann of Louisiana State University Department of Sociology to assist with the economic analysis of the data gathered from the various sources. As discussed in the introduction, the quantity and quality of the gathered data was limited, so meaningful comparison between the projects was not possible. The only data that was supplied in sufficient detail, and involving enough personnel, was that supplied by Gulf Island Fabrication, Inc. in Houma, Louisiana. Gulf Island built the hull of the Sir Douglas Morpeth mini-TLP for British Borneo, although their actual contract was with Atlantia. They also fabricated the structure of the deck, and assembled the components onto it.

Other labor data was supplied (e.g., Shell supplied a significant quantity of data on the operational aspects of Ursa, as discussed previously) but the number of persons employed on any specific aspect was insufficient to have a meaningful impact on the local labor market. This may be an inherent problem with the type of analysis that was intended for this project: the effect on labor markets outside the Gulf Coast may not individually be large enough to quantify. The majority of the U.S. fabrication will inherently be close to the coast (for transportation reasons) so it is only as one considers the smaller component parts that there is an increasing involvement from areas away from the Gulf. However, these components will be spread increasingly thinly as one looks at increasingly small components. There are some possible exceptions if some specific component happens to be manufactured in a small community that has a single industry, but generally, the components for an offshore platform are associated with relatively heavy industry.

This following discussion provides information about the labor demand generated by the fabrication of the Morpeth platform. We will first describe the amount of labor and occupations that went into the fabrication of Morpeth. We then show how this labor demand relates to the labor supply in the labor market area around Houma in which the company is located. Finally, we show what other costs were incurred by the Morpeth project, and in which states those costs occurred.

3.1. AMOUNT OF LABOR AND ITS OCCUPATIONAL COMPOSITION OF THE MORPETH PROJECT

Most of the onsite fabrication for the Morpeth project in the Houma area was carried out during April 1997-August 1998. The project required a total of 423,874 nonmanagerial hours during that time period, for an overall labor cost of $6.7 million. Tables 6 and 7 summarize the amount of total hours and percent of wages for nonmanagerial work on the Morpeth project during the period April 1997-August 1998. Most project tasks were carried out by welders and fitters, painters, electricians, equipment operators, riggers, and sand blasters. (The category "Extra Work" consists of various tasks that the client asked for during the fabrication stage. The documentation for the fabrication process does not permit an allocation of these tasks to specific occupations.) Fitters and welders account for two thirds of all hours that went into the fabrication of the Morpeth platform. The pay for the various occupations required for the platform construction ranges from about $13 to $28 per hour. Clearly, that pay level makes those jobs very attractive, especially in the Houma labor market area.

Table 6

Percent Hours and Percent of Wages for Morpeth Project

Occupation	Hours	% Total Hours	% Total Wages
Brace Rack—Welders/Fitters	4,532	1.1	1.0
Confined Space Watch— Technicians	1,912	0.5	0.3
Dimensional Control—Technicians (Quality Assessment)	840	0.2	0.2
Electrical—Electricians	2,600	0.6	0.5
Equipment—Equipment Operators	42,546	10.0	12.3
Field Fitting—Fitters	48,644	11.5	9.8
Field Welding—Welders	58,328	13.8	14.0
Loadout/Lofting—Riggers	6,004	1.4	1.5
Material Moving—Laborers	5,621	1.3	1.3
Painting—Painters	13,878	3.3	3.5
Pipe Field Fitting—Fitters	41,784	9.9	10.8
Pipe Field Welding—Welders	12,214	2.9	3.2
Pipe Support—Fitters/Welders	1,588	0.4	0.4
Pipe Rack—Fitters/Welders	681	0.2	0.2
Pipe Shop Fitting—Fitters	6,238	1.5	1.2
Pipe Shop Welding—Welders	10,084	2.4	2.3
Pipe Supports—Fitters/Welders	9,160	2.2	2.1
QualityControlDocumentation—Clerical	840	0.2	0.1
Quality Control Paint Inspection—Painters	311	0.1	0.1
Reblasts Welds—Sand Blasters	475	0.1	0.1
Safety Training—Safety Training	1,561	0.4	0.3
Sandblasting/Prime—Sand Blasters	26,462	6.2	6.6
Shop Fitting—Fitters	51,925	12.3	10.3
Shop Welding—Welders	39,269	9.3	8.6
Extra Work	32,839	7.7	8.4
TOTAL	423,874	100.0	100.0

Table 7

Summary of Hours and Percent of Wages for Morpeth by Discipline

Occupation	Hours	%Total Hours	%Total Wages
Welders/Fitters	15,961	3.8	3.6
Welders	119,895	28.3	28.1
Fitters	148,591	35.1	32.2
Technicians	1,912	0.5	0.3
Technicians (Qual. Assess.)	840	0.2	0.2
Electricians	2,600	0.6	0.5
Equipment Operators	42,546	10.0	12.3
Riggers	6,004	1.4	1.5
Laborers	5,621	1.3	1.3
Painters	13,878	3.3	3.5
Painters (QC)	311	0.1	0.1
Clerical	840	0.2	0.1
Sand Blasters	26,937	6.4	6.7
Safety Training	1,561	0.4	0.3
Extra Work	36,377	8.6	9.2
Total	423,874	100	100

Figure 28 shows the man-hour distribution of labor over the duration of the project. This again brings out the preponderance of effort put in by the welders and fitters throughout the project. Hours on assembly tend to be weighed towards the latter part of the project, as would be expected. Painting is weighed towards the second half of the project, but not specifically towards the end. Figure 29 shows the cumulative hours spent by all labor on the Morpeth project at Gulf Island Fabrication.

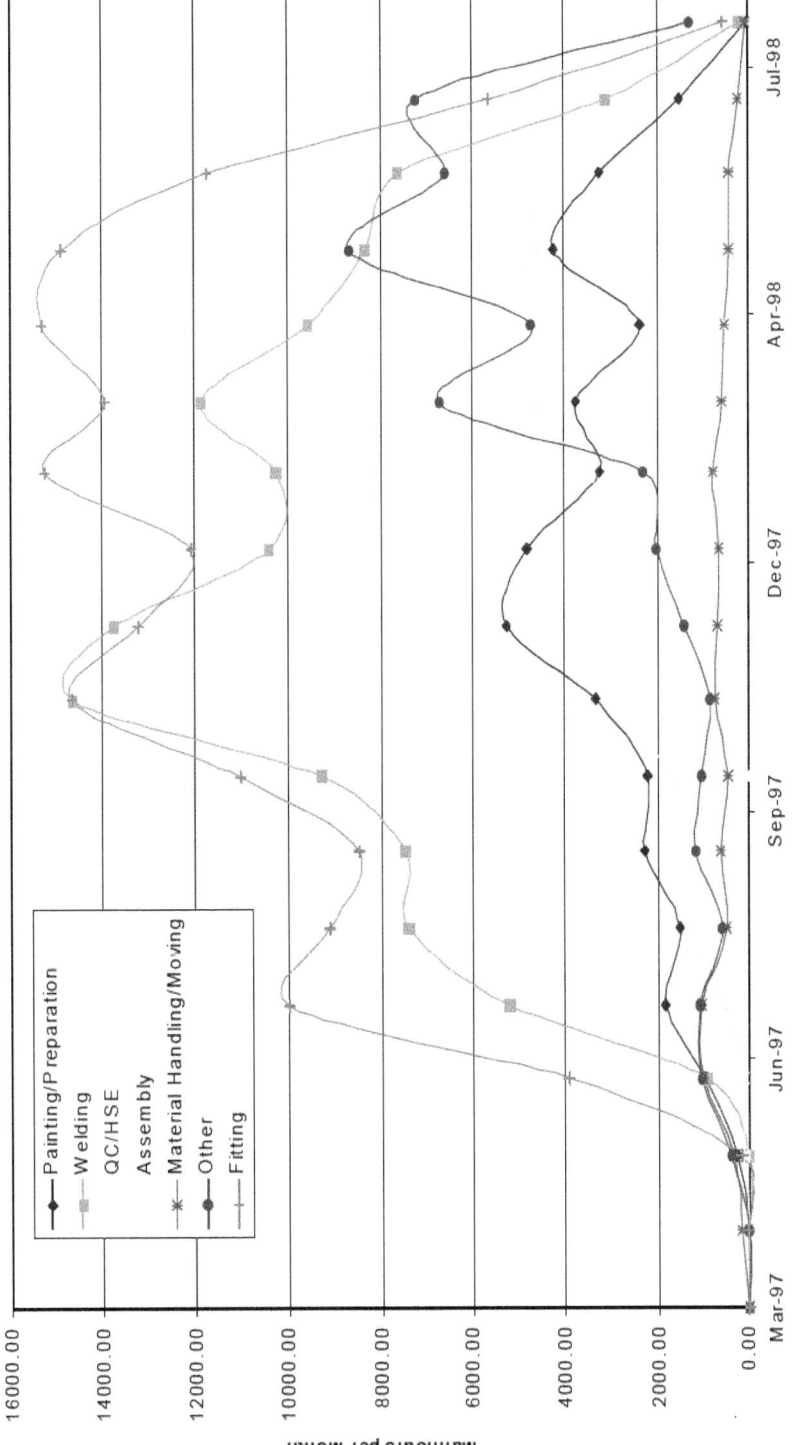

Figure 28. Man-hour Labor Distribution on Morpeth at Gulf Island Fabrication.

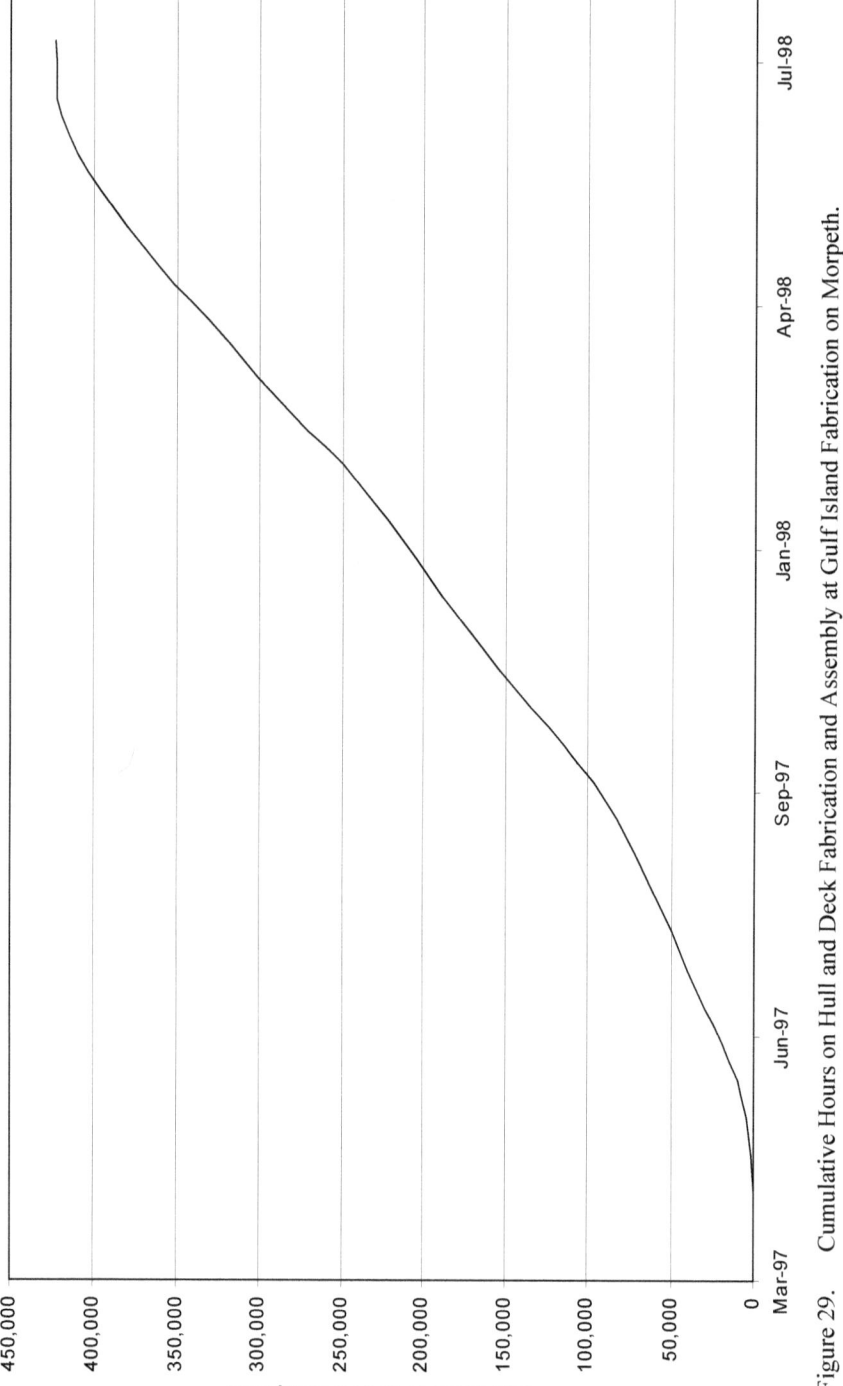

Figure 29.   Cumulative Hours on Hull and Deck Fabrication and Assembly at Gulf Island Fabrication on Morpeth.

40

Table 8 presents our estimates of the average number of persons employed for the various project tasks during the 16-month duration of the fabrication. We combined all tasks that essentially required the same type of occupations. According to those estimates, the fabrication project employed a total of 662 persons working a standard work week every month during the length of the project. This includes a total of 444 fitters and welders, 66 equipment operators, and 22 painters for those 16 months.

Table 8

Number of Full-Time Equivalent Workers

Occupation	Total Hours	FTE per Month
Welders/Fitters	15,961	25
Welders	119,895	187
Fitters	148,591	232
Technicians	1,912	3
Technicians (Qual. Assess.)	840	1
Electricians	2,600	4
Equipment Operators	42,546	66
Riggers	6,004	9
Laborers	5,621	9
Painters	13,878	22
Painters (QC)	311	0.5
Clerical	840	1
Sand Blasters	26,937	42
Safety Training	1,561	2
Extra Work	36,377	57
Total	423,874	662

Note: We estimate FTE employment by dividing the total number of hours worked by the standard work week (40 hours) and the duration of the project (16 months).

3.2. OCCUPATIONAL STRUCTURE OF THE HOUMA LABOR MARKET AREA

A key objective of this research project is an estimation of the effect of platform fabrication on the local labor market area. What is the demand for labor from this fabrication, and how is it related to the supply of labor in that local labor market area? To answer that question, we will first present a brief summary of the occupational structure in the Houma labor market area, to be followed by the impact of occupation-specific labor demand in this area that results from fabrication work for the Morpeth platform.

A major methodological problem for the estimation of the effect of labor demand on a local labor market area in 1998 is the lack of industry-specific occupational information for that year. Essentially, occupation-by-industry data are available from the U.S. Bureau of the Census every 10 years. Unfortunately, the 1990 census data are likely to have a substantial error term, yet the 2000 census data for industry and occupation will not become available until late 2003. Given these data constraints, we chose three datasets for our analysis of the effect of the Morpeth project on the Houma labor market area: (1) the 1998 Occupational Employment Statistics (OES) Survey from the Bureau of Labor Statistics of the U.S. Department of Labor for the Houma Metropolitan Statistical Area (Lafourche and Terrebonne Parishes). (2) A special tabulation of 1990 industry by occupation data (STIO) from the U.S. Bureau of the Census that was commissioned in conjunction with the Socioeconomic Database for the Gulf of Mexico Region 1930-1990 sponsored by MMS; those data are also for the Houma Metropolitan Statistical Area (Lafourche and Terrebonne Parishes). And (3) Occupational Employment Statistics from the Louisiana Department of Labor (OES-LA) for 1998 (and projections for 2008), covering Louisiana's regional labor market area No. 3 that includes Assumption, Lafourche, and Terrebonne Parishes.

Each of these three datasets has advantages and shortcomings. By presenting datasets with different advantages and disadvantages, we hope to minimize any systematic error in relating Morpeth-generated labor to the Houma labor market area. While the OES data cover 12 months of the Morpeth project in 1998, they are only for occupations and do not permit the identification of occupational data within the fabrication industry. However, since many welding skills can be transferred among various industries, we decided that these data do have informational value for the present analysis of labor demand. The 1990 STIO data have the disadvantage that they are somewhat dated, but they permit us to examine the relationship between specific occupations involved in the Morpeth project and the supply of those occupations within the two industries relevant for fabrication: Standardized Industry Code (SIC) 353 = Construction and related industries, and SIC 373 = Ship and boat building and repairing. Finally, the OES-LA data have the same advantage and disadvantage as the STIO data, but they cover a different geography (regional labor market area vs. metropolitan statistical area), and they also include employment projections to 2008 that might be useful for some policy makers who wish to view the Morpeth generated labor demand in the context of those projections. Occupational information from those three datasets are presented in Tables A1.1-A1.3 and A2.1-A2.3.

3.2.1. OES Data for Houma MSA

The 1998 OES data (see Table A1.1) showed 5,148 workers in the Houma Metropolitan Statistical Area (MSA) who were employed in the occupational categories of Welders (Occupation Code=93914), Shipfitters (89121), Riggers (85935), Painters (87402), Sheetmetal (89132), Assemblers and Fabricators (93956), and Operators (92998). The Morpeth fabrication project employed about 11 percent of workers in those occupations. (These occupations make up 88% of all workers for the Morpeth fabrication project.) Morpeth workers tended to have slightly higher hourly wages than other workers in the same occupations in the Houma MSA; thus, the Morpeth project accounted for about 15 percent of the total payroll for these occupations in the Houma MSA.

3.2.2. STIO Data for Houma MSA

The 1990 STIO data for the Houma MSA (see Table A1.2) show a total of 4,742 workers in these same occupations (Occupation Codes 579, 725, 777, 779, 783, 759, 785 and 859). The number of workers in these occupations who worked on the Morpeth project in 1998 amounts to 12 percent of that 1990 figure, which is comparable to what was shown above for the OES data.

The 1990 STIO data permit a differentiation of occupations by industry for the Houma MSA (see Table A1.2). Considering only the two industries of construction and related machinery and ship and boat building and repairing, 1,227 persons worked in the above occupations in 1990. By 1998, Morpeth's employment of 583 workers with the same occupational skills made up 48 percent of employment in the construction and ship building industries. This is an indicator of the substantial impact of Morpeth on employment in those specific occupations within the construction and ship building industries.

3.2.3. OES-LA Data for Louisiana RLMA 3

The 1998 OES-LA data cover Louisiana's regional labor market area (RLMA) No. 3, which includes Assumption, Lafourche, and Terrebonne Parishes. According to Table A2.1, there were 4,510 workers in the same occupations as specified in the section on OES data. Morpeth in 1998 accounted for 13 percent of that employment.

3.2.4. STIO for Louisiana RLMA 3

To compare the same geography with the OES-LA data, we also aggregated the STIO data to the same RLMA by adding Assumption to the Houma MSA. For the La. RLMA 3 in 1990, the STIO data show an employment level of 5817 in the occupations referenced in the STIO-HOUMA-MSA section (see Table A2.2). Morpeth's employment of personnel in the same occupations was 10 percent of that total. Considering only the two industries of construction and ship building, Morpeth's 1998 employment represents 40 percent of the corresponding 1990 employment for Louisiana's RLMA 3 (see Table A2.3).

Comparing the impact of Morpeth's labor demand on the Houma MSA and Louisiana's RLMA 3, using the three datasets as specified above, it becomes apparent that

1. Morpeth had a substantial impact on the demand for those occupations that are required for the fabrication of platforms (at least of the Morpeth type);

2. this impact is especially large within the industry of the company where the fabrication took place; and

3. there is not very much demand for those kinds of occupations in Assumption Parish, since the impact of Morpeth does not differ much between the Houma MSA and Louisiana's RLMA 3.

4. CHRONOLOGY OF FIELD DEVELOPMENT

The following section describes the processes by which a field is acquired and developed. In practice, there are many variations in the details, and probably some in the fundamentals, but this outline has been written with the intent of giving an overview of the process, especially for people unfamiliar with the offshore industry. Since this project was started, and the original report written, there have been a number of documents published that cover some of the information contained here. However, there are still sufficient gaps in the literature for this document to fill.

4.1. PRELEASE ACQUISITION

The profit potential of an oil lease is the overriding factor in determining an oil company's interest in it, whether or not they develop it themselves. In some less developed areas of the world this may mean that sufficient acreage is offered at a sufficiently low price to make a bid attractive. In the Gulf of Mexico, an attractive price is typically not enough incentive by itself. The lease area must be studied, through the development and interpretation of geologic and seismic data, to determine if economically recoverable reserves exist.

Though it is no longer a deciding factor, companies prefer that a field lies within or near an area in which they have existing infrastructure, so it can be serviced from an existing supply base and have good access to existing pipelines (particularly their own). For leases outside a company's area of interest, the magnitude of the expected reserves must be greater in order to pay for the additional expense of establishing bases and infrastructure.

Even at this early stage, companies need to consider how they would develop the field, in broad terms, were they to be successful in winning the lease and finding the expected reserves. There is little point in having a major discovery if it cannot be economically developed. One alternative to make the profit potential more attractive is to take on a lease with the intent of selling it outright or selling an interest in it, after having assessed its capability.

4.2. PARTNERS AND OPERATOR

Depending on the results of the initial assessment of the lease, partners may be taken on or encouraged to buy in. It may be that a particular area looks considerably more attractive when the existing infrastructure of a potential partner is considered. The reasons for partnering are to spread the risk, and to improve the consortium's capabilities in certain areas. It may be that one potential partner has expertise in a specific area that would be of value to a specific development option, so they may be encouraged to join in order to gain additional knowledge. Equally, a company may join a venture in part to learn how another company acts as the operator. For example, Shell had a financial interest in Morpeth and is reported to have taken an active interest in how a minor operator developed the field. This may not have been their primary purpose, but it was certainly an added benefit.

Additional partners may be taken on later in the process as the need and opportunity arises. In a limited number of cases drilling contractors have taken a working interest in lieu of payment for drilling the exploratory wells, but this has always been after the lease has been acquired. Drilling contractors have never got into the position of competing with the oil companies at the lease bid stage. Drilling contractor involvement has had limited success because they are somewhat risk averse: they like a steady income from their assets, while oil companies are inherent risk takers.

4.3. BIDS TO MINERALS MANAGEMENT SERVICE

As with any competitive bid process, bids made to the MMS for the leases attempt to keep a balance between paying a low price and winning the bids on the blocks that are important. Clearly, the value is based on all the same factors that were used to decide where to consider bidding. But there may also be specific strategic issues, such as a desire to be seen as a major deepwater operator at the forefront of technology, which can influence the magnitude of a bid. But the aim is always to get the bid for the lowest possible price.

4.4. MORE DETAILED SEISMIC

Having obtained the lease, the next step is to get a more detailed understanding of the potential reserves. Normally, unless already available from pre-lease acquisition activities, a more detailed seismic study is performed. This 3D seismic data, and its subsequent interpretation, gives the best available data on any potential hydrocarbon reservoir structures in the lease area short of actually drilling wells. Reserve estimates are made from this data though it cannot confirm the presence of hydrocarbons. Gas can be seen sometimes, but it is extremely difficult to distinguish between oil and water[16]. Fluid densities are easier to determine in shallow formations, but even in these, the level of data processing to ascertain the differences is considerable. In addition, the salt of salt domes can seriously degrade the quality of returned seismic signals.

4.5. EXPLORATORY DRILLING

No drilling can be undertaken prior to lease acquisition, but the 3D seismic results provide a good idea of where one should drill once the bid has been accepted. The cost of drilling is relatively high. A deepwater semi-submersible will cost around $200,000 per day (more for a drillship), and the consumable/transportation costs are approximately another $100,000 per day[17]. Given an exploratory well, excluding well testing or any drilling problems, may take 60 days to complete, the cost for an exploratory well will be on the order of $15 to $20 million. If significant hydrocarbon is found, then well testing may cost another $5 million, although there will be some return through sales of produced hydrocarbon.

The number of wells drilled will depend considerably on what is found. If everything appears to confirm what had been expected, then the number of exploratory wells will be minimized; but should there be surprises, then it may be necessary to drill more wells to gather additional information.

4.6. FIELD DELINEATION

Field delineation through exploratory drilling is an expensive exercise so it will tend to be minimized. If a field is relatively homogenous and can clearly be economically developed, then there is little need to determine its exact boundaries. Conversely, if the field is made up of multiple thin pay zones and complex geology, it may be necessary to drill more wells to confirm the presence of hydrocarbon in the potential pay zones. It may be impossible to access all the relevant areas by directional drilling, so determination of the field layout will significantly impact how the field is to be developed: from a central facility, or a series of subsea facilities tied back to one point.

The economics of additional exploratory drilling and field delineation are very much in dispute, and there are those who suggest that too much time is spent determining to too fine a level the field properties. In addition to the cost of more exploratory wells, the process delays production start up. The earlier the decision to develop is made, the earlier a company sees a return on its investment. It may even be

---

[16] After time, and experience with a field, it can be possible to distinguish between oil and water, but this is generally true only for fields that have had a history of seismic signatures run.

[17] Rig day rates vary considerably, depending on the capability of the drilling rig, and market demand. When this project was started in early 2000, the day rates were as quoted in the text. Since then, the rates for deepwater semi-submersibles in the Gulf of Mexico have dropped to around $50,000 per day in 2003, or approximately one-third of what they were three years ago.

economic to have two vessels working the field, one drilling and the other, at a much lower day rate, completing the wells.

4.7. WELL TESTING

All the fields included in this study performed some well testing, but not for very long. Well testing is a compromise for all parties, including the MMS. The oil company wants to get realistic data on reservoir flow rates, but does not want to deal with the produced gas. The MMS does not want the operator to flare, and hence waste, the gas. The operator wants to get some return on the well testing by flowing into a barge, but the economics are marginal, at best. The end result is that most of the wells considered in this study were flow tested for a maximum of a few days, many much less.

A well that is producing 10,000 bpd will generate $200,000 to $300,000 per day. But the cost of the semisubmersible, with all its associated costs, will be around $200,000 per day, so the margin is small. There are some deepwater drillships available that have limited onboard storage capability, and can easily be set up for either early or extended well testing. Their use may alter the economics, but given their day rate is higher than a conventional deepwater semisubmersible, it is not immediately apparent how this would work in the Gulf except for early well testing.

4.8. DECIDE TO DEVELOP

At some point a decision to develop must be made. As presented here, it is a linear process from lease acquisition to this point. In reality there is a combination of forward thinking about how to develop, and what development will entail and backward assessment of what facilities exist. Certainly it will be necessary to define the recoverable reserves, estimate the rate of recovery, and assess the expected cash flow. This must be compared to the cost of development and operations which themselves are dependent on the development option chosen.

Most of the projects included in this study decided on the type of development relatively early on by considering the various factors discussed in the following section (Factors Affecting Development Options). Depending on how these factors are evaluated a specific development option may become apparent or several will be considered. For example, a company may evaluate the advantages of a spar versus a mini-TLP for a given development, while another may decide on a specific development option and search for a suitable field to meet its demands.

It may transpire that even if a field appears to be economic, it is better to farm-out or sell the explored lease than to develop it, as was the case for Shell on Morpeth when they sold it to British Borneo. Sometimes a smaller company can develop a field more economically than a large one.

4.9. FACTORS AFFECTING DEVELOPMENT OPTIONS

There is a long list of reasons why one particular development option is chosen over another, and the major ones are discussed in the following section. Generally there is a strong logic behind why a particular route is taken, but it is not uncommon for circumstances to dictate that a company moves forward with a particular development option before they have had time to fully assess all the options. Consequently, the development decision becomes a best compromise at the time.

The development decision is typically an iterative process as various factors are considered and choices evaluated. The layout of this report suggests a linear process of field discovery, decision to develop, choice of development option, development, etc. While there is a clear linear component to the process, as with any complex problem, it is not always reasonable to move forward without consideration of the steps ahead: it may be reasonable to decide to look for oil in ultra-deepwater, but without development options, one is not likely to start delineating the field. Without this process of thinking ahead, one can arrive at a situation where there has been so much commitment to a project that it is unstoppable, even though it may be economically dubious.

Oil companies will often use consultants to help them assess the various development options. As an example, Amerada Hess spent about $2 to $3 million on preliminary engineering to assess the possible options for the Baldpate development. These studies included floating production options, TLP, and the compliant tower. For a number of reasons they relatively quickly decided that the tower was the way forward, but still had to study the type of tower, and the various options. While these studies tend to be at a high level, they need to consider all aspects in order to be beneficial. One development option may appear to be the best, but if it means the use of, say, subsea wellhead, then well intervention techniques and costs must be included.

4.9.1. Water Depth

Generally the first factor considered when evaluating development options is the water depth at the proposed site. Not only does this affect the overall cost of development, but it also limits the development options. In shallow water (less than 200 feet) there are many fixed structure options including converted jack-up, caissons, lean-to-well-protectors, other minimal structures, and conventional jackets. Subsea development is probably feasible, but would not normally be considered because of the necessity to either bury the wellhead, or install some trawl protection so that it would not snag fishing nets.

As the water depth increases, some of the minimal platforms become infeasible, but subsea becomes a possibility for individual wells. These can then be tied together and produced to a shallow water hub platform for processing. There is still a large array of minimal platforms designed for intermediate water depths, but there is a limit to the number of wells and process equipment they can support. Beyond 500 feet water depth the number of minimal platforms available sharply decreases. A conventional jacket structure becomes more expensive as the size must increase in order to withstand the higher environmental loads; consequently they tend to be economic only if they are producing a large number of wells.

Beyond 500 feet water depth it is possible to use converted semi-submersible drilling units. The first of these was installed in the North Sea in 260 feet of water, but they have been used in over 2,000 feet water depth in the Gulf of Mexico, and over 3,000 feet offshore Brazil.

It is at around 1,000 feet water depth that the various deepwater options will be considered: compliant tower, spar, TLP, FPSO, etc. There are water depth limits to the compliant tower, and TLPs are not well suited to the shallower end of the deepwater spectrum. The limits of each option are discussed in greater detail in the section on types of structure.

4.9.2. Size of Field and Number of Wells

The number of wells, and how they will be drilled, has a major influence on the type of installation chosen. Each well takes up a certain amount of physical space on the platform, so the more wells, the larger the platform has to be. Also, if the wells are to have dry trees, then the structure needs to be able to support all of the additional weight. If the field is highly fragmented, then subsea development may be the best option since it may be difficult to drill all the needed wells from the central facility. Conversely, if the wells can all be clustered, then a single central structure will offer the advantage of being able to complete all the wells using a rig package rather than having to use a deepwater semisubmersible. The difference in price will be well in excess of $100,000 per day.

4.9.3. Expected Production Rate

A high production rate will necessitate larger separators and other processing equipment leading to higher deck load. In addition the export risers will need to be larger, as will all the onboard piping. The development option chosen would have to accommodate both the space for the equipment and its weight. It would be possible to undersize the equipment if the high production rate was expected for a short time only, but the economics would have to be carefully assessed.

4.9.4. Type of Crude

Subsea developments are generally best suited to wells with low workover/intervention requirements and with good flow assurance (i.e., wells that will not get fouled with paraffins, etc.). Though these limitations can be offset with chemicals and the application of other technologies, it may not be economic or practical to do so. These considerations may push the development option in a different direction.

4.9.5. Quantity of Gas

If a field has very large quantities of gas, particularly at high pressure, then the size of the processing equipment will increase. As with the impact of high production rates and a large number of wells, some of the smaller development options may not be reasonable in this case if they cannot support the deck load of the larger structures.

4.9.6. Financial Risk

The speed with which any option can start bringing a return on investment is an important consideration in any development decision. Look at these examples:

- The economics might dictate that a quick development via a subsea tie-back to an adjacent structure may be attractive if the short time to first oil and the low capital costs offset the higher operating expenses.

- A smaller company may wish to install a less costly structure to quickly develop known reserves, without the additional expense of having to accurately delineate the field. Should later drilling show that the field is larger than expected, additional tie-backs can be installed. The downside to this approach is that the platform may not be installed in the best place, and additional expense may be required to either move it or use other drilling options. A major oil company may be in the position to fund far more detailed assessments of the field, but this may make the development less economically viable.

4.9.7. Politics

Government, corporate and industry politics may all play a role in influencing a development decision. Governments can affect how a field is developed through local content requirements, restrictions on particular development options, health, safety and environment regulations, etc. Corporate politics may arise through the influence of corporate perceptions that specific development options are higher risk than others. Additionally, past experience with specific contractors may lead a development team to favor a specific development option, not necessarily because it is the best option, but because of a trust in that contractor to produce a quality product on time and budget.

4.9.8. Local Infrastructure

The presence and ownership of local infrastructure influences the ability to economically export the produced hydrocarbons. The viability of a new facility can be compromised if sufficient infrastructure is not available. As an example, subsea completion options may not be feasible (because of maintenance costs associated with cleaning lines fouled with paraffin and hydrate deposits) if pipelines are longer than about 20 miles for oil and 70 miles for gas[18]. Conversely, it may be that the installation of infrastructure will allow adjacent fields to become economically viable which can make up for the added expense either through direct development of those fields or through fees paid by other operators to process their crude on your facility. Rates vary depending on the market, type of crude, location, etc., but would likely be in the range of approximately $2.50 per barrel of oil, and $0.50 per 1,000 cubic feet of gas.

4.9.9. Length of Field Life

Field life normally only affects the decommissioning considerations, since some development options can be reused at other fields. As an example, one of the reasons for choosing a spar for the Neptune development was that the structure would need to be moved to an adjacent field in order to continue production. This would be practically impossible with a fixed base structure. A TLP could be moved, but there would be considerable expense associated with obtaining new tendons, and installing new piles. A spar moored using conventional drag-embedment anchors can be relocated a short distance (e.g., about

---

[18] These estimates are based on discussions with industry representatives as well as data in the May 2002 edition of *Offshore* magazine.

100 miles) with relative ease (although longer distances would involve considerable complications because it must be towed vertically at slow speeds).

4.9.10. Possible Re-Use of Platform as a Hub

When the wells associated with an installation have paid out, a decision needs to be made regarding what to do with the structure. Decommissioning is discussed below, but an alternative is to use the facility as a "hub" for other fields with operating wells. A hub facility may continue to produce from other wells that have been tied back into it, act as a gathering point for hydrocarbons for piping to shore, or act as a maintenance point for pigging the pipelines. As a hub, the installation can become an integral part of the OCS infrastructure, with an extended life generating cash for the operator through fees for processing, flow-through, and maintenance.

4.9.11. Need for Workover

All wells need maintenance that requires entry into the well (intervention). Some well intervention can be accomplished using a coiled tubing unit; other wells require the tubing to be pulled in order to develop a new or different pay zone. If the facility has drilling equipment on board, or the ability to install a rig package, then the cost of these well interventions is relatively low. Subsea developments are somewhat more complicated because some type of vessel, such as a conventional deepwater drilling unit, is needed for any required well intervention. Since these vessels can cost around $250,000 per day, it is an expensive option. There are well intervention vessels that are much less expensive than drilling units, but their capabilities are limited (e.g., it is unlikely that they would be capable of re-completing a well). Consequently, there is a trade-off between capital expenditure, operating expenditure, and potential downtime, all of which need to be considered when making a development option choice.

4.9.12. Decommissioning Costs and Technology

Decommissioning is becoming increasingly important. In the early 1980s little consideration was given to what should be done with the old platforms in the Gulf, and around the world, when they reached the end of their useful life. By the early 1990's it had become common to reuse shallow water platforms (i.e., removing them from site, refurbishing them, and then re-installing them at new locations), some even being transported overseas to new fields. In addition, the rigs-to-reefs program became well established.

However, as an issue of importance to the development team, decommissioning was not given much weight until attention was brought to the issue by the Brent Spar in the North Sea. Shell had decided to sink the old platform in the North Atlantic, and had obtained permission to do so from the British Government. They then ran into problems with Greenpeace, leading to public outcry and boycotting of Shell gas stations around Europe. This raised the issue from one of technical and economic considerations to one of public policy. While still not as important a consideration in the U.S. as in Europe, decommissioning is now a serious issue for any development decision.

A number of companies approached concerning this study have indicated that it is not exactly clear what will be required of them when the time comes to decommission their offshore facilities in the Gulf of Mexico. They assume that all the wells will need to be plugged and abandoned, but are not sure of the requirements for the remaining structure. Floating units (TLP's, spars, semisubmersible based systems, etc.) are relatively easily decommissioned down to the subsea equipment. Clearing all the equipment off the seabed would be complicated and expensive, but probably not outside present technology.

The difficulty comes with the bottom-founded structures (i.e., jackets and compliant towers in the Gulf, and including gravity based structures in other areas of the world). In shallow water the piles can be cut, and the jackets lifted onto a barge for reuse or shore-based dismantling. In deepwater it would be possible to sever the base using explosives and topple them in place, but recovering the structure would be extremely difficult. Structure recovery systems are being proposed for use in the North Sea, but, though they must lift heavy structures, they do not have to operate in such deep water or recover such tall, and often skinny structures as in the Gulf.

Based on responses from industry representatives, the whole area of decommissioning has not been fully addressed by many of the companies involved in the Gulf OCS. There is uncertainty as to what will be required, and what is feasible, and, consequently, the issue is not being fully incorporated into the development decision process. There have been attempts to organize effective education on these issues but the required knowledge has not necessarily filtered down to the project level at the time development options are considered. The issue is not one of lack of regulations, but a need for more open discussions as there have been in other areas of the world.

4.10. DEVELOPMENT OPTIONS

4.10.1. Conventional Jacket Based Structures

The conventional jacket based offshore structure is what most people think of when they think of an offshore platform. Jackets have evolved over the years from the early platforms built on location offshore to the modern engineered structures of today, but they are still, in many respects, the same as they were over forty years ago -- fixed steel structures constructed of tubular members welded together and founded on driven steel piles.

Some modifications to the basic concept have come about. In the middle 1970's a two-piece jacket was installed in the Santa Barbara Channel off California. And in 1980, Cognac, a three-piece jacket, was installed in the Gulf of Mexico. Both of these were attempts to extend what is basically a shallow water technology into deeper water depths. Later jackets, such as Pompano and Virgo, were installed in deep water in a single section, but these represent the water depth limit in practical and economic terms for jacket technologies at present.

Jacket structures are normally installed in two stages: first the jacket is piled to the seabed, then a deck structure, prefitted with all the process equipment and accommodation, is lifted atop and welded in place.

4.10.1.1. Limitations

Jacket structures are limited to specific water depths. This is not necessarily because one cannot design a jacket for deeper water, but because the fabrication, transportation, and installation become impractical, and their weight makes them uneconomic. In the Gulf of Mexico, approximately 1,500 feet water depth is commonly considered the limit, although this would likely be significantly less in harsh environments (e.g., North Sea and East Canada) and possibly a little more in benign areas such as West Africa.

4.10.1.2. Advantages

The main advantage of a jacket type structure is that based on the long experience with such facilities in the Gulf of Mexico, in shallow enough water depths (i.e., less than about 350 feet) one gets a stable platform that is not too sensitive to topsides weight for a well understood price. Other advantages include

- Construction Experience. Jacket construction is relatively simple and well understood around the Gulf Coast, with many yards having extensive experience. Hence the potential for cost overruns is very much reduced. This is extremely important on most projects. (In the case of shallow water platforms it is possible to get lump sum fixed price bids for an installed facility, with little chance of significant change orders increasing the cost.)

- Short Transportation. This expensive and high-risk task is minimized since jackets are normally built close to the installation site.

- Installation Experience. Whether lifting or launching, jacket installation techniques are well established; hence the risks are better known and can be better controlled.

- High Production Capacity. If a large number of wells and export risers are needed to develop a field, the increase in weight and other loads can be designed within a fairly broad range.

- Expansion Capability. As with the ability to accommodate a fairly large production capacity, if it transpires that additional processing capacity is required at a later date, it is likely that simple modifications will allow the addition of more process equipment, conductors, risers, etc.

- Deck Installation. The deck can simply be lifted into place with few hook up problems.

- Drilling Flexibility. The structure can normally be designed for the installation of a "rig package" to complete the wells perform workovers. In shallower water depths (up to approximately 350 feet) it may be possible to use a jack-up for workover, which could considerably reduce costs.

- Low Tolerances. The deck and jacket can adjust to reasonable lack-of-fit (compared to other options), so tolerances do not have to be tight and are within the capability of many yards.

- Robust Structures. Jacket structures are relatively robust and can withstand considerable damage (through collision, overload, etc.) without collapsing.

- Hub Capabilities. Jackets are ideally suited for extended use as a processing hub after the platforms associated wells have dried up. Maintenance costs are relatively low as long as corrosion is kept under control and large topsides payloads can usually be accommodated.

- Inspection Ease. Experience has shown where underwater damage is most likely to occur, so periodic inspection is simplified.

- Export Pipelines. The cost of export pipelines is significantly lower than on a floating platform that uses, for example, steel catenary export risers.

4.10.1.3. Disadvantages

The greatest disadvantage of a conventional jacket is the limited water depth in which it can be installed. Other issues include

- Water Depth. At greater water depths, jacket costs and weight are high for the supported topsides as compared to other options.

- Repair Costs. While jackets can withstand considerable damage without collapsing, they are very expensive to repair. Underwater repairs are expensive (e.g., some require special chambers to allow dry welding) and dangerous, and the structure cannot be removed from location and taken to a yard for repairs.

- Decommissioning. Jackets are expensive to decommission and remove from location once their useful life has been reached.

4.10.1.4. Fabrication

The jacket part of the platform, so called because it surrounds the well conductors, involves relatively simple construction. Jackets are fabricated from tubes forming a braced structure of typically 4, 6, or 8 legs. Each face is normally fabricated flat on the ground and then "rolled up" into the upright position, with larger jackets fabricated on their sides. The intermediate bracing is then welded into place. The main skills and equipment required are the equipment to cut the tubular intersections, and welders to weld the individual tubes together. While some higher strength steel may be used, most of the structure can be built using standard "mild" steel. This keeps the cost of the steel down, but also means that welders do not have to be so highly qualified. Welding high strength steel requires extremely good quality control, and the welding rods need to be kept in an oven until ready for use in order to avoid "hydrogen embrittlement" which can cause the welds to crack.

Because of the relatively simple construction, and potential risks associated with transportation, jackets are normally fabricated in the same general area were they are to be installed. There are some exceptions (frequently West Africa jackets are built in the U.S. or South America, and some of the large

West Coast jackets were built in Japan) but they do not apply to the Gulf of Mexico. There are many small yards that will fabricate shallow water jackets, but there are a limited number of yards that can handle jackets large enough for deep water. As an example, the base section of Cognac was built in Morgan City, Louisiana. Photographs of that being transported through the bayous show how little clearance there was on each side. Water depth for the tugs and barges can also be an issue. Also, rolling up the sides of a large jacket needs plenty of crane capacity, and adequate space for a large jacket lying on its side (see Figure 30).

Figure 30. Pompano Jacket at Harbor Island Yard during Side Roll-Up
(Courtesy of J. Ray McDermott).

The platform deck structure (the part of the structure that starts approximately 20 feet above the water line) is normally fabricated and assembled in a yard under a different contract than the jacket. While there is a significant structural component to deck fabrication, there is also a very significant assembly component. It is the responsibility of the deck fabricator to assemble and install all the modules that will have been fabricated by other vendors. Such modules would include the accommodation, power supply, pump skids, separator modules, etc. that are used for the operations of the facility. This could involve modules from over 50 major vendors. The structural aspects of the deck will be highly dependent on the type of support structure (jacket, TLP, etc.) but the assembly aspect will be comparable regardless of platform type. Deck fabrication can lead to schedule bottlenecks because some components and modules require significant lead time (some in excess of a year).

4.10.1.5. Load-out, Transportation, Installation, and Piling

As stated above, most large jackets are fabricated on their side. Once they are completed, they need to be loaded onto a transport barge and towed to site. This is normally achieved by skidding the jacket along a "skid rail" onto the transport barge. The barge will be brought alongside the fabrication yard and aligned with the skid rails, both vertically and laterally. The jacket is then pulled onto the barge with a combination of winches and hydraulic rams. Normally, once the jacket has started to move, the winches are sufficient to keep it moving. As the jacket starts to move onto the barge, ballast has to be adjusted in order to keep the overall deflections of jacket and barge within reasonable limits as determined by analyses. Alternatively, if the jacket is small enough and the crane capacity great enough, a jacket may be lifted onto the barge.

Once the jacket is loaded onto the barge it is "seafastened" to the barge to prevent it from sliding or rolling off during transportation. For short tows, as would be normal in the Gulf of Mexico, these seafastenings are designed assuming a relatively short exposure to severe weather. For jackets built in remote locations and requiring longer, open ocean tows, the design of the seafastenings can be highly complex. Figure 31 shows the Shell Bullwinkle jacket just prior to launch.

Figure 31. Shell Bullwinkle Jacket Just Prior to Launch (Courtesy of Shell Exploration and Production Co.).

Transportation is frequently one of the highest risk operations undertaken for an offshore structure (see the section on Transportation). The fact that most Gulf of Mexico jackets are built on the Gulf Coast significantly reduces this risk. Having loaded the jacket onto the barge, and seafastened it, it is ready to be towed to site. A jacket won't be loaded onto the barge until the site is ready to receive it because a jacket on a barge is in a vulnerable condition even if it has not left the yard. Because of its size, it is extremely difficult to effectively moor a jacket-loaded barge in high winds. If a hurricane were to strike, it is very exposed, and salvaging a jacket off a grounded or damaged barge, once the storm surge has abated is not simple.

The barge is then towed out to the site, and, if all is ready, the seafastenings will be cut. The barge is then ballasted down at the stern until the jacket launches itself (see Figure 32). Earlier engineering analyses will have ensured that the jacket has sufficient buoyancy to float, that it will not dive too deep and hit the seafloor, and that all the members are sufficiently strong not to collapse under the hydrostatic pressure. Once the jacket has stabilized in the water it will be "up-ended" into the final vertical orientation by flooding certain sections, positioned accurately on the design location, rotated to the correct alignment, and ballasted onto the seabed. The jacket is now relatively safe, as long as it is not exposed to any large waves, which could tip it over before the piles are driven.

Figure 32. Bullwinkle Jacket during Launch (Courtesy of Shell Exploration and Production Co.).

On shallow water jackets the piles are normally driven through the center of the individual legs, and then welded off above the waterline. On larger jackets this is uneconomic, so the piles are driven, underwater, through pile sleeves that are located around the base of the jacket. By using an underwater hammer, one does not have all the extra pile steel reaching from the seabed up to the surface. After piling, the deck structure is transported out to the jacket, lifted onto the jacket, and welded in place (see Figure 33 and Figure 34). Proper planning and execution is critical to keep the offshore work to an absolute minimum in order to reduce costs.

Figure 33. Jacket Deck Arriving on a Barge.

Figure 34. Lifting a Deck onto Jacket with Two Cranes on
One Derrick Barge.

4.10.2. Compliant Tower

A compliant tower uses many of the same features of a conventional jacket, steel tubular members, welded frame construction, etc. However, rather than remaining rigid in the face of environmental forces (wind and waves), a compliant tower is built to be flexible, absorbing the energy of the environment by deflecting. There are a number of different options for compliant towers. The main distinction is between guyed (as in Exxon Lena) and free standing, as in Baldpate and Petronius, but there are variations within the freestanding design as well.

4.10.2.1. Limitations

The maximum water depth for compliant towers is generally accepted to be approximately 3,000 feet, but there is also a minimum (roughly 1,000 feet), below which it is difficult to get a structure that has a long enough natural period to achieve compliance. There have been relatively shallow water equivalents to the compliant tower (e.g., the Elf Oscillating Tower that was installed in the early 1970's) but they are likely to be of very limited application.

4.10.2.2. Advantages

The main advantage of a compliant tower is that it takes relatively conventional jacket structure technology and construction techniques and, through careful modification, applies it to deepwater. For this reason many of the advantages of jacket structures apply to compliant towers

- Deep Water Capable. Compliant towers extend the water depth capability of jacket type construction to approximately 3,000 feet water depth.

54

- Lower Cost. Relative to other deep water options, compliant towers offer an inexpensive method of developing the shallower end of the deepwater spectrum (1,000 to 3,000 feet).

- Construction Experience. Construction of most of the tower is similar to that used for jackets, is relatively simple, and well understood around the Gulf Coast. Hence there are many yards that have the fabrication capability, assuming sufficient space, even if they lack the actual compliant tower fabrication experience.

- Short Transportation. This expensive, high-risk task is short since towers can be economically fabricated on the Gulf Coast.

- Installation Experience. Launch installation is well proven and established technology, hence the risks are better known and should be controllable. There is a slight increase in risk over a jacket because the compliant tower is narrower and more flexible.

- Deck Installation. As with conventional jackets, the deck can be simply lifted into place with few hookup problems.

- Drilling Flexibility. The structure can normally be easily designed to support the installation of a "rig package" to complete the wells, and for workover.

- Low Tolerances. The deck and jacket can adjust to reasonable lack-of-fit; hence construction tolerances do not have to be extremely tight.

- Robust. The structure is flexible enough to be able to absorb significant collision energy without collapsing, as long as the colliding vessel is moving slowly (see disadvantages below).

- Export Pipelines. The cost of export pipelines is significantly lower than on a floating platform that uses, for example, steel catenary export risers.

4.10.2.3. Disadvantages

The disadvantages of a compliant tower include

- Production Limits (size and weight). Because the structure depends on maintaining a specific range of dynamic characteristics, the size and weight of the deck are limited which leads to limits on production equipment and capacity. This also limits future expansion so if field flow characteristics have been underestimated during design it may be difficult to find the space or weight capacity to expand the facilities.

- Production Limits (space). The relatively small plan area of the structure limits the number of wells that can be produced through the conductor framing, and load capacity limits the number and size of remote tie-ins and export risers.

- Impact Vulnerable. While the structure is capable of absorbing large quantities of energy at low speeds, the slow response time means that higher speed impacts could cause considerable damage.

- Repair Costs. As with jackets, underwater repairs are expensive (e.g., some require special chambers to allow dry welding) and dangerous, and the structure cannot be removed from location and taken to a yard for repairs.

- Decommissioning. Towers are expensive to decommission and remove from location once their useful life has been reached.

4.10.2.4. Fabrication

The details of fabrication will be different than those for a conventional jacket, but the overall scheme will be very similar – a compliant tower looks like a very tall slender jacket. The tower structure may be built in one or more parts (e.g., Baldpate comprised a lower "jacket base section" and an upper "jacket tower section") and these parts may be built in different fabrication yards (as was the case with the Baldpate tower).

The deck section is very similar to that of a conventional jacket, albeit somewhat smaller.

4.10.2.5. Load-out, Transportation, Installation, and Piling

The various installation phases are similar to those of a conventional jacket, with a few changes. On a guyed compliant tower, a derrick barge will normally install the moorings prior to tower arrival. Once the tower is installed, the moorings will be pulled in to the tower and connected. The tower portion of the process proceeds much as for a conventional jacket with the pieces loaded onto a barge, towed to site and launched, upended and lowered into place.

The Baldpate tower, which is freestanding, was installed in two major parts, the jacket base section (JBS) and the jacket tower section (JTS). The JBS was lowered over two docking piles that ensured the correct location (within ± 2 ½ inches of location relative to center well) onto four leveling piles that ensured the JBS was sufficiently level (within 1 degree). The JBS was then piled into place. Next, the JTS was towed out, lowered and locked to the JBS. This installation procedure minimized the exposure of an un-piled structure to damage due to inclement weather. The JBS was deep enough that had a storm arisen during installation it would have been relatively safe from wave action.

There were some differences between the launch of the JTS and a conventional jacket, but they involved technicalities of overhang, stability, floating level, etc., not methodology.

Deck installation was in a single lift, as for many other offshore structures.

4.10.3. Tension-Leg Platform (TLP)

Unlike the previously discussed options (jackets and towers) that are pile founded, large steel frames made of tubular members, a TLP (see Figure 35) is a watertight, buoyant hull that floats at the surface and is connected to the seafloor via tendons, or "tension legs," that have been attached to driven piles. The topsides facilities sit atop this hull, subject only to slight horizontal movements caused by wind, waves and currents, and operate much like conventional platform structures. A TLP hull usually consists of four columns up to 100 feet in diameter connected by pontoons around the perimeter.

Figure 35. Ursa TLP after Installation of Deck at Curacao (Courtesy of Shell Exploration and Production Co.).

4.10.3.1. Limitations

The TLP concept works by keeping the tendons in tension at all times. In other words, the buoyant force of the hull must always exceed the forces acting to compress the tendons: wind, wave, tide, ballast water, riser load, CG tolerance, and payload effects. The TLP design restricts operations to maintain the minimum tension limit state, and there is little ability to increasing payload capacity. In short, the TLP is a very weight sensitive structure. The practical TLP water depth ranges from 1,000 feet to 5,000 feet.

4.10.3.2. Advantages

The main advantage of a TLP is that the structure can operate in deeper water depths than conventional jackets.

- Construction Ease. Construction is relatively simple, and the engineering is well understood around the Gulf Coast, with many yards having extensive experience. Hence the potential for cost overruns is very much reduced.

- Wide Footprint. Unlike some other development options, a TLP has a large internal space in which to run risers to the topsides because support columns are moved to the perimeter.

- Mobility. The hull and topsides can be towed to a new location though the tendons cannot be reused.

- Dry Trees. Because of their motion characteristics, TLP's can use dry trees, as opposed to subsea wells, for well completions.

4.10.3.3. Disadvantages

The greatest disadvantage of a TLP is the limited water depth in which it can be installed compared to other floating options. Other issues include

- Hull Cost. Because of its size and complexity, a TLP hull is significantly more expensive than a mini-TLP or a spar.

- Foundation. The seafloor piles are more complex than that of other offshore mooring systems.

- Riser Cost. Compared to jackets and towers using traditional riser technology, the steel catenary export risers necessary for a TLP are expensive.

- Tendon Costs. The TLP tendons are relatively unique items, which makes them expensive. And they are designed only for the depth at original location so a relocated TLP will require new tendons.

4.10.3.4. Fabrication

The TLP fabrication consists of separate hull and topsides construction, often at different locations. The hull is built from four upright airtight cylinders (columns), up to 100 feet. in diameter, with tendon guides at the base corners. These columns are connected by pontoons at their base. Fairly standard steel plate construction methods common to shipbuilding are used.

The tendons are typically 24 inches or more in diameter and comprise 40 percent or more of the hull and mooring costs. In conjunction with the tendons there may also be a subsea template fabrication for the foundation and for drilling. Foundation templates would include guides for the driving of piles and attachments for the tendons.

Topsides construction is typical of that used for conventional jackets and compliant towers, although will often be installed in components on larger TLP's (see Figure 36).

Figure 36. Deck Installation on Ursa (Courtesy of Shell Exploration and Production).

4.10.3.5. Load-out, Transportation, Installation, and Piling

If templates are used for either drilling or foundation, these will be constructed onshore, loaded onto a barge via a crane and towed to the installation site. Depending on the template size, either a MODU or heavy lift vessel will be required to lift and lower the templates in place. For foundation templates, piles will be driven using an underwater hammer to secure the foundation. An alternative to driving the piles is to drill, install and grout the piles in place. This will depend on the pile strength needed, the soil conditions and the available equipment.

If the hull has been constructed near the installation site, it can be towed from the construction yard to the location. However, if a longer distance is required (e.g., a TLP hull constructed in Italy) would normally be transported "dry" using a heavy lift vessel or large barge (see Figure 37).

Figure 37. Ursa TLP Dry Towed from Italy (Courtesy of Shell Exploration and Production).

If the topsides are to be installed before towing the completed platform to site, this will be completed at a shore-based facility with adequate lifting capacity. Figure 38 shows a wet tow of Ursa once the topside had been installed. Otherwise, both the topsides and hull will be towed separately to the installation site and mated on location. Factors affecting this decision are construction locations of the hull and topsides, available equipment for towing to site and installing the platform, and budget and time restraints.

Generally, at least some of the tendons will have been attached to the template or piles prior to the hull arrival. Those pre-installed tendons will then be attached to the hull prior to installing and attaching the remaining tendons, if any.

Figure 38. Wet Tow of Ursa from Curacao to Site (Courtesy of Shell Exploration and Production Co.).

4.10.4. Mini-TLP

There are alternatives to the typical TLP design, for instance the MOSES design (minimum offshore surface equipment structure), that are known as mini-TLP's. These alternatives are tension leg platforms, but they differ from the larger TLP's by hull configuration and they have greater weight limitations. A mini-TLP (see Figure 39 and Figure 40) has similar production capacity to a spar, but due to equipment constraints, less than a full-sized TLP. The practical mini-TLP water depth ranges from 1,000 feet to 5,000 feet.

Figure 39. El Paso Prince TLP (Courtesy of MODEC
Int. LLC).

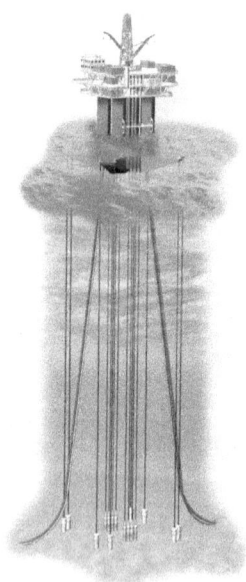

Figure 40. Anadarko Operated Marco Polo TLP Owned
by El Paso & Caldive (Courtesy of MODEC
Int. LLC).

4.10.4.1. Limitations

The main limitation of the mini-TLP is in the total load it is able to support. The mini-TLP cannot hold as much production and drilling equipment as a spar or a full-size TLP.

4.10.4.2. Advantages

The main advantage of a mini-TLP, just like the full-size TLP, is that the structure can operate in deeper water depths than conventional jackets. Additionally,

- Construction Ease. The construction is relatively simple, and the engineering is well understood around the Gulf Coast, with many yards having extensive experience.

- Cost. The mini-TLP hull is a relatively inexpensive option compared to a spar or a full-size TLP.

- Arrangement. Risers run along the external edge of the hull, allowing for greater capacity for production and subsea risers.

- Dry Trees. Because of their motion characteristics, mini-TLP's can use dry trees, as opposed to subsea wells, for well completions.

4.10.4.3. Disadvantages

Unlike a Spar, a mini-TLP's topsides and hull must be separated before it can be moved to a new location. In addition,

- Tendon Costs. The seafloor piles and the tendon system are more expensive than a Spar's mooring system.

- Mobility. Though it can be moved to a new location (if the hull and topsides are separated) its tendons are designed for a single water depth and cannot be reused.

- Drilling Capability. Though mini-TLP's can and do incorporate workover drilling capability, full drilling capability is generally not suited to the lower weight capability of these systems.

4.10.4.4. Fabrication

Like a full-size TLP or a spar, mini-TLP fabrication consists of separate hull and topsides construction, often at different locations. The hull is built in quadrants that form a mono-column, leading to a submerged base. The base consists of 3 or 4 watertight arms, extending from the base of the mono-column, forming a "Y" or a cross. These arms provide stability and are used as the connection point for the tendons. The main column of a mini-TLP can measure up to 100 feet in diameter and 360 feet in length, and the tendons may be up to 24 inches in diameter. In conjunction with the tendons there may also be a subsea template fabrication for the foundation. Foundation templates would include guides for the driving of piles and attachments for the tendons.

Like the other deepwater structures, a mini-TLP employs separately built topsides, containing multiple decks. These decks are built in stages, with separate modules or "skids," blocks of production equipment, control facilities, crew accommodations, etc. Once all of these blocks are built, they are brought to a common location and placed upon the decks according to function.

4.10.4.5. Load-out, Transportation, Installation, and Piling

Similar to the full-size TLP, templates may be used for either drilling or foundation and are typically installed first. Depending on the distance between the construction site and the installation site, the hull will be transported dry (on a heavy lift vessel) or wet using tugs (see Figure 41). The topsides will be transported using a heavy lift vessel (unlike a full-size TLP, the option to install the topsides on the hull prior to towing to the site is not available for the mini-TLP).

61

Figure 41. Morpeth Hull Transportation to Site (Courtesy of Atlantia Offshore Ltd.).

Generally, at least some of the tendons will have been attached to the template or piles prior to the hull arrival. Those pre-installed tendons will then be attached to the hull prior to installing and attaching the remaining tendons, if any. Once all the tendons have been secured, the topsides can be lifted in place (see Figure 42).

Figure 42. Lifting Deck of Morpeth into Place (Courtesy of Atlantia Offshore Ltd.).

4.10.5. Spar

As with most other deepwater options, a spar is a floating system. Similar to the TLP and mini-TLP designs, a spar consists of a watertight, buoyant hull supporting the production topsides. However, a spar hull is cylindrical, like an upright tube or buoy, connected to the seafloor via heavy, low-tensioned, spread mooring lines that radiate from the submerged section of the hull (see Figure 43). There are some variations to the basic hull design (e.g., a truss-spar with a lower truss section replacing part of the cylindrical hull minimizing the effects of "loop" currents) but the overall concept remains the same (see Figure 44).

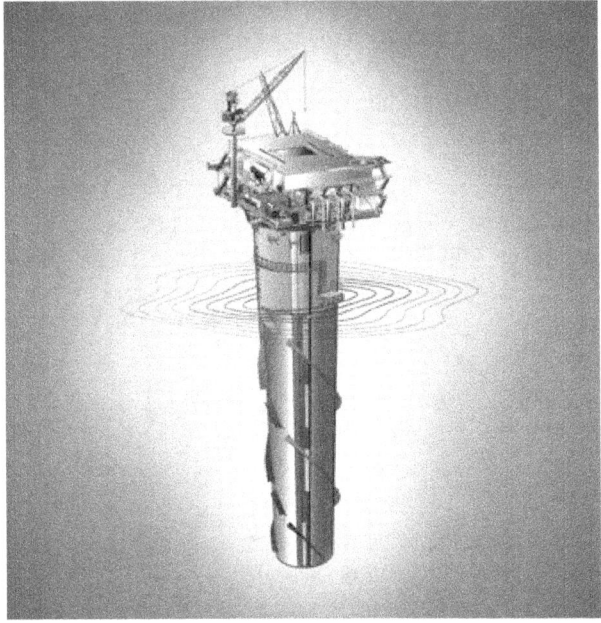

Figure 43. Neptune Spar (Courtesy of Kerr-McGee Oil and Gas Corp.).

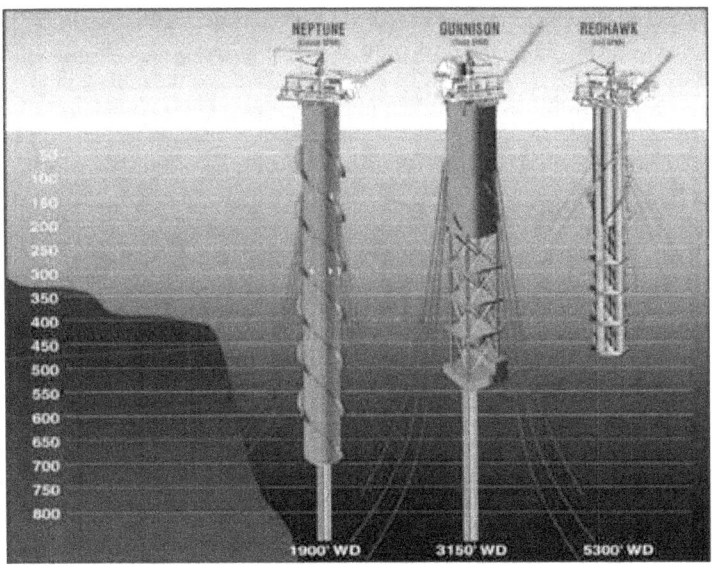

Figure 44. Three Spar Configurations as Used by Kerr-McGee (Courtesy of Kerr-McGee Oil and Gas Corp.).

4.10.5.1. Limitations

As with most of the floating development options, strict weight limitations exist. Because the spar hull is long and narrow, and uses buoyancy cans for riser tensioning, there is a limited centerwell space for risers. The spar also has less equipment capacity than a full-size TLP. Spars can be installed in a great range of water depths, up to 10,000 feet.

4.10.5.2. Advantages

The greatest advantage of the spar is its range of applicable water depths, which exceed those of most other deepwater development options. Other advantages include

- Production Capacity. The spar has greater equipment and production capacity than a mini-TLP.

- Cost. A spar is generally less expensive than a full-size TLP.

- Mobility. A spar can be moved in an upright tow position up to approximately 100 miles to a new location and the mooring system may be reused at depths up to that of its original location.

- Stability. The spar design is inherently stable, as the center of buoyancy is located above the center of gravity.

- Dry Trees. Because of their motion characteristics, spars can use dry trees, as opposed to subsea wells, for well completions.

4.10.5.3. Disadvantages

Spars are generally more susceptible to heave motion than TLP's, making hydraulic riser tensioning systems necessary. In addition, the deep draft of a spar hull can make the structure subject to loop currents and vibration issues, which must be accounted for in design.

4.10.5.4. Fabrication

Spar fabrication consists of separate hull and topsides construction, often at different locations. The hull is built using a truss, rolled up and covered to form a watertight column. The lower portion of the steel truss frame can be constructed and left bare so as to allow stressful currents to flow through. The upper hull portions contain the riser buoyancy cans and sealed, watertight ballasts.

The topsides is typically built using three integrated decks, each consisting of 'skids.' Skids are large blocks of production or drilling equipment, built in advance and later placed upon the decks and connected in accordance with functionality. These skids also contain the crew's control rooms, office space, and living/dining areas.

4.10.5.5. Load-out, Transportation, Installation, and Piling

Typically, a drilling rig will pre-drill one or more of the necessary wells, and export pipelines are laid and buoyed for later hookup. Prior to installation, a survey is performed to define the mooring lay down area and a derrick barge will install the anchor piles using an ROV and a free-riding hydraulic hammer. The mooring lines are laid out and connected to a recovery line for later recovery and hull attachment.

Once the hull is completed, typically in Finland, it is shipped to the Gulf of Mexico on a heavy-lift vessel, sometimes in two sections due to weight and size constraints. The hull can be connected and held at an onshore GOM location until it is ready to be transported to site. Typically, it can be towed to this location using oceangoing tugs. Once in position, the ballast tanks in the hull are filled as necessary, and the structure upends (this takes approximately two minutes). Then a derrick barge places a temporary work deck on the hull to facilitate utility hook up, mooring line attachment, and riser installation. Tugs put the hull in position, the mooring lines are reeled in and attached.

The topsides are later transported to the site via material barge, and placed onto the hull by a heavy lift crane on the derrick barge. Finally, the buoyancy cans are lifted off the material barge and placed into the centerwell bay, and ballasted to production deck requirements.

4.10.6. Converted Semisubmersible

Semisubmersible platforms are used all over the world as mobile work structures for drilling, lifting and other operations. Their hulls are similar to the hull of the TLP in that they are vertical column-based floating systems with pontoons (see Figure 45, which shows the Laffit Pincay, a converted semisubmersible that at the time of the photograph was stacked in Pascagoula, Mississippi). These mobile units have been converted to permanently moored platforms as an alternative to some of the other relatively deepwater development options. This is advantageous since the hull requires little retrofit and with a mooring system and upgraded topsides can relatively quickly and inexpensively be used as a production platform. One of the first converted units was the Transworld 58, which was converted and used to produce the first oil in the United Kingdom sector of the North Sea from the Hamilton Argyll field. PETROBRAS in Brazil operates about 15 semisubmersible production platforms.

Figure 45. Converted Semisubmersible Laffit Pincay.

4.10.6.1. Limitations

Similar to a spar, semisubmersibles have a wide range of practical water depth applicability, up to 10,000 feet, but most of the semisubmersibles capable of being operated in such a water depth would be too expensive to purchase to consider suitable for conversion. The best candidates for conversion are older units that have water depth limits of around 2,000 feet. They are only suited to developments with subsea completions since their motion properties, and to a certain extent mooring system reliability, make them unsuitable for dry trees.

These limitations do not apply to the purpose built large deep draft semisubmersibles such as is being used to develop Thunder Horse for BP in the Gulf of Mexico.

4.10.6.2. Advantages

Their suitability to a wide range of water depths and the relatively simple conversion from mobile drilling unit to permanently moored facility are two important advantages. Other advantages include

- Risers. Semisubmersible units can handle a large number of risers compared to other development options.

- Relatively inexpensive if the correct candidate can be found for conversion when the market is down.

- Can be moved easily from one location to another if the wells pay out.

4.10.6.3. Disadvantages

The motion characteristics of semi-submersibles make them less stable than TLP's, and spars, although their motions should be significantly better than many converted tankers. Additionally

- Storage. Semisubmersibles have little if any storage capability.

- Likely to be very sensitive to weight. There is always a tendency for production equipment to get heavier as a project progresses. Weight control when converting a semisubmersible is critical.

- May not be ideally suited to the location, so may have to compromise during the conversion.

- Much of the installed equipment may need to be replaced because it is technically obsolete (i.e., it may still be operational, but it does not do what is now required, and it may not be possible to get the parts to repair it).

- May require considerably more conversion than expected. Whenever converting a vessel, there are almost always unexpected surprises. These may include unexpected corrosion, cracking in critical areas, higher usage of fatigue life than expected, etc.

4.10.6.4. Fabrication

Development of a converted semisubmersible platform begins with identifying a suitable drilling unit for the conversion. Depending on the existing demand for mobile drilling facilities, this may be a difficult task since an operator may be able to make considerably more money from drilling contracts than from selling the asset, hence one is often stuck in the position of either having to pay too much, or getting a considerably less than optimum unit. Once located, the facility will be taken to a shipyard to be converted. This involves outfitting the topsides facilities with the necessary production and processing equipment, installing equipment for the mooring system, etc. Any yard capable of constructing or servicing semisubmersible drilling units are generally capable of a conversion such as this.

4.10.6.5. Transportation, Installation, and Anchoring/Piling

Generally, the completed unit, including topsides, will be towed to the installation site rather than towing the hull, installing it and then installing the topsides, which has been transported separately. These vessels were designed to be mobile in their life as a drilling unit so this process is normally relatively straightforward. Prior to the transportation of the facility, the mooring lines will have been installed with either drag anchors or one of the various pile configurations available. The lines will have been attached and readied for hookup with the hull when it arrives on station. It may be that the rig's original mooring system can be used, but it would require very careful inspection, and even with this, there is a reasonable chance that defects will be missed. Once this has been accomplished, commissioning can begin since the topsides are already in place.

4.10.7. Deep-Draft Semisubmersible

This deepwater option is similar to a converted semisubmersible platform, but is purpose-built for use as a production platform. In most respect its properties are the same as any semisubmersible, but its hull design allows deeper draft and greater stability for the overall system. Because they are purpose built, they tend not to have some of the disadvantages of a converted semisubmersible, but at a considerably higher price.

4.10.7.1. Limitations

Similar to a spar, semisubmersibles have a wide range of practical water depth applicability, up to 10,000 feet.

4.10.7.2. Advantages

The deep-draft motion characteristics of these facilities allow the use of dry tree well completions, although they do not necessarily use them. The main advantages are

- can be designed for almost any water depth and load carrying capability required;

- capable of huge deck and very large process capacity;

- can handle large number of wells;

- large deck area;

- can store crude in the lower hull (although this would not normally be used for export, simply to back-flush the flow lines before or after a shutdown; and

- can choose a range of construction materials (there are some concrete semisubmersible production units).

4.10.7.3. Disadvantages

Although a semi-submersible can be designed for the required load capability, weight growth during fabrication can still be a problem, as with any floating installation. Other disadvantages include the following:

- Cost will likely be expensive.

- Best suited for very large developments where other options are not as attractive.

- Mooring system is likely to be expensive, and may require the use of new materials (e.g., polyester) that are very expensive, and have not had the extent of field testing as conventional wire and chain.

- Need to use a shipyard that understands building a vessel with all the concomitant ballast and weight control systems.

- Transportation may be complicated for large units.

4.10.7.4. Fabrication

Fabrication of deep-draft semisubmersibles needs to be undertaken at a proper shipyard that knows how to build marine equipment. This is not necessarily a serious limitation, but few facilities around the Gulf Coast have the experience of facility size to build a large, deep-draft semisubmersible.

4.10.7.5. Load-out, Transportation, Installation, and Piling

Transportation may be a significant issue. Most deep draft semisubmersibles will be large, or an alternative option will have been used. But there are limits to the size of cargo that can be carried on either a barge or self propelled ship. One does not want to be in the position that there is only one vessel that is capable of transporting the unit: the costs will likely be very high, and there is no back-up should the ship/barge sink. To a certain extent, the same applies to the installation: everything will be big, so will take a long time and use expensive equipment. If using polyester line, and one mooring line is dropped, then is there a replacement available to complete the installation. Likely there will not be, unless such an eventuality has been built into the project, thereby again increasing the costs.

4.10.8. Floating Production, Storage, and Offloading System (FPSO)

An FPSO is a vessel with the capabilities inherent in its name: production, storage, and offloading of oil and gas. While there are an increasing number of purpose-built FPSO's, the majority of facilities in use today are converted tankers that have been modified to execute these functions in deepwater environments.

A tanker-based FPSO usually has a length of approximately 1,000 feet and a breadth of 200 feet (see Figure 46). The conversion requires installation of a mooring system (often using a turret placed in the forward section of the vessel near the bow) and production facilities on the ship's main deck. Unless the FPSO is moored in a relatively benign environment, a turret is used to anchor the vessel to the mooring system while allowing the vessel to pivot according to the prevailing weather (i.e., weathervane). Production risers are also run through the turret system. If a turret is not required, a spread mooring system is installed with mooring lines attached directly to anchor points on the vessel's deck, typically at the fore and aft ends of the vessel.

Besides choosing between spread moored and turret moored systems, there are two other options for an FPSO mooring system: fixed and disconnectable. The majority of FPSO's employ a fixed mooring design which is intended to keep the vessel on station for the duration of its life at that location. In some instances, it is desirable to have the ability to move the vessel off station during its service life (e.g., to avoid icebergs), and this requires a disconnectable mooring system allowing the vessel to leave its mooring lines behind, move off station, and then return and reconnect the mooring lines.

Figure 46. Pemex Ta'Kuntah FSO (Courtesy of MODEC Int. LLC).

A few of the more modern designs use dynamic positioning (DP), a system of thrusters in concert with global positioning systems or a similar technology to hold to a precise position. The DP enabled FPSO's still require a mooring system to maintain the vessel on station with the DP system providing minute corrections.

4.10.8.1. Limitations

Unlike other production facility options, an FPSO does not make use of export pipelines to direct its production to shore or to other facilities. An FPSO depends on shuttle tankers to allow it to offload produced oil from its storage tanks (see Figure 47). If shuttle tankers are unavailable for whatever reason and the FPSO storage tanks are full, production must stop until its tanks can be offloaded.

Figure 47. Pemex Ta'Kuntah FSO Simultaneous Offloading (Courtesy of MODEC Int. LLC).

4.10.8.2. Advantages

The primary advantage of an FPSO is its suitability to a wide range of water depths. Though most of the units have been installed in water depths less than 3,000 feet, they have also been successfully employed in greater depths, such as in Petrobras' Marlin Sul Field (about 4,700 feet water depth). Other advantages include the following:

- Weight Insensitive. Compared to its other deepwater floating counterparts, an FPSO is not particularly sensitive to the weight of its production equipment.

- Infrastructure Free. The FPSO's need not be installed in areas with existing infrastructure since they don't depend on export pipelines.

- Hull Experience. Because even new-build FPSO's rely on a typical ship-shaped hull, there is a large depth of experience with fabrication around the world.

- Storage Capacity. The FPSO's, by design, can carry significant volumes of produced oil in its storage tanks, much more than other deepwater options.

- Deck Space. Unlike other deepwater facilities, there is a large deck area to use for production trains. This allows greater expansion options and reduces the risk of vapor cloud explosions since equipment is more spread out.

- Mobility. It is possible to relocate an FPSO, even great distances since its typical ship shape makes it suitable for open ocean transport.

4.10.8.3. Disadvantages

The primary disadvantage for an FPSO is the significant inspection costs particularly associated with the storage tanks. Unlike other deepwater systems, the main structural system is also used to store produced oil and ballast water. Cleaning and inspecting the tanks is expensive and dangerous and impacts production operations, but is vital to maintaining the facility.

4.10.8.4. Fabrication

Whether the FPSO is a new build or a conversion, the hull work will be completed in a shipyard and follow the path very similar to that of a tanker fabrication. For a conversion, the primary hull work will involve replacing existing steelwork that has corroded or become damaged, reinforcing support points for topsides equipment, and installing a turret or other mooring attachment structures. If a turret mooring system is used, the turret will be either delivered from the fabricator as a unit to be installed or will be fabricated by the shipyard depending on the contract arrangements.

The topsides equipment and supports are installed in the shipyard. A process deck is installed on top of the ship main deck to provide clearance (typically about 10 feet) and to protect the process from wave impact in high seas. All the equipment, piping, etc. will be installed and readied before the unit is taken to the installation site.

4.10.8.5. Load-out, Transportation, Installation, and Piling

Whether spread moored, or turret moored, the mooring lines (composed of wire rope, chain, connectors and anchors) will be installed before the arrival of the FPSO unit. The anchors will be set in their proper location with the attached mooring lines and readied for retrieval.

As with any ship-shaped vessel, the unit will be launched from the shipyard. No lifting, upending, flooding, etc. are required as with most other floating production options since this behaves much like an ocean-going ship. However, the FPSO will typically not have the ability to move on its own (though some are equipped with dynamic positioning systems). They require tugs to tow them from the fabrication yard to the site. Once the unit is towed to the installation site, the mooring lines are retrieved and attached to the turret or the deck mounted anchor points.

4.10.9. Subsea Tieback

This is the most basic development option and is used in conjunction with some other deepwater development option (e.g., TLP or spar) or a shallower water host platform. A subsea system is a minimal structure that houses a variety of equipment (e.g., wellheads and manifolds) at the seafloor. It is designed strictly to protect the wells and direct their flow to other locations.

4.10.9.1. Limitations

Subsea tiebacks require some other production facility to receive its flow and process it. They cannot process the product and must be maintained remotely.

4.10.9.2. Advantages

The primary advantage of subsea systems is their relatively low cost (compared to installing a complete production platform) that allows them to access reserves that could not be economically exploited otherwise.

4.10.9.3. Disadvantages

Unlike some of the other deepwater development options, any well maintenance must be handled using a MODU or other drilling vessel. This leaves them subject to the prevailing rates and availability of such equipment.

4.10.9.4. Fabrication

Often, a subsea system will make use of a template. The template is essentially a steel frame that is used to house the subsea production equipment and may serve as a drilling guide. If used, the template is fabricated in an onshore facility and equipped appropriately. All the equipment, manifolds, production trees, piping, etc., is usually sourced from various manufacturers. Often the specifications of this equipment are customized to suit the particular needs of the project rather than use "stock" items.

4.10.9.5. Load-out, Transportation, Installation, and Piling

If a template is to be used for the system and it is needed as a drilling guide, it will be taken to the site and lowered to the seabed with some type of lift vessel. Typically, the template is piled in place using either driven or grouted piles.

With or without the template, drilling takes place using a drillship or semisubmersible. The wellheads, templates, flowlines, etc. are installed to complete the wells and tie back the production to a host facility.

4.11. Financing

The type of financing method used is subject to significant variation based on many factors including oil company size, cost of development, novelty of development, who the partners are, availability of cash, etc. The following section briefly discusses the most commonly used options, but it must be realized that new financing methods are being developed continually: some may be variations of existing methods, some completely new. In addition, there have been some relatively recent changes in the way partnering works. In the past it was normal for two or more oil companies to cooperate to explore and develop a specific field. Now, although with some limited success, some of the larger drilling contractors are becoming partners in a field by helping with the exploration costs, while others have subsidiaries that are acting in some respects as independent oil companies.

Not all the partners involved with a development will use the same method of financing, and the method may change during the project, or after installation. It is normal for all parties to have an agreement as to how the moneys are to be raised so that all liabilities are known by all parties.

4.11.1. Company Cash

The simplest method by which an oil company might develop a field is with cash that they have on hand, or is generated by profits as needed. This is an eminently suitable method for relatively inexpensive developments, but is not normally viable for smaller companies, or large deepwater projects. Through partnering the costs of some high value projects can be brought within the reach of smaller companies. Examples of company cash deals include Shell's commitment in Ursa (45% working interest of $1.45 billion) or British Borneo's commitment to a shallow water installation ($500,000). This is not meant to imply that Shell could immediately come up with the cash for such a project, but planned over time, they could meet the required draws on funds.

4.11.2. Stock Issues

Another way to raise money to finance a major project is through stock issues. As an example, British Borneo raised U.K. £54 million (about $80 million) in early 1996 and an additional U.K. £167 million (about $270 million) in July 1997 through rights issues. This money was to help fund their expansion into such projects as Morpeth and Allegheny, although there were other expansions going on at the same time. This method is particularly useful to smaller companies whose stock prices are increasing. This is not normally a project specific way of raising funds.

4.11.3. Bond Issues

Companies can issue bonds as a way of raising money to pay for major projects. None of the projects studied for this paper used bond issues as a way of raising funds.

4.11.4. Bank Loans

One or all of the partners approach a bank, or consortium of banks to finance a project, somewhat akin to taking out a mortgage. Morpeth was partially funded by bank loans. The bank will normally insist that there is an independent engineer's "due diligence" study undertaken to verify the feasibility of the venture. Assuming nothing untoward is found, the lead bank will find additional partners to help fund the project. The details of the loans, and required guarantees vary from case to case. Some structures, like a spar or a TLP, have a potential for reuse after the field has paid out, so the bank has a real collateral interest in the structure as well as the field. In the case of a jacket-based structure, the collateral is more in the field than in the structure as the potential for reuse is extremely limited. Consequently, the thrust of the due diligence study may change depending on the type of structure being financed.

4.11.5. Sale-Leaseback

In a sale-leaseback the oil company finances the particular venture through other means, but at some stage after completion of the project, sells it to a third party, and leases it back. This releases capital to fund another project and is particularly useful for companies that are expanding relatively slowly, and want to finance a limited number of projects at a time. Additionally, the cost of money influences the attractiveness of a sale-leaseback deal. Because of U.S. tax laws, it is cheaper to effectively borrow money via a sale-leaseback than through conventional means.

A sale-leaseback arrangement can also be valuable for projects that use relatively new technology. Sometimes these projects are difficult to fund through conventional loans because the banks perceive them as increased risk, and even if they will finance them, the rate may be high. To help offset this, the project is funded by other means, and once it has proved itself in operation, it can be easier to find a prospective purchaser to undertake a sale-leaseback. This purchaser will not normally be a bank, but some structured finance corporation.

The terms of the sale-leaseback vary depending on the circumstances, but normally the value of the installation is paid off, plus some effective interest, over the period of the leaseback. At the end of the period the structure must have some value within a specific range, for tax purposes. The lessee then has the option to either buy the structure back at some agreed value, normally determined by an independent appraiser, or to renew the lease. As an example, Philip Morris owns a number of offshore installations that are leased back to their operators.

It is possible for a company to raise funds through a sale-leaseback of their interest in a field, without them being the sole owner. Amerada Hess's interest in Baldpate is an example of this.

4.11.6. Hedging

Hedging is a method of protecting revenue by agreeing to sell a percentage of output at a specific rate, regardless of what happens to the world price. By protecting the sale price, hedging ensures cash flow to pay off incurred debt. For example, British Borneo hedged by selling a percentage of its production from Morpeth at a rate of approximately $16 per barrel. As it happened, the price of oil increased sharply during the hedging period, so the company missed out on a significant amount of income, however, they protected themselves from a potential drop in prices.

An alternative to selling a percentage of production is to sell a fixed quantity at a specified price. This works as long as the price does not rise and production does not fall to below the agreed quantity to be supplied. In this situation, the company that hedged is required to buy oil at a high price and sell it at the hedging price in order to meet their commitment. Clearly this can potentially lead to very large losses.

4.12. PRELIMINARY ENGINEERING

In many cases there will be significant preliminary engineering at the decision to develop stage. The economics of the project will depend on the cost of development, and these will, in turn, depend on the preliminary engineering. In other cases, there will have been less detailed work at the earlier stage, and additional preliminary engineering will be needed to ensure technical feasibility prior to advancing. If this is the case, the purpose of the preliminary engineering is to generate sufficient information to allow the detail design to be put out to bid.

It is possible that preliminary engineering at this stage will be an extension of some of the concept assessments undertaken earlier in the project, but frequently non-design companies will be used for the concept assessment in order to prevent any conflicts. The amount of preliminary engineering, and who undertakes the work, will often depend on the type of bid sought, and how the project is planned to progress. Sometimes the oil company may undertake the work themselves. Conversely, the work may be undertaken as a steady refinement of a plan, allowing a stop at any point without too significant an expenditure.

4.13. MODEL TESTING

Floating structures move with the seas, and it is important for the safe and efficient operation of an installation to know how much it will move. There are computer programs that can predict vessel motions in a sea state, but these do not necessarily work particularly well with non-ship-shaped objects. They can be good at predicting the effects of changes in certain parameters, but normally need to be calibrated to a "base case." In addition, there is a need to know what the loads will be resisted by the moorings or tendons, and if they will vibrate at any unexpected frequencies. These loads can be complicated and influenced by the low frequency response of the moored object. The best way to answers these questions is through model tests.

A model of the structure is made at as large a scale as practical, normally in excess of 1 to 100. Figure 48 shows a model of a mini-TLP being tested in a wave basin. The model will include tendons (for a TLP) or moorings (for a spar or semisubmersible) that accurately represent their properties. The model will then be placed into a model basin that is capable of generating waves and currents. The tank where tests were undertaken on Ursa, Neptune, and Morpeth, located at Texas A&M University, is 150 feet long, 100 feet wide, and 20 feet deep, with a deeper pit of 55 feet. The cost of the tests varies depending on modeling detail, number of parameters considered, etc., but were in the range of $200,000.

Figure 48. Model of a Mini-TLP being Model Tested in a Wave Basin
(Courtesy of Atlantia Offshore Ltd.).

4.14. DETAIL ENGINEERING

If a concept has been decided upon in some detail prior to bidding, then there may be a separate contract for detailed engineering. For example, Hudson Engineering (part of McDermott) did the detail engineering on the Baldpate compliant tower although they did not win all of the construction bids. In other cases, the oil company may put the concept out for bid, to include design and fabrication.

4.15. BIDDING OPTIONS

There is a broad range of bidding options for the oil company, from complete project turnkey to a detailed managed project. Some of these possibilities are discussed below.

4.15.1. Whole Project Turnkey

Turnkey contracts are common in shallow water, and occasionally in deep water. The oil company puts out a bid request for a structure capable of producing specific field characteristics. They may give some specifications for the type of structure (frequently this is implied by whom they request to bid) or may leave it very open. It is significantly less common in deep water because few companies are capable of undertaking such a project from either the risk or technical standpoint.

4.15.2. Major Packages

This is probably the most common type of contract in deep water. The operator gives a number of major turnkey or cost plus packages. A common split is Hull, Topside Design, Topside Fabrication, Pipelines, and Installation. The operator administers each package, although they may designate a specific company to act as liaison to ensure that weight and dimensional controls are maintained. The individual packages may be either fixed price or cost plus based on an estimate. On fast track projects the operator may order some of the major components, which require a longer lead time, in advance in order to prevent delays. They may also split out other items that they want to control more strictly, either based on past experience, or because of known quality issues.

4.15.3. Cost Plus

The Morpeth mini-TLP structure was let as two contracts, one for installation, and the other for the completed SeaStar mini-TLP. This was a risky move by British Borneo. In the past they had worked with Atlantia on a number of shallow water turnkey contracts in which minimal platforms were installed. When they decided to move into deepwater, they formed an alliance with Atlantia to develop the SeaStar design from concept to a reality. After various original cost estimates, Atlantia was contracted on a cost plus basis to fabricate a SeaStar mini-TLP. Some of the original cost estimates were low, but the main reason for these underestimates was that the size of the TLP kept growing along with the required production equipment. This was a case of a cost plus contract based on past experience, confidence in the product, and reasonable expectations of a well managed project.

Notwithstanding Morpeth, it is unusual to have cost plus contracts because of the uncertainty of the final cost, and the high potential for cost overruns. These types of contracts are most common on time-critical projects, which are let before the design has been finalized, hence the details of scope are not known. These projects are hardest to control, and hence cost overruns most likely.

4.16. CONTRACTORS

Price is very important in choosing a contractor, but it is rarely the only consideration. Clearly there is the question of experience, capability, and other factors as discussed below.

4.16.1. Schedule

Schedule is extremely important on deepwater projects. Given the magnitude of the investments, considerable money can be spent on interest alone before production starts, and any delay can alter how a company performs financially in any given year. When considering a contractor it is important not only to ensure that they can meet the schedule, but that they can compensate for any delays that may occur. As an example, a specific yard may be capable of building a structure on schedule with its normal labor force, but delays may require an increased labor force to "make up time" that may either be unavailable in the local labor market or be unworkable if the yard does not have sufficient infrastructure to support more workers. It is not that the yard cannot meet the schedule, but they have no ability to compensate for delays that are outside their control.

4.16.2. Project Management

It is critical that the chosen yard has excellent project management skills. This extends into the areas of material traceability, weight control, scheduling, etc. Without these basics, a simple project can be brought to a halt.

4.16.3. Labor Force

There are obviously the issues discussed above about having sufficient available labor to compensate for delays, but the stability of the labor force must also be considered. Does the yard have a dedicated labor force supplemented as needed? If the yard is unionized, are all the relevant contracts in place for the duration of the required fabrication period? Could changes in government affect the labor force? If so, how stable is that government?

4.16.4. Material Supply

It can be difficult to get certain materials in some yards, particularly on short notice. European designs will often use materials that are not readily available in the U.S., and vice versa. To compound the problem, steel specifications change from country to country, and it can be difficult to get an exact match. This can lead to additional work in verifying compatibility. If only metric materials are available for an imperial designed structure, there may be an increase in weight because of the need to compensate for plate sizes. Since weight control is extremely important on most deepwater structures, this can lead to serious problems later on. These issues are not insurmountable, but need to be considered.

4.16.5. Transportation

Transportation is one of the highest risk operations. There have been a large number of structures lost over the years due to problems in transportation: recently one of the Mighty Servant semisubmersible transport ships sank with a high value deck as cargo. It was due for installation by Chevron in West Africa. These vessels are considered a "safe" means of transportation, but the delays due to the loss of that deck will have cost Chevron millions of dollars. Closer is not necessarily better, but as a general rule it is safer.

4.16.6. Safety Systems

A fabrication yard's safety policy and procedures can significantly affect their suitability, particularly when it comes to the oil company's field surveyors.

4.16.7. Weather

The weather can affect the ability of a yard to meet specifications, and to complete work. If the yard has enclosed facilities for fabrication, then they are less affected by the weather, but high humidity can have a serious impact on the ability to produce high quality welds, and high quality painting. There is also the risk of hurricanes or other storm events causing delays in schedule and damage to the facility.

4.17. QUALITY CONTROL

There are a number of different groups involved with the quality control on a deepwater development project. These all have the same basic aim, but with different emphasis. The fabrication yard wants to produce a quality product, but for the minimum cost (assuming lump sum pricing). They will have specifications that establish how much non-destructive testing (NDT) they do on welds, the tolerance on construction, the types of materials, the methods for ensuring that correct materials are used in the right places, etc. They need to produce a quality product to protect their name, and encourage future work, but they also need to keep costs down. The fabrication certified verification agent (CVA) will be doing a similar task, but with the aim of ensuring the project meets a set of standards acceptable to the appropriate regulatory agency. The owner's representative will want to get the best quality product achievable from the yard, however they are not necessarily tied to the specifications. They have the option to interpret the specifications, and decide that certain things outside the specification may be acceptable (i.e., they are allowed judgment). If there is a classification society surveyor involved (e.g., if the vessel is to be classed) then they will be ensuring that the structure is built to their own rules.

4.18. TRANSPORTATION

As mentioned in previous sections, transportation activities are some of the riskiest tasks undertaken as part of an offshore development, and the deeper the water the higher the risk. This is in part due to the unpredictability of weather conditions (especially in open ocean) but also due to the lack of control and recovery available should something go wrong. At sea, there are few options available if serious problems arise and the entire load (costing millions of dollars and months of work) can be lost.

However, with proper planning and execution, transportation of platforms, topsides and equipment can and is successfully undertaken. Transportation is typically discussed in terms of dry and wet. A dry tow involves a vessel large enough to transport the cargo entirely out of the water while a wet tow is performed with the cargo (e.g., a spar hull) in the water pulled by tugs.

Depending on the size of the cargo and the distance to be traveled, there are many transportation options. An ocean transport of significant size will require a heavy lift vessel to transport it. A smaller cargo over a shorter distance may only require an ocean going barge pulled by tugs (see Figure 49). In any case, proper seafastenings are required, planning of the route and coordination among the crew to handle the operation.

Figure 49.   Shallow Water Gulf of Mexico Jacket under Tow in Bayous.

4.19. ASSEMBLY

Like transportation operations, assemblies on site are also risky. While the likelihood of an error occurring may be low, the consequences of a problem can be quite high from a safety and operational standpoint. But, as with any activity, proper planning and execution can overcome the obstacles.

The most common assembly activities on site include topsides installation, riser hookup, mooring or tendon attachment, and pile driving. Most of these activities require a vessel with lift capability. The availability and cost of such a piece of equipment will depend on the size of the load and its location. Based on the development option considered, these factors will have been taken into account at the planning stage.

4.20. INSTALLATION

Listed and described below are some of the physical components necessary for a given offshore development installation.

4.20.1. Template

A template is a fabricated structure, typically rectangular in shape, that houses subsea equipment such as trees, manifolds, and pigging and may also provide guides for drilling. The template sits on the sea floor and can range from 10 to 150 feet in length, 10 to 70 feet wide, and 5 to 30 feet high, depending on the range and the amount of equipment it houses. Templates that provide the capability of linking several wells in a building block fashion are known as "Host Templates."

4.20.2. Tendons

The TLP's use tendons to secure their buoyant hulls to the seafloor. They are attached to the seafloor using concrete or steel piles, which are driven into or grouted to the seafloor. Each of these piles can be as large as 10 feet in diameter and 400 feet long. One disadvantage to this type of mooring is that the tendons for a TLP are designed for a specific depth (i.e., they cannot be reused at other locations requiring different depths) and are relatively expensive compared to other mooring systems.

4.20.3. Tendon Connectors

Tendon connectors are specially designed hardware used to attach the tendons to the anchor points at the sea floor and at the hull.

4.20.4. Jacket

As described in more detail in the sections on conventional jackets and compliant towers, a jacket is a welded steel frame made of tubular steel members which is almost completely submerged and supports the topsides structure and equipment as well as protecting the conductors and risers. Jackets are primarily pile founded though there are also gravity base structures that rest on the sea floor and are stabilized by their own weight. Jackets are typically four and eight leg structures though six and three leg alternatives are not uncommon.

4.20.5. Deck

The deck is the above-water structure of any offshore development platform. Like a jacket, it is a welded steel frame with a mix of tubular members and other structural shapes. Typically, decks are built with several (two or more) vertical levels to support various equipment packages. The arrangement and orientation of the deck will depend on the production requirements and the supporting structure (e.g., jacket, TLP, spar, etc.).

4.20.6. Moorings

Moorings as found on semisubmersibles, spars and FPSO's are different from tendons used for TLP's. Moorings do not run vertically from hull to seabed, but typically radiate away from the structure for some distance. Moorings are usually composed of heavy chain and wire rope and are anchored in a variety of ways (e.g., drag anchors, driven piles, grouted piles, suction piles, etc.). Moorings are less expensive than tendons since they are not such a specialized piece of equipment.

4.20.7. Pipelines

Pipelines allow production from wells to be directed to platforms, hubs, terminals, etc. Unless shuttle tankers will be used exclusively to transport the hydrocarbons from the field, every offshore installation requires some sort of pipeline connection to another facility. Just as with onshore pipelines, offshore lines are steel tubular members of various sizes and carry oil, gas or a mixture from one location to another. Pipelines typically refer to only that portion of the flowline that rests on the seafloor, as opposed to risers, which are discussed below.

4.20.8. Risers

A riser is the portion of a flowline that runs from the pipeline on the seafloor up to the platform production area. For a jacket installation, risers are run along the outer face of the steel frame and supported at intervals with clamps. For deepwater installations, special types of risers are used due to the long distances they travel. Steel catenary risers are one type of special riser used in deepwater installations. Spars typically require risers with special buoyancy cans at the top in order to support their weight. Whatever system is used, risers are part of the flow of hydrocarbons from one installation to another.

4.20.9. Subsea Wells

Subsea wells have their wellheads at the seafloor (either as part of a subsea template or alone) as opposed to dry wellheads that sit above the water on platforms. For wells away from the production facility that cannot be reached by directional drilling, subsea wells are the only way to produce the hydrocarbons.

4.21. Commissioning

Commissioning is the process of completing and testing the installation and function of the operations side of the facility—as opposed to its structural side.

4.21.1. Topsides

Once the facilities have been transported to site and installation is complete, the commissioning process begins. All the production and processing facilities must be hooked up and tested to assure their proper function. Transportation and installation are considered in their design, but these activities may cause problems with these systems, e.g., fittings that have worked loose, supports that have been damaged, etc. Addressing these issues is part of the commissioning that must take place before the facility becomes operational.

4.21.2. Pipelines

As discussed in earlier sections, pipelines are the primary means of transporting produced hydrocarbons from wells to the platform and from the platform to other facilities (either offshore hubs or onshore terminals). Whether installed prior to the facility installation or after its arrival, the pipelines must be commissioned just as the topsides facilities. Connections to risers must be completed and functionality tests run. This may involve the use of "pigs," which are run through the lines to determine its fitness.

4.21.3. Risers

Risers connect the topsides production facilities with the pipelines at the sea floor. Like pipelines, the risers must be connected and tested after installation of the facility to allow production to begin. Depending on the development option used, some risers may be preinstalled with the structure to facilitate this commissioning process. Otherwise, the risers must be installed on site once the facility is in place.

4.22. Development Drilling

Earlier in this document, exploratory drilling was discussed as a method of defining, in greater detail, the production prospects of a field. Development drilling is the more involved process of drilling the production wells for the field. Depending on the development option chosen, the development drilling activities will be accomplished from the platform itself, or using a mobile offshore drilling unit or drill ship. Platforms, compliant towers, TLP's, mini-TLP's, spars and deep-draft semisubmersibles are capable of having dry tree wells with drilling operations taking place from the topsides. Other development options require a drilling vessel to drill and complete the wells.

If drilling is to be completed using a drilling vessel, these wells may be completed before the installation of the facility. All commissioning activities must be coordinated with the development drilling activities since both activities must be accomplished before production can begin on a facility.

4.23. Operations

While the earlier stages of the development chronology are important to a project's success, the operations are the money producing activities that last from first oil until decommissioning. Successful and efficient operations are key to the profitable development of a field. These operations encompass a wide range of activities from drilling, production and processing to maintenance, repairs and upgrades.

4.23.1. Production and Processing

Ensuring the regular flow of hydrocarbons from the wells and processing the production so it can be transferred to other facilities is the primary function of the platform operations. Production activities include water and gas injection for those wells that are not free flowing, flow assurance activities such as flowline maintenance, etc. Processing primarily involves separation of the production into water, oil and gas, compression of gas production to facilitate transport, re-injection of produced water, etc.

4.23.2. Well Maintenance

If the development option allows it, well maintenance may be performed from the production facility. This activity must be coordinated carefully with the ongoing production activities since some drilling and production activities should not be performed at the same time due to the risk to personnel and equipment. Fewer limitations exist when the well maintenance activities occur from a drill vessel, which would be the case for remote wells, or development options that don't support drilling activities.

4.23.3. Maintenance and Inspection

In order to keep the facility operating efficiently and effectively, a comprehensive maintenance and inspection program is necessary. These activities should be focused on proactively addressing maintenance needs to minimize the need for repairs and replacements. Inspections are an important part of this process and include both above and below water visual and non-destructive testing techniques.

4.23.4. Supply Boats

The most efficient method of delivery the large amounts of consumables and other supplies needed by a large offshore development platform is through the use of supply boats. The increasing need for more capable vessels to service deepwater facilities has led to improvements in the supply boats themselves and the crews that operate them. This has been made possible, in part, by the long-term contracts given to supply operators allowing them the revenue stream to invest in assets and training. Improvements include more reliable better maintained vessels, more use of dynamic positioning systems, larger and better trained crews, and greater cargo capacity (see Figure 50).

Figure 50. Supply Vessel Amy Chouest at Dock.

4.23.5. Crew Changes

Deepwater development operations involve fairly large crews (50 persons or more). Because of the logistical challenges and the size of the crews, crew changes are minimized as much as possible by extending the shifts served by each crewmember. Helicopters are the primary method of facilitating crew changes for deepwater operations because they offer greater speed and flexibility than crew boats.

5. SHALLOW WATER VS. DEEPWATER

Based on the different economic, technological, operational and safety factors involved in offshore operations, there are significant differences between how a shallow water facility and a deepwater facility are planned, built, installed and operated. This section addresses the differences seen in specific areas of an offshore development when operating in shallow water versus deepwater.

5.1. MANNING

The driving factors behind manning levels in shallow water versus deepwater are distance and production. Because many shallow water platforms are close to shore, they can economically be manned during the day only, with crews coming aboard via helicopter or even supply boats. The distances required to reach deepwater platforms make this kind of partial manning impractical both from a cost and an operational standpoint.

Production is the overriding factor determining manning requirements. Many shallow water platforms have no processing capacity at all, or minimal capacity and act merely as well protectors with the production redirected to hub platforms or to shore-based facilities. There is no need for a crew on these facilities and they are typically only visited for maintenance purposes. On a deepwater facility this is never the case. In order to be feasible economically, the production rates must be high and there must be processing capability to handle the hydrocarbons. This requires manning on a 24-hour basis with a significant crew size (e.g., 50 or more). Additionally, more maintenance is required for the significantly larger and more complex facilities found in deepwater compared to shallow water structures. This also requires a dedicated work force.

5.2. SUBSEA

Subsea systems (e.g., wellheads, manifolds, etc.) are useful for producing wells that can't be reached by more conventional methods. However, they add more complexity to the process of installation, production and maintenance, and this increased complexity brings increased cost. The typical shallow water production in the Gulf of Mexico does not generate enough return to offset this increased cost, so subsea systems are less attractive in this environment.

For deepwater production, the greater production levels make the use of subsea more economical. It may be relatively straightforward to install a minimal structure (e.g., a caisson or well protector) in shallow water to develop a field not accessible from existing infrastructure. But in deepwater, the subsea systems are the only minimal structures available. The cost of a new development structure for deepwater may not be justified by the potential production, but a subsea system could be installed at much lower cost and tied back to an existing facility.

5.3. PIPELINES AND GAS

The primary means of directing production from offshore facilities to onshore facilities is through the use of pipelines. Every potential field development must consider the availability and suitability of pipelines to handle the produced hydrocarbons.

For shallow water developments, there is a network of pipelines available that has been installed over the more than 40 years of Gulf of Mexico production. If the company does not own their own pipelines, fees can be paid to the owners for their use in what have become fairly standard arrangements. Typically, only a short pipeline is required in order to tie the new production into the existing network. While any pipeline work is costly and requires specialized equipment, it is a fairly straightforward process and can be completed by a number of contractors.

Deepwater developments are no different in their need to transport their product, but their options are more limited and more costly. There are far fewer deepwater developments compared to shallow water, and the existing network of pipelines that serve them is smaller and more spread out. In order to tie into this network, or create a new path to a hub platform in more shallow water is costly in terms of time, materials and equipment.

Besides the cost differences between deepwater and shallow water pipeline systems, there are other considerations somewhat unique to deepwater operating environments. Hydrostatic pressure, temperature, and material weight are important considerations. The system design must address the large pressures that can crush the material. Temperatures in deepwater environments can cause flow restrictions inside the pipelines. And the large volume of materials required to connect subsea systems to platforms, and deepwater production to hubs, involve weight that cannot be carried by more conventional shallow water systems. Though these effects also must be considered in shallow water developments, they are not as critical.

5.4. INFRASTRUCTURE

Over the many years of production in the Gulf of Mexico, a significant infrastructure has been built up along the Gulf Coast to serve the industry. Companies of all sorts (e.g., diving, repairs, equipment, food services, etc.) thrive in a relatively competitive environment giving operators a choice of provider for most of the services they require. But the bulk of these companies operate almost exclusively in the shallow water arena. The number of companies with the capability and experience to operate in deepwater is much smaller. As a result, shallow water facilities have an advantage in being able to obtain a more competitive price for these services than deepwater facilities.

As an example, look at underwater inspection services. All facilities in the Gulf of Mexico have inspection requirements that must be met and there are a number of companies that can offer those services. The bulk of underwater inspections for shallow water facilities can be accomplished by divers operating from a dive boat in one or two days. These services can be contracted months in advance or, if available, only days in advance using a "vessel of opportunity." However, for deepwater facilities, many underwater inspections must be accomplished using remote operated vehicles (ROV) that can descend much further than a diver. These operations can be accomplished by a far fewer number of companies and require much more planning and expense.

5.5. DRILLING

As with most of the comparisons between shallow and deepwater facilities, the differences in drilling are driven by costs. Shallow water facilities are serviced by a number of experienced drilling contractors that offer a well-understood service. Operators can draw upon a fairly large equipment base (e.g., jack-up rigs). All of these things work to keep costs within a fairly manageable range which is necessary given the relatively low production rates generated by shallow water developments. Deepwater drilling contractors are fewer in number, their equipment is less plentiful, and their costs in time, materials and manpower are greater.

5.6. PLATFORMS

The advantages and disadvantages of the different types of platforms available for a deepwater development have been discussed earlier in this document. The same sorts of factors used to differentiate deepwater options can also be used to differentiate shallow water options from deepwater options. In shallow water it is possible to install a minimal platform, capable of producing five wells for around $1 million. Such a facility would be tied back to some other complex, so it would not be manned and would be fitted with only minimal processing equipment. Such a facility would probably produce up to about 5,000 bbls/day. Given the relatively low cost of these platforms, it may be cheaper to install a few of these, connected by pipelines, rather than installing a larger platform producing from directional wells. Figure 51 shows a "large scale" minimal platform that has been designed for up to 650 feet water depth, and up to 25,000 BOPD; however, the cost would be closer to $10 million than $1 million.

Because everything in deepwater is more expensive, the type of scenario described above would not be feasible in a deepwater environment. A platform producing only 5,000 bbl/day would not produce sufficient return to make a profit in deepwater. To exploit the larger reserves needed for a deepwater development platforms need to be capable of carrying larger process equipment, with more throughput and the fewer platforms required the better.

To connect several structures in shallow water via pipelines requires a simple pipelay barge at a cost of around $30,000 per day. In deepwater, a semisubmersible installation vessel would be needed that may cost over $300,000 per day. So directional drilling becomes more attractive in deeper water to allow production of more wells from a central platform. Those that are too far away, or too complex to drill, may be produced through a subsea wellhead that is connected to the platform via a flowline. In the end, to make the investment pay off you're more likely to end up with a single platform, manned 24 hours a day, producing close to 50,000 bbl/day. And the cost for such a platform may be in the area of $150 million.

This is a broad example used to illustrate a point and there are exceptions. The Cantarell field in the Bay of Campeche (Southern Gulf of Mexico) is mainly located in 150 feet water depth, but because of the huge size of the reservoir, and the extremely high production rates, these shallow water platforms are large and clumped together to form bridge-connected complexes (see Figure 52). Also, in harsh environment areas, the arguments do not hold true as each platform is more expensive, and more likely to need to be permanently manned. (The risk and cost of using day visits is too high, and may often be prohibited by the weather.)

Figure 51. SeaHarvester Minimal Platform (Courtesy of Sea Horse Platform Partners Ltd.).

Figure 52. Platform Complex in Cantarell Field, Mexico.

5.7. WORKOVER

A producing well will normally require some maintenance during its life. For example, the well may penetrate various production zones, and, as one is depleted, the oil company will want to start producing from others. It may not be possible to complete and produce from multiple zones at the same time as they may be at different pressures which would result in hydrocarbons flowing from the higher pressure reservoir to the lower pressure one, with a consequent reduction in total production at the surface. In addition, the zones may be producing different products that the company may not want to "co-mingle." Maintenance of an existing well may necessitate re-perforating (breaking up the rock formation around the well in order to allow the oil to flow into the production tubing) or other methods of stimulating recovery. All this requires workover.

On a shallow water platform in the Gulf of Mexico, it is normal to bring a jack-up drilling rig alongside the platform, cantilever the derrick over the stern of the jack-up and out over the platform, and allow the derrick direct access to the wells, with all the drilling support equipment[19] being contained on the jack-up. Given that all this equipment is supported on the jack-up, the platform does not have to be designed for the additional drilling weight, hence it can be much smaller and cheaper. The jack-up may cost in the range of $20,000 to $50,000 per day, depending on its size and the going rates, but that is inexpensive in comparison to the extra cost that would be associated with building a platform capable of supporting all the personnel and equipment required to work on the wells. Indeed, this ability to get access to the wells with a jack-up is one of the reasons that it is economic to use a relatively large number of small platforms in shallow water.

In deepwater, there are a number of alternative solutions to the workover issue. The large platforms, like full-size TLP's and most of the spars, have a drilling package mounted on the platform. This drilling package does most of the development drilling, and may be permanently mounted so that it can do the necessary workover. On the Baldpate compliant tower, a drilling package was installed soon after tower installation to complete the wells, but the intent was to remove it after these had been completed. To achieve this, Amerada Hess hired a drilling contractor to install their drilling rig and undertake the work. If at a later stage it is necessary to do additional drilling, then the rig can be brought back out to the platform, and re-installed. This way they are not saddled with the cost of purchasing and running a drilling package that will only be useful for a limited time. The rental cost for a platform rig will vary depending on the size of the equipment, complexity of the wells, etc., but will normally be in the range of $20,000 to $40,000 per day. This approach of a platform mounted drilling rig is often used in water depths that are too deep for a jack-up, although in some cases the platform rig will be supported by equipment mounted on a drilling tender, a barge that floats next to the platform. The disadvantage of using a drilling tender is that there is an increase in the amount of downtime due to weather, particularly in the winter months.

The small TLPs, and some of the other minimal deepwater development options, use a floating mobile offshore drilling unit (MODU) to do their development drilling and workover. In the case of the Sir Douglas Morpeth mini-TLP, the wells were located approximately 1,500 feet south of the facility. The hydrocarbons are produced through flexible flowlines that run from subsea completions up to the platform. After processing, they are exported through steel catenary risers (SCR) to export pipelines to a shallow water production facility. If the wells need maintenance, a semisubmersible is brought in to re-enter them, and carry out the additional work. The great advantage of this approach is that, like the shallow water platform, the structure does not need to be designed for the additional weight of the drilling package. The downside is that the cost of a deepwater semisubmersible drilling unit is much higher than the cost of a platform rig. A semisubmersible will likely cost between $50,000 and $120,000 per day depending on water depth and availability. In deepwater there are significantly fewer units capable of doing the drilling work, so their rates tend to be higher, but also subject to availability. Given that a

---

[19] This may be the full set of equipment required to drill a well, including mud pumps, shale shakers, blowout prevention equipment, electrical power generation, storage of all the consumables in both the sack store and bulk store, drilling crew and accommodation, drill pipe, etc.

deepwater well on a small platform may be producing at 20,000 bbd, downtime for that well will cost $300,000 per day at $15 per bbl[20], so delays caused by unavailable rigs can be very expensive.

5.8. BLOWOUTS

The potential for deepwater blowouts is a much-studied issue. The MMS has funded the first stage of a study being undertaken by Global Petroleum Research Institute (GPRI), the Offshore Technology Research Center (OTRC), and Texas A&M University to look at some of the issues associated with a deepwater blowout. It has been suggested that in the OCS there is one blowout for every 285 wells[21]. So far there have been no deepwater blowouts, although there have been a number of cases of sub-surface cross flow, where hydrocarbons have migrated from one formation to another because of downhole problems. However, there is no real reason to believe that there will not be a blowout, and the question then becomes, how it can be controlled.

In shallow water there are a number of alternative control measures available depending on the circumstances of the blowout, and plenty of drilling units available for use in shallow water. Conversely, in deepwater not only are the options more limited, there are few units capable of operating at the required water depths. It may be that there are only one or two drillships capable of drilling in 10,000 feet water depth in the Gulf of Mexico at any given time, so the availability of a unit to undertake a dynamic kill[22] is extremely limited, not counting the time taken to drill the intersecting well (which may be 25,000 feet below the seabed).

The issue of deepwater blowouts is complicated, and starting to get the serious study that it deserves. The intent of this very brief discussion is to establish that there are significant differences between shallow water blowouts and deepwater blowouts, but not to go into great detail. There are many other potential differences that are being studied. For example, a relatively large percentage of blowouts in shallow water "bridge over"[23] (approximately 40%). It may be that the same could be said for deepwater wells, but it is not clear that that is true. The issue is complicated because the pressure gradient inside a deepwater well will be much lower than in a shallow water well, and a high pressure gradient leads to high flow rates, and an increased potential for bridging. Combine that with the different formations, and their propensity to collapse, and it is certainly not clear how deepwater wells would react in the event of open flow.

5.9. EVACUATION

The issue of evacuation has been debated many times over the years. There are those who swear that the reason offshore installations are evacuated dates back to the early days of the industry when the offshore workers were needed onshore to help their families prepare for the hurricane's arrival, or even evacuate the area. There are others who state that the perceived reliability of early offshore structures was

---

[20] There is always discussion regarding the effects of "loss of production." There are those who argue that production is not lost, only delayed. Since the oil is in the ground, you can just get it out later. The other side of the argument is that the facility has been cost modeled based on certain production rates. If those rates are reduced for any reason, there is a cash flow crunch – all the debt associated with the installation needs to be serviced, but there is no money flowing in to service it. This is a real loss, and may cause the costs associated with the debt to increase, hence there is potentially an actual loss due to the delayed production.

[21] Podio Study of 1996. The statistics were presented at a deepwater blowout industry workshop on 15th August 2002. Details of the presentation can be found at http://pumpjack.tamu.edu/gpri/index html.

[22] A hole is drilled to intersect the well that is blowing out, normally close to where the hydrocarbons are entering the hole. Water is then pumped down the hole at a very high rate such that the back-pressure induced as the water flows up and out of the blowing well causes the hydrocarbons to stop flowing into the well.

[23] Bridging is simply the case where the well gets blocked with formation rock that flows into the well with the blowing out hydrocarbons. The pressure gradient is change in pressure, with respect to the distance, between the bottom of the hole, and the "surface." In shallow water the "surface" may actually be at atmospheric pressure. In a deepwater well, the "surface" will be at the seabed, under 10,000 feet of water. If the deepwater and shallow water wells are at the same depth below the seabed, then the pressure gradient will likely be much greater on the shallow water well.

too low, and that evacuation was needed to protect the offshore workers. Yet others state that regulators mandate evacuation. Regardless of the real reasons, there are certain facts about all precautionary hurricane evacuations from offshore platforms:

- In the event that a platform is hit by a hurricane, there is little that a crew could do onboard a platform, FPSO, or other installation apart from being inside a protected area. The wind force on a man in a 60-knot wind (about 70 mph) is roughly 70 pounds. This increases to approximately 200 pounds in a wind of 100 knots (115 mph). In addition, any loose objects will be flying around making open areas extremely dangerous. All processing should have been shut-in before transit of the storm, so little assistance could be given there. There is a possibility that on certain moored vessels, some limited actions could be taken to reduce the probability of a mooring failure.

- Precautionary evacuations are associated with some risk – there have been people killed and injured during these evacuations. It is not to be inferred that staying offshore is necessarily safer than evacuation to shore, but there are inherent risks associated with any movement of personnel.

- The potential for legal action by injured parties needs to be very carefully considered when discussing the merits or otherwise of precautionary evacuation.

- As structures move further offshore, there is an increased need to plan evacuations such that those furthest offshore do not get stranded as those closer in are evacuated. This is discussed in greater detail below.

Most of the shallow water Gulf of Mexico is relatively close to land such that a helicopter can fly out to a platform and back to land on a single tank of fuel. This is important because whenever a helicopter takes off, it must always have sufficient fuel to get back without having to take on additional fuel. This is to allow for unexpected eventualities that disallow landing at the expected destination (e.g., severe weather, fog, fire at the facility, etc.). Most shallow water facilities are located close enough that as long as they have a refueling facility, they meet this criterion. The same cannot be said for many of the deepwater facilities. In order to fly out to these, the helicopter must take on fuel part way out in order to have sufficient for the return flight.

Consider now a platform that is used as the refueling station for another platform further offshore. If the refueling platform is threatened by a hurricane, it is necessary to evacuate both the nearshore platform, and the deepwater platform that it "serves." In addition, the deepwater platform has to be evacuated first so that there are personnel on the inshore platform to refuel the helicopter. While this is not complicated for a few platforms, a major hurricane threatening a large area of the Gulf could lead to relatively complex logistical issues. In addition, there is a possibility that the near shore platforms could be evacuated by supply and crew boats. The boats will generally want to run for shelter in the event of severe weather (unlike large ships which will often put to sea when threatened by hurricanes), but can often help with the evacuation of close in platforms. Given that most supply boats will have a cruising speed of only about 12 knots, and the speed of a rapidly moving hurricane may be close to 12 knots, they will generally not want to wait offshore for too long before heading for home.

There has been talk about having offshore bases that could be used for supplies, and as evacuation "ports" in the event of a hurricane. The intent would be that personnel are evacuated to these facilities, but remain offshore through the storm. While such a facility may be used in the future, none exist at present, so evacuation, and precautionary evacuations need to be carefully planned for the far offshore deepwater facilities.

References

The following is a list of some of the more important documents accessed during the course of this project. Many of the papers were published at various Offshore Technology Conferences where new technology is often given an entire sessions, with six or more papers dedicated to the one subject. Much of the unreferenced information used was supplied directly by the companies approached, and hence cannot be given a public reference. Individuals closely associated with the particular projects supplied additional information. Some information was obtained off the Internet; but in most cases, this was subject to confirmation prior to its use. Some companies (particularly Shell) directed the authors to their web site as an official source of information. In these cases, the information was not subject to additional confirming research. Only a limited number of newspaper/periodical articles have been included, and only those that were found to be of particular relevance. Clearly, the authors are continually reviewing the trade press and much background information is gleaned from it.

Beckmann, M.M., M.L. Byrd, J. Holt, J.W. Riley, C.K. Snell, C. Tyer, and D. Brewster. 1996. Pompano subsea development: Template/manifold, tree & ROV intervention systems. Paper No. 8205, presented at the Offshore Technology Conference, Houston, TX.

Bevan, J. 1997, July 20. Miracle man from British Borneo city profile – Alan Gaynor has turned a quirky little shell company into Britain's third largest independent oil producer. *The Sunday Telegraph*, London.

Burke, R.G. 2000, February. Back to the cradle. Offshore Engineer, 22(4 pages).

Business Wire. 1997, October 1. Gulf Island fabrication announces letter of intent for British Borneo's Allegheny field SeaStar TLP.

Carminati, J.R., L.F. Eaton, K.A. Folse, and R.E. Sokoll. 1999. Ursa TLP well systems. Paper No. 10758, presented at the Offshore Technology Conference, Houston, TX.

Davies, K. and M. Srivareerat. 1999. Morpeth SeaStar: foundation and tendon systems. Paper No. 10856, presented at the Offshore Technology Conference, Houston, TX.

de Koeijer, D.M., D. Renkema, J.C. Edel, C.H. Willis, and D. Payne. 1999. Installation of the Baldpate Compliant Tower. Paper No. 10919, presented at the Offshore Technology Conference, Houston, TX.

Digre, K.A., R.M. Kipp, R.J. Hunt, S.Y. Hanna, J.H. Chan, V. Rosen, and C. van der Voort. 1999. Ursa TLP, tendon & foundation design, fabrication, transportation and TLP installation. Paper No. 10756, presented at the Offshore Technology Conference, Houston, TX.

Edel, J.C., S. Thibodeaux, F. Sezer, J.D. Payne, and C.H. Willis. 1999. Fabrication of the Baldpate compliant tower. Paper No. 10918, presented at the Offshore Technology Conference, Houston, TX.

Ganguly, P., L. Goldberg, and B. Wood. 1997. The Pompano subsea inspection. Paper No. 8469, presented at the Offshore Technology Conference, Houston, TX.

Gatlin, M.E. 1999. Operations role in the design and commissioning of the Ursa TLP. Paper No. 10759, presented at the Offshore Technology Conference, Houston, TX.

Glanville, R.S. 1996. The Oryx spar Vioska Knoll Block 826. Society of Naval Architects and Marine Engineers Offshore Symposium, Texas Section.

Glanville, R.S. and R.D. Vardeman. 1999. The Neptune spar – performance over the first two years of production. Paper No. 11073, presented at the Offshore Technology Conference, Houston, TX.

Gottung, P.W., K.A. Digre, R.A. Hughson, M.S. Lindsay, and H. Schipper. 1999. Ursa TLP topside-module installation and hull-deck-rig integration. Paper No. 10757, presented at the Offshore Technology Conference, Houston, TX.

Grimond, M. 1997, July 17. British Borneo to raise pounds 167 m from shareholders. Independent, London, Page 23.

Hart's Daily Petroleum Monitor. 1998, October 21. British Borneo field onstream.

Hosey, J. 1996, October/November. A mate's life on a Gulf supply boat. Professional Mariner, 21:11.

Hunt, M. and L. Gary. 2000, January. Gulf of Mexico fabrication yards build 5,500 platforms over 50 years. Offshore, 60(1): 94.

Jefferis, R.G., K.A. Digre, and J.P. Haney. 1999. Ursa – team-based project management – overcoming adversity in 4000 ft. of water. Paper No. 10753, presented at the Offshore Technology Conference, Houston, TX.

Kennefick, J., P. Lang, and D. Harvey. 1999. Morpeth export system. Paper No. 10859, presented at the Offshore Technology Conference, Houston, TX.

Kibbee, S.E, S.J. Leverette, K.B. Davies, and R.B. Matten. 1999. Morpeth SeaStar Mini-TLP. Paper No. 10855, presented at the Offshore Technology Conference, Houston, TX.

Knott, T. 2000, January. SAW cuts against the grain. Offshore Engineer, 28 (2 pages).

Kocaman, A., E. Verdin, and J. Toups. 1997. Neptune project: spar hull, mooring and topsides installation. Paper No. 8385, presented at the Offshore Technology Conference, Houston, TX.

Kypke, D.A. 1995. Tension leg platforms, in the beginning... Society of Naval Architects and Marine Engineers Offshore Symposium, Texas Section.

Le Blanc, L. 1996, November. Spar-shaped drilling unit designed for 8,000-10,000 ft depth corridor. Offshore, 56(11):30

Lehtinen, T. 1997. Spar hull construction. Society of Naval Architects and Marine Engineers 5th Offshore Symposium, Texas Section.

Lochte, G., T. Dean, D. Gray, C. Kochenower, C. Loper, and O. Tarlton. 1999. Morpeth subsea production system. Paper No. 10858, presented at the Offshore Technology Conference, Houston, TX.

Major, R.A., G.R. Frazer, J.E. Taylor, and J.A. Mercier. 1999. World's fifth TLP to achieve classification. Paper No. 11072, presented at the Offshore Technology Conference, Houston, TX.

Means, E. and B. Wright. 2000, January 14. Aker and J Ray kill off spars. Upstream, 5(02):7.

Oil & Gas Journal. 1994, September 5. BP installs big pompano platform in Gulf of Mexico, 92(36):34.

Oil & Gas Journal. 1995, March 13. Economics and technology spark deepwater projects in Gulf, 93(11):25.

Oil & Gas Journal. 1996, September 9. Deepwater experience, prospects outlined, 94(37):35.

Preston, S.M., T.D. Caldwell, M.M. Beckmann, R.F. Coffman, D. Hanks, and C.L. Hebert. 1996. Pompano subsea development: An example of how successful client/contractor relationships result in effective project execution. Paper No. 8204, presented at the Offshore Technology Conference, Houston, TX.

Professional Mariner. 2000, December/January. Gulf coast mariners have a new voice, 45:16.

Redfern, I.J., D.E. Calkins, and R.B. Matten. 1999. Morpeth SeaStar installation. Paper No. 10857, presented at the Offshore Technology Conference, Houston, TX.

Rigden, D. 2000, February 11. Sinking Borneo sends a mayday. Upstream, 5(06):31.

Simon, J.V., J.C. Edel, and C. Melancon. 1999. An overview of the Baldpate project. Paper No. 10914, presented at the Offshore Technology Conference, Houston, TX.

Smith, P.L., S.B. Hodges, and K.A. Digre, B.A. Sarwono, and H. Schipper. 1999. Ursa TLP hull design, fabrication, and transportation. Paper No. 10754, presented at the Offshore Technology Conference, Houston, TX.

Upstream. 2000, January 21. Pompano opens door for Mica. 5(03).

Wall Street Journal. 1994, November 10. Oryx Energy to use a floating system in Gulf of Mexico.

William, J., F. Roach, V.C. Knight, G.E. Lochte, S.E. Kibbee, and N. Mackintosh. 1999. Morpeth field development overview. Paper No. 10854, presented at the Offshore Technology Conference, Houston, TX.

Wright, B. 2000, February 11. McDermott hits Typhoon jackpot. Upstream, 5(06):12.

Wright, B. and E. Means. 2000, January 7. Statoil heads for deep-water exit. Upstream, 5(01):2.

Vardeman, D., S. Richardson, and C.R. McCandless. 1997. Neptune project: overview and project management. Paper No. 8381, presented at the Offshore Technology Conference, Houston, TX.

Zimmer, R.A., R.F. Figgers, J.F. Geesling, H. Kim, D.H. Yeung, Z. Banatwala, G.A. Sidwell, J.A. Stout, B.W. Harris, and M. van Vught. 1999. Design and fabrication of the Ursa TLP deck modules and TLP hull upper column frame. Paper No. 10755, presented at the Offshore Technology Conference, Houston, TX.

Appendix

GEOGRAPHY

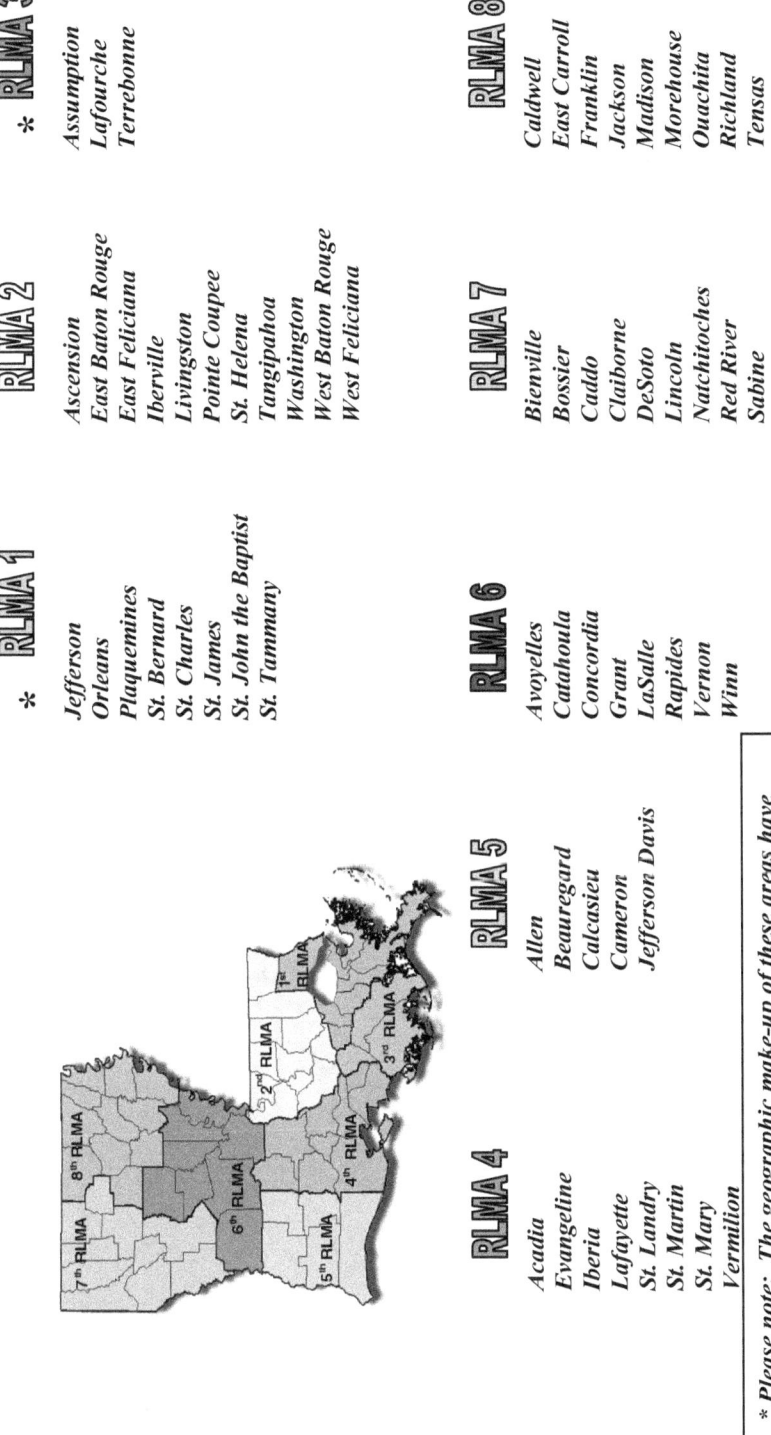

* RLMA 1

Jefferson
Orleans
Plaquemines
St. Bernard
St. Charles
St. James
St. John the Baptist
St. Tammany

RLMA 2

Ascension
East Baton Rouge
East Feliciana
Iberville
Livingston
Pointe Coupee
St. Helena
Tangipahoa
Washington
West Baton Rouge
West Feliciana

* RLMA 3

Assumption
Lafourche
Terrebonne

RLMA 4

Acadia
Evangeline
Iberia
Lafayette
St. Landry
St. Martin
St. Mary
Vermilion

RLMA 5

Allen
Beauregard
Calcasieu
Cameron
Jefferson Davis

RLMA 6

Avoyelles
Catahoula
Concordia
Grant
LaSalle
Rapides
Vernon
Winn

RLMA 7

Bienville
Bossier
Caddo
Claiborne
DeSoto
Lincoln
Natchitoches
Red River
Sabine
Webster

RLMA 8

Caldwell
East Carroll
Franklin
Jackson
Madison
Morehouse
Ouachita
Richland
Tensas
Union
West Carroll

* Please note: The geographic make-up of these areas have been redefined; therefore, data are not comparable to previous projections. (RLMA 1 now includes the parishes of St. Charles, St. James, and St. John the Baptist. RLMA3 now excludes parishes St. Charles, St. James and St. John the Baptist.)

Figure A-1. Data for the 1998-2008 Employment Projections Cover the State of Louisiana and the Eight Regional Labor Market Areas (RLMA's).

GEOGRAPHY

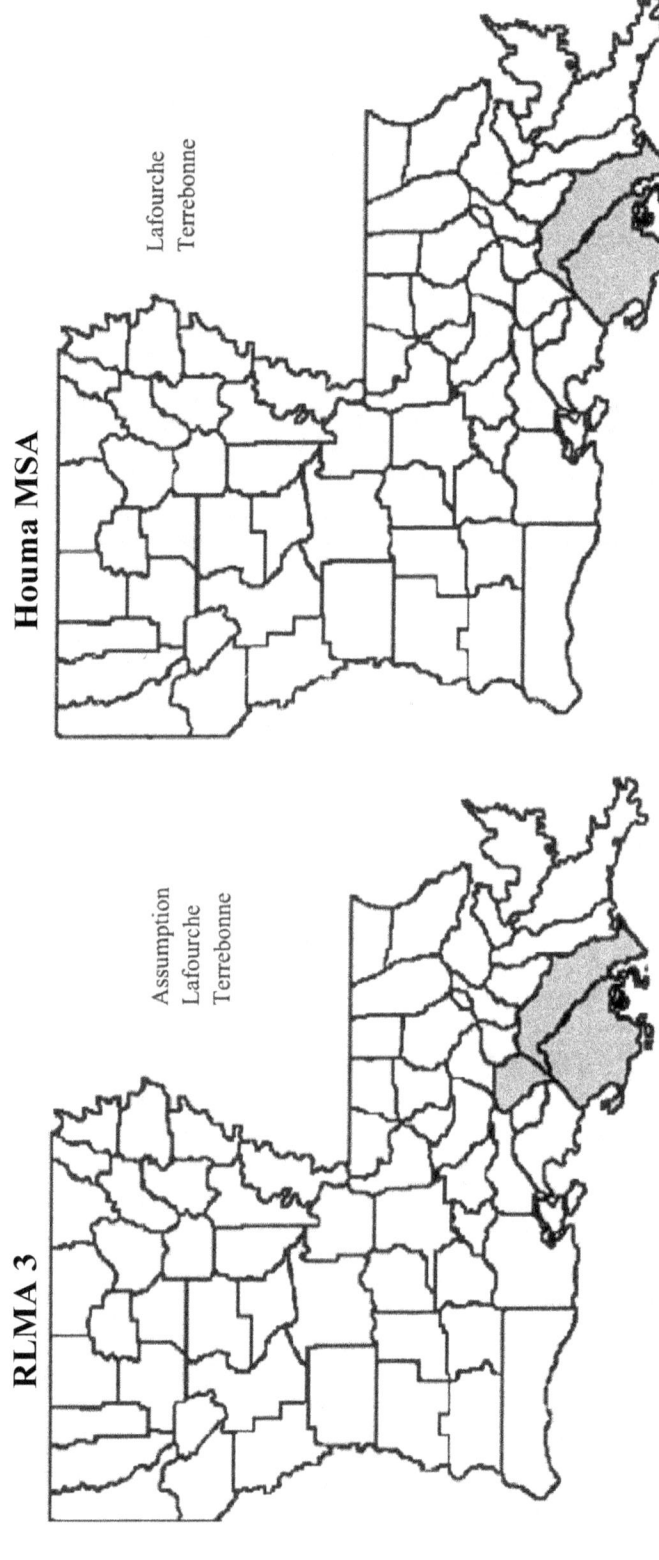

Figure A-2. Houma Metropolitan Statistical Area (MSA) Includes Lafourche and Terrebonne Parishes Compared to Regional Labor Market Area 3 (RLMA 3), which also Includes Assumption Parish.

Table A-1

Regional Labor Market Area and Houma Metropolitan Statistical Area—1999 Wage Comparison

SOC-Code	Occupational Title	RLMA 3						Houma MSA					
		Total # Empl.	Mean ($/hour)	Entry ($/hour)	Median ($/hour)	Experience ($/hour)	Annual $	Total # Empl.	Mean ($/hour)	Entry ($/hour)	Median ($/hour)	Experience ($/hour)	Annual $
Management Occupations													
11-1011	Chief Executives	280	41.18	23.88	32.80	>70.00	85,657	270	39.75	22.95	30.49	>70.00	82,690
11-1021	General & Operations Managers	1,820	25.39	16.90	21.62	32.30	52,804	1,720	25.08	17.21	21.21	31.57	52,160
11-1031	Legislators	*	5.96	5.75	6.17	6.58	12,398	*	**	5.55	5.95	6.35	11,960
11-2011	Advertising & Promotions Managers	30	36.77	24.64	35.79	42.69	76,477	30	35.47	23.77	34.54	41.18	73,780
11-2021	Marketing Managers	50	22.86	17.34	23.35	26.23	47,540	50	22.05	16.73	22.53	25.30	45,870
11-2022	Sales Managers	390	28.25	17.10	25.44	35.39	58,756	390	27.25	16.50	24.54	34.14	56,690
11-3011	Administrative Services Managers	110	18.09	10.18	17.20	24.49	37,624	110	17.14	9.74	15.48	22.54	35,660
11-3021	Computer & Information Systems Managers	40	23.72	18.60	21.48	26.20	49,343	40	22.88	17.94	20.72	25.28	47,600
11-3031	Financial Managers	180	26.81	13.90	21.37	33.93	55,764	170	26.13	13.34	20.91	33.57	54,340
11-3040	Human Resources Managers	60	24.05	17.92	22.99	31.37	50,020	60	23.05	17.16	22.01	29.76	47,940
11-3051	Industrial Production Managers	110	25.71	18.60	25.12	34.26	53,474	110	24.70	17.73	24.11	32.83	51,370
11-3061	Purchasing Managers	80	21.58	13.85	19.66	29.64	44,882	70	20.67	13.29	18.76	28.22	42,990
11-3071	Transportation, Storage, & Distribution Managers.	50	19.40	16.09	19.30	22.51	40,354	50	18.72	15.52	18.63	21.73	38,930
11-9021	Construction Managers	80	24.23	19.60	22.31	26.11	50,392	80	23.37	18.91	21.52	25.19	48,620
11-9041	Engineering Managers	70	29.34	21.44	30.68	35.60	61,019	*	29.14	21.08	29.94	36.33	60,620
11-9051	Food Service Managers	130	12.23	8.50	10.41	15.67	25,449	130	11.81	8.20	10.04	15.12	24,560
11-9061	Funeral Directors	30	13.82	8.60	13.82	16.99	28,733	30	13.32	8.30	13.33	16.39	27,710
11-9081	Lodging Managers	*	13.56	12.23	13.31	14.98	28,203	N/A	N/A	N/A	N/A	N/A	N/A
11-9111	Medical & Health Services Managers	*	18.61	10.37	17.66	24.77	38,702	N/A	N/A	N/A	N/A	N/A	N/A
11-9141	Property, Real Estate, & Community Association Managers	*	17.61	7.97	9.15	12.44	36,641	N/A	N/A	N/A	N/A	N/A	N/A
11-9151	Social & Community Service Managers	20	23.87	22.95	25.09	27.22	49,652	N/A	N/A	N/A	N/A	N/A	N/A
11-9199	Managers, All Other	220	20.62	15.64	18.78	25.60	42,885	220	19.65	15.04	17.74	24.35	40,860

Table A-1

Regional Labor Market Area and Houma Metropolitan Statistical Area—1999 Wage Comparison

SOC-Code	Occupational Title	RLMA 3						Houma MSA					
		Total # Empl.	Mean ($/hour)	Entry ($/hour)	Median ($/hour)	Experience ($/hour)	Annual $	Total # Empl.	Mean ($/hour)	Entry ($/hour)	Median ($/hour)	Experience ($/hour)	Annual $
Business and Financial Operations Occupations													
13-1021	Purchasing Agents & Buyers, Farm Products	*	15.50	11.90	13.67	19.73	32,233	N/A	N/A	N/A	N/A	N/A	N/A
13-1022	Wholesale & Retail Buyers, Except Farm Products	30	15.08	12.63	14.17	18.00	31,365	30	14.47	12.27	13.61	17.00	30,100
13-1023	Purchasing Agents, Except Wholesale, Retail, & Farm Products	100	16.15	11.92	14.75	20.44	33,590	100	15.34	11.45	14.10	19.30	31,910
13-1031	Claims Adjusters, Examiners, & Investigators	10	21.74	16.20	18.90	29.64	45,219	N/A	N/A	N/A	N/A	N/A	N/A
13-1051	Cost Estimators	80	24.12	17.70	22.29	27.78	50,162	80	22.62	16.77	21.01	24.94	47,050
13-1061	Emergency Management Specialists	10	23.03	13.51	21.46	31.66	47,898	N/A	N/A	N/A	N/A	N/A	N/A
13-1071	Employment, Recruitment, & Placement Specialists	10	15.98	13.59	15.80	18.24	33,250	N/A	N/A	N/A	N/A	N/A	N/A
13-1072	Compensation, Benefits, & Job Analysis Specialists	20	13.53	11.20	12.99	16.54	28,142	N/A	N/A	N/A	N/A	N/A	N/A
13-1073	Training & Development Specialists	*	18.35	14.66	17.19	22.09	38,154	*	17.70	14.14	16.58	21.31	36,810
13-1199	Business Operations Specialists, All Other	210	22.96	12.64	25.70	31.98	47,754	210	22.15	12.19	24.80	30.86	46,070
13-2011	Accountants & Auditors	330	18.24	13.26	16.54	21.00	37,955	330	17.83	12.75	16.39	20.49	37,090
13-2072	Loan Officers	50	17.54	15.11	17.55	20.24	36,474	50	16.92	14.58	16.93	19.53	35,180
13-2099	Financial Specialists, All Other	50	11.56	9.30	10.26	14.62	24,030	50	11.14	8.97	9.90	14.10	23,180
Computer and Mathematical Occupations													
15-1021	Computer Programmers	10	16.90	12.14	15.95	20.34	35,142	N/A	N/A	N/A	N/A	N/A	N/A
15-1041	Computer Support Specialists	*	17.32	12.26	13.32	17.08	36,039	*	16.62	11.76	12.78	16.39	34,580
15-1051	Computer Systems Analysts	50	21.56	16.60	21.10	26.26	44,837	50	20.69	15.93	20.24	25.20	43,020
15-1099	Computer Specialists, All Other	20	17.47	15.56	17.06	19.40	36,326	N/A	N/A	N/A	N/A	N/A	N/A
Architecture and Engineering Occupations													
17-2111	Health & Safety Engineers, Except Mining Safety Engineers & Inspectors	20	26.90	21.21	25.13	31.63	55,966	*	28.21	20.76	28.99	37.42	58,690
17-2112	Industrial Engineers	30	26.19	24.06	26.02	27.98	54,474	30	25.13	23.08	24.96	26.84	52,260
17-2199	Engineers, All Other	80	30.34	26.18	30.94	34.80	63,117	*	29.11	25.12	29.68	33.39	60,550
17-3011	Architectural & Civil Drafters	*	13.45	10.51	13.52	16.09	27,961	N/A	N/A	N/A	N/A	N/A	N/A

Table A-1

Regional Labor Market Area and Houma Metropolitan Statistical Area—1999 Wage Comparison

SOC-Code	Occupational Title	RLMA 3						Houma MSA					
		Total # Empl.	Mean ($/hour)	Entry ($/hour)	Median ($/hour)	Experience ($/hour)	Annual $	Total # Empl.	Mean ($/hour)	Entry ($/hour)	Median ($/hour)	Experience ($/hour)	Annual $
17-3022	Civil Engineering Technicians	*	18.35	11.38	17.02	24.16	38,157	*	17.61	10.92	16.32	23.18	36,620
17-3099	All Other Drafters, Engineering, & Mapping Technicians	40	18.18	13.05	16.63	28.55	37,814	40	17.01	11.44	15.23	23.03	35,380
Life, Physical, and Social Science Occupations													
19-4099	Life, Physical, & Social Science Technicians, All Other	20	19.49	17.56	20.20	23.10	40,547	N/A	N/A	N/A	N/A	N/A	N/A
Community and Social Service Occupations													
21-1013	Marriage & Family Therapists	*	9.91	9.44	10.04	10.62	20,618	N/A	N/A	N/A	N/A	N/A	N/A
21-1014	Mental Health Counselors	*	14.98	14.17	15.52	16.89	31,164	*	14.37	13.59	14.89	16.20	29,900
21-1021	Child, Family, & School Social Workers	60	14.84	11.95	13.88	17.58	30,880	60	14.24	11.46	13.32	16.87	29,620
21-1022	Medical & Public Health Social Workers	*	9.55	6.01	6.66	15.17	19,854	*	9.01	5.76	6.37	14.43	18,740
21-1093	Social & Human Service Assistants	90	9.20	6.95	8.85	11.05	19,149	90	8.90	6.60	8.69	10.70	18,510
21-9099	All Other Counselors, Social & Religious Workers.	80	12.97	7.88	12.44	16.29	26,965	80	12.44	7.56	11.93	15.63	25,880
Legal Occupations													
23-1011	Lawyers	50	16.00	6.83	13.36	19.93	33,272	50	15.37	6.55	12.83	19.14	31,960
23-2091	Court Reporters	20	13.35	12.04	13.33	15.17	27,777	N/A	N/A	N/A	N/A	N/A	N/A
Education, Training, and Library Occupations													
25-3021	Self-Enrichment Education Teachers	*	17.23	14.88	17.35	19.88	35,834	*	16.53	14.28	16.65	19.07	34,380
25-4021	Librarians	*	17.44	13.55	17.27	20.79	36,264	*	16.44	12.68	16.32	19.75	34,190
25-9041	Teacher Assistants	*	**	**	**	**	15,148	*	**	**	**	**	13,560
Arts, Design, Entertainment, Sports, and Media Occupations													
27-1024	Graphic Designers	20	12.40	9.27	14.23	15.97	25,807	N/A	N/A	N/A	N/A	N/A	N/A
27-4013	Radio Operators	30	10.69	7.62	9.61	12.87	22,255	*	10.27	7.26	8.99	12.42	21,360
27-4021	Photographers	*	7.83	5.97	6.92	9.65	16,283	N/A	N/A	N/A	N/A	N/A	N/A
Healthcare Practitioners and Technical Occupations													
29-1051	Pharmacists	90	29.15	24.22	30.45	37.65	60,644	90	27.46	22.66	28.14	35.00	57,120
29-1111	Registered Nurses	270	19.78	16.64	19.21	22.57	41,145	250	18.92	15.90	18.36	21.54	39,350
29-1123	Physical Therapists	*	37.58	27.46	36.59	50.68	78,163	*	35.90	26.22	34.85	46.36	74,680

Table A-1

Regional Labor Market Area and Houma Metropolitan Statistical Area—1999 Wage Comparison

SOC-Code	Occupational Title	RLMA 3						Houma MSA					
		Total # Empl.	Mean ($/hour)	Entry ($/hour)	Median ($/hour)	Experience ($/hour)	Annual $	Total # Empl.	Mean ($/hour)	Entry ($/hour)	Median ($/hour)	Experience ($/hour)	Annual $
29-2041	Emergency Medical Technicians & Paramedics	30	11.38	8.88	11.40	13.93	23,666	*	10.92	8.52	10.94	13.36	22,700
29-2051	Dietetic Technicians	-	9.65	8.39	9.61	10.72	20,075	N/A	N/A	N/A	N/A	N/A	N/A
29-2052	Pharmacy Technicians	130	7.71	6.58	7.67	8.79	16,035	130	7.36	6.23	7.32	8.44	15,300
Healthcare Support Occupations													
29-2061	Licensed Practical & Licensed Vocational Nurses	360	11.80	9.77	11.01	13.29	24,540	*	11.32	9.36	10.54	12.74	23,550
29-2071	Medical Records & Health Information Technicians	10	8.98	8.06	9.09	10.14	18,697	N/A	N/A	N/A	N/A	N/A	N/A
29-2081	Opticians, Dispensing	*	9.10	7.72	9.55	10.43	18,918	*	8.73	7.42	9.16	10.01	18,150
31-1012	Nursing Aides, Orderlies, & Attendants	590	6.63	5.96	6.52	7.14	13,798	590	6.38	5.78	6.28	6.87	13,260
31-9091	Dental Assistants	250	9.13	7.20	8.22	10.94	18,993	*	8.80	6.94	7.92	10.53	18,300
31-9099	Healthcare Support Workers, All Other	*	10.20	9.50	10.16	10.84	21,225	*	9.83	9.15	9.79	10.44	20,450
Protective Service Occupations													
33-1012	First-Line Supervisors/ Managers of Police & Detectives	30	16.91	12.77	15.76	18.09	35,167	30	16.29	12.29	15.18	17.42	33,890
33-3021	Detectives & Criminal Investigators	70	15.02	10.72	12.67	16.13	31,247	*	14.48	10.33	12.21	15.54	30,110
33-3051	Police & Sheriff's Patrol Officers	310	11.53	9.85	11.15	13.27	23,975	*	11.41	9.69	10.96	12.89	23,720
33-9032	Security Guards	390	8.00	6.26	7.17	9.31	16,634	390	7.75	6.07	6.94	9.11	16,110
33-9099	Protective Service Workers, All Other	*	6.29	5.77	6.20	6.62	13,092	*	6.06	5.56	5.97	6.38	12,610
Food Preparation and Serving Related Occupations													
35-1012	First-Line Supervisors/ Managers of Food Preparation & Serving Workers	320	11.66	7.65	10.68	15.41	24,234	310	11.42	7.49	10.76	14.96	23,740
35-2011	Cooks, Fast Food	940	6.05	5.74	6.08	6.51	12,591	940	5.78	5.66	5.92	6.28	12,030
35-2012	Cooks, Institution & Cafeteria	470	8.13	6.16	6.96	9.72	16,911	*	7.82	5.95	6.70	9.39	16,270
35-2014	Cooks, Restaurant	*	7.56	6.10	7.33	8.94	15,726	*	7.26	5.94	7.06	8.61	15,090
35-2015	Cooks, Short Order	*	6.26	5.94	6.39	6.92	13,016	60	5.90	5.72	6.10	6.56	12,270
35-2021	Food Preparation Workers	740	6.38	5.81	6.29	6.76	13,288	*	6.19	5.61	6.07	6.53	12,870
35-3011	Bartenders	120	6.22	5.66	5.96	6.26	12,938	120	6.23	5.69	5.98	6.55	12,970

Table A-1

Regional Labor Market Area and Houma Metropolitan Statistical Area—1999 Wage Comparison

SOC-Code	Occupational Title	RLMA 3						Houma MSA					
		Total # Empl.	Mean ($/hour)	Entry ($/hour)	Median ($/hour)	Experience ($/hour)	Annual $	Total # Empl.	Mean ($/hour)	Entry ($/hour)	Median ($/hour)	Experience ($/hour)	Annual $
35-3021	Combined Food Preparation & Serving Workers, Including Fast Food	700	6.34	5.65	5.95	6.25	13,200	700	6.02	5.66	5.86	6.06	12,520
35-3022	Counter Attendants, Cafeteria, Food Concession, & Coffee Shop	80	7.09	6.09	6.72	8.26	14,754	80	6.51	5.81	6.33	6.88	13,540
35-3031	Waiters & Waitresses	860	6.43	5.77	6.14	6.68	13,358	860	6.14	5.69	5.97	6.44	12,780
35-9011	Dining Room & Cafeteria Attendants & Bartender Helpers	*	6.01	5.80	6.19	6.63	12,493	*	5.77	5.64	5.98	6.39	12,000
35-9021	Dishwashers	190	6.07	5.78	6.23	6.66	12,622	190	5.85	5.57	6.00	6.42	12,160
35-9031	Hosts & Hostesses, Restaurant, Lounge, & Coffee Shop	130	6.29	5.81	6.22	6.85	13,075	130	6.02	5.70	6.02	6.60	12,530
Building and Grounds Cleaning and Maintenance Occupations													
37-1011	First-Line Supervisors/ Managers of Housekeeping & Janitorial Workers	50	11.76	7.58	9.62	11.14	24,452	50	11.33	7.30	9.27	10.73	23,560
37-1012	First-Line Supervisors/ Managers of Landscaping, Lawn Service, & Groundskeeping Workers	*	12.69	11.76	12.70	13.65	26,406	30	12.19	11.29	12.20	13.11	25,360
37-2011	Janitors & Cleaners, Except Maids & Housekeeping Cleaners	980	7.04	6.00	6.68	7.96	14,634	970	6.65	5.82	6.39	7.47	13,840
37-2012	Maids & Housekeeping Cleaners	330	6.93	6.01	6.80	8.01	14,413	310	6.67	5.87	6.57	7.74	13,870
37-3011	Landscaping & Groundskeeping Workers	250	9.02	7.31	8.37	9.91	18,751	*	8.56	6.91	7.83	9.17	17,800
37-9099	All Other Building & Grounds Cleaning & Maintenance Workers	60	7.50	6.14	6.92	8.45	15,604	60	7.21	5.90	6.65	8.11	14,990
Personal Care and Service Occupations													
39-1021	First-Line Supervisors/ Managers of Personal Service Workers	30	10.06	6.55	10.76	12.84	20,925	30	9.69	6.31	10.37	12.37	20,160
39-5012	Hairdressers, Hairstylists, & Cosmetologists	120	7.85	7.13	7.92	8.70	16,331	120	7.57	6.87	7.63	8.38	15,740
39-9011	Child Care Workers	90	6.40	5.70	6.04	6.48	13,321	90	6.09	5.68	5.91	6.24	12,670
39-9031	Fitness Trainers & Aerobics Instructors	*	5.97	5.76	6.18	6.59	12,414	N/A	N/A	N/A	N/A	N/A	N/A
39-9032	Recreation Workers	80	6.15	5.82	6.25	6.70	12,798	80	5.90	5.58	6.01	6.43	12,280

Table A-1

Regional Labor Market Area and Houma Metropolitan Statistical Area—1999 Wage Comparison

SOC-Code	Occupational Title	RLMA 3						Houma MSA					
		Total # Empl.	Mean ($/hour)	Entry ($/hour)	Median ($/hour)	Experience ($/hour)	Annual $	Total # Empl.	Mean ($/hour)	Entry ($/hour)	Median ($/hour)	Experience ($/hour)	Annual $
Sales and Related Occupations													
41-1011	First-Line Supervisors/ Managers of Retail Sales Workers	870	13.59	9.79	12.26	16.58	28,270	800	13.72	9.97	12.27	16.53	28,540
41-1012	First-Line Supervisors/ Managers of Non-Retail Sales Workers	40	15.75	11.59	13.18	17.19	32,775	40	15.19	11.17	12.70	16.57	31,590
41-2011	Cashiers	2,330	6.56	5.84	6.29	6.92	13,636	2,140	6.32	5.78	6.12	6.68	13,150
41-2021	Counter & Rental Clerks	120	8.29	6.14	7.14	9.38	17,249	120	7.99	6.02	6.88	9.04	16,620
41-2022	Parts Salespersons	240	10.41	7.50	9.44	12.79	21,654	240	10.05	7.25	9.12	12.34	20,900
41-2031	Retail Salespersons	2,390	8.78	6.08	6.88	9.19	18,265	2,380	8.50	5.94	6.64	8.94	17,680
41-3011	Advertising Sales Agents	*	14.99	9.98	12.38	15.93	31,189	*	14.46	9.62	11.93	15.34	30,080
41-3021	Insurance Sales Agents	160	26.51	20.03	28.30	32.26	55,154	*	25.55	19.30	27.27	31.09	53,150
41-3041	Travel Agents	30	8.68	6.27	9.25	10.49	18,043	30	8.36	6.13	8.91	10.11	17,400
41-4011	Sales Representative, Wholesale & Manufacturing, Technical. & Scientific Products	80	17.62	11.97	17.18	22.42	36,650	80	16.93	11.48	16.55	21.62	35,220
41-4012	Sales Representative, Wholesale & Manufacturing, Except Technical & Scientific Products	720	19.10	11.55	17.86	23.99	39,740	720	18.44	11.14	17.24	23.13	38,350
41-9022	Real Estate Sales Agents	*	9.38	5.84	6.34	6.83	19,511	N/A	N/A	N/A	N/A	N/A	N/A
41-9031	Sales Engineers	60	27.63	21.03	25.62	38.28	57,475	60	26.63	20.27	24.70	36.89	55,400
41-9099	Sales & Related Workers, All Other	*	9.57	6.01	6.68	9.33	19,904	*	9.22	5.79	6.44	8.99	19,180
Office and Administrative Support Occupations													
43-1011	First-Line Supervisors/ Managers of Office & Administrative Support Workers	470	14.43	9.92	12.05	16.66	30,002	470	14.20	9.46	12.37	16.63	29,530
43-2011	Switchboard Operators, Including Answering Service	80	8.14	6.56	8.01	9.51	16,937	*	7.77	6.27	7.65	9.09	16,160
43-3011	Bill & Account Collectors	100	10.03	7.96	9.82	11.66	20,863	*	9.61	7.63	9.41	11.17	19,990
43-3021	Billing & Posting Clerks & Machine Operators	120	10.67	8.08	9.60	12.37	22,185	120	10.27	7.78	9.25	11.91	21,360
43-3031	Bookkeeping, Accounting, & Auditing Clerks	1,270	9.57	7.13	8.76	11.43	19,898	1,250	9.19	6.82	8.40	11.03	19,120

Table A-1

Regional Labor Market Area and Houma Metropolitan Statistical Area—1999 Wage Comparison

SOC-Code	Occupational Title	RLMA 3						Houma MSA					
		Total # Empl.	Mean ($/hour)	Entry ($/hour)	Median ($/hour)	Experience ($/hour)	Annual $	Total # Empl.	Mean ($/hour)	Entry ($/hour)	Median ($/hour)	Experience ($/hour)	Annual $
43-3051	Payroll & Timekeeping Clerks	40	12.15	9.59	11.89	13.95	25,282	40	11.59	9.13	11.27	13.30	24,100
43-3061	Procurement Clerks	20	10.56	8.37	10.26	12.67	21,972	N/A	N/A	N/A	N/A	N/A	N/A
43-4051	Customer Service Representatives	270	9.62	7.79	9.42	11.10	20,019	*	9.22	7.46	9.02	10.63	19,180
43-4071	File Clerks	*	7.41	6.33	7.31	8.42	15,412	*	7.05	6.09	6.98	8.04	14,670
43-4081	Hotel, Motel, & Resort Desk Clerks	80	7.31	6.21	6.88	8.31	15,198	80	7.00	5.96	6.60	7.96	14,550
43-4111	Interviewers, Except Eligibility & Loan	70	8.94	7.40	8.73	10.46	18,579	*	8.55	7.06	8.38	10.03	17,790
43-4131	Loan Interviewers & Clerks	60	10.41	9.16	10.42	11.97	21,647	*	9.97	8.78	9.98	11.47	20,740
43-4151	Order Clerks	*	15.28	11.95	15.26	16.95	31,779	*	14.64	11.45	14.62	16.24	30,440
43-4999	All Other Financial, Information, & Record Clerks	*	9.67	6.12	6.87	14.90	20,101	N/A	N/A	N/A	N/A	N/A	N/A
43-5032	Dispatchers, Except Police, Fire, & Ambulance	270	13.10	9.73	11.09	16.47	27,255	270	12.56	9.31	10.63	15.84	26,130
43-5041	Meter Readers, Utilities	*	9.61	7.63	9.71	11.72	19,997	*	9.21	7.31	9.30	11.23	19,160
43-5061	Production, Planning, & Expediting Clerks	240	13.42	10.70	12.70	15.44	27,919	240	12.82	10.26	12.16	14.70	26,670
43-5071	Shipping, Receiving, & Traffic Clerks	250	9.76	7.62	8.77	10.89	20,297	250	9.37	7.31	8.41	10.49	19,500
43-5081	Stock Clerks & Order Fillers	1,010	8.26	6.15	7.12	9.46	17,176	1,010	7.90	5.96	6.84	9.06	16,440
43-5111	Weighers, Measurers, Checkers, & Samplers	40	12.50	6.89	9.95	17.17	26,010	N/A	N/A	N/A	N/A	N/A	N/A
43-4161	Human Resources Assistants, Except Payroll & Timekeeping	30	11.75	8.42	10.79	13.44	24,455	30	11.05	8.04	10.23	12.66	22,990
43-4171	Receptionists & Information Clerks	780	8.29	7.02	8.25	9.54	17,236	770	8.07	6.95	8.02	9.24	16,780
43-5199	All Other Material Record, Scheduling, Dispatching, & Distributing Workers	*	12.19	11.18	12.32	13.42	25,367	*	11.68	10.71	11.80	12.87	24,300
43-6011	Executive Secretaries & Administrative Assistants	340	12.53	9.79	11.71	14.88	26,052	340	12.03	9.39	11.29	14.33	25,030
43-6013	Medical Secretaries	*	9.84	8.54	9.86	11.36	20,476	*	9.43	8.18	9.45	10.88	19,620
43-6014	Secretaries, Except Legal, Medical, & Executive	2,440	11.16	8.32	11.57	13.61	23,207	2,390	10.75	8.02	11.15	13.07	22,350
43-9011	Computer Operators	90	10.40	7.01	9.12	11.93	21,616	90	9.85	6.66	8.57	11.00	20,480
43-9021	Data Entry Keyers	130	7.83	6.29	7.48	9.29	16,294	130	7.45	6.04	7.11	8.86	15,500
43-9022	Word Processors & Typists	40	8.26	6.52	7.75	10.03	17,179	*	7.87	6.22	7.27	9.54	16,370

Table A-1

Regional Labor Market Area and Houma Metropolitan Statistical Area—1999 Wage Comparison

SOC-Code	Occupational Title	RLMA 3						Houma MSA					
		Total # Empl.	Mean ($/hour)	Entry ($/hour)	Median ($/hour)	Experience ($/hour)	Annual $	Total # Empl.	Mean ($/hour)	Entry ($/hour)	Median ($/hour)	Experience ($/hour)	Annual $
43-9041	Insurance Claims & Policy Processing Clerks	20	14.20	12.11	13.00	13.88	29,529	N/A	N/A	N/A	N/A	N/A	N/A
43-9061	Office Clerks, General	1,440	9.32	6.81	8.41	10.78	19,391	1,440	8.91	6.51	8.05	10.31	18,530
43-9999	All Other Secretaries, Administrative Assistants, & Other Office Support	70	13.81	11.33	13.92	16.15	28,727	70	13.21	11.02	13.41	15.44	27,480
	Farming, Fishing, and Forestry Occupations	N/A	N/A	N/A	N/A	N/A	N/A	N/A	N/A	N/A	N/A	N/A	
	Construction and Extraction Occupations												
47-1011	First-Line Supervisors/ Managers of Construction Trades & Extraction Workers	1,490	17.48	15.12	18.16	20.40	36,352	1480	16.80	14.55	17.47	19.62	34,950
47-2031	Carpenters	460	10.55	6.67	10.68	13.60	21,940	460	10.16	6.42	10.28	13.10	21,130
47-2051	Cement Masons & Concrete Finishers	*	8.01	5.92	6.49	9.97	16,665	*	7.72	5.70	6.25	9.60	16,050
47-2061	Construction Laborers	60	7.79	6.23	7.13	8.48	16,196	60	7.48	5.98	6.85	8.14	15,550
47-2073	Operating Engineers & Other Construction Equipment Operators	110	12.94	10.23	12.14	14.54	26,924	110	12.33	9.76	11.47	14.18	25,640
47-2111	Electricians	270	13.80	11.96	13.24	15.64	28,713	260	13.28	11.50	12.73	15.04	27,620
47-2121	Glaziers	*	8.72	6.23	9.08	11.37	18,155	*	8.41	6.00	8.74	10.95	17,480
47-2141	Painters, Construction & Maintenance	420	11.97	11.28	12.36	13.43	24,915	420	11.53	10.86	11.90	12.93	23,990
47-2152	Plumbers, Pipefitters, & Steamfitters	1,000	14.87	12.41	15.03	16.78	30,943	1,000	14.31	12.00	14.47	16.12	29,770
47-2221	Structural Iron & Steel Workers	*	15.02	13.87	15.29	16.63	31,227	*	14.46	13.36	14.72	16.01	30,070
47-3012	Helpers--Carpenters	30	9.39	6.98	8.54	11.95	19,541	*	9.03	6.70	8.21	11.49	18,770
47-4011	Construction & Building Inspectors	20	16.64	12.12	15.38	21.04	34,614	*	7.58	6.26	7.28	8.40	15,760
47-4999	All Other Construction Trades & Related Workers	*	10.76	8.50	10.54	13.13	22,377	30	10.40	8.56	11.22	12.36	21,630
	Installation, Maintenance, and Repair Occupations												
49-1011	First-Line Supervisors/ Managers of Mechanics, Installers, & Repairmen	300	18.45	14.28	18.65	22.40	38,388	300	17.77	13.75	17.96	21.57	36,960
49-2091	Avionics Technicians	10	8.05	6.18	7.01	8.83	16,744	N/A	N/A	N/A	N/A	N/A	N/A
49-2094	Electrical & Electronic Repairmen, Commercial & Industrial Equipment	140	21.78	17.40	23.34	26.03	45,310	140	20.97	16.75	22.47	25.06	43,630

Table A-1

Regional Labor Market Area and Houma Metropolitan Statistical Area—1999 Wage Comparison

SOC-Code	Occupational Title	RLMA 3						Houma MSA					
		Total # Empl.	Mean ($/hour)	Entry ($/hour)	Median ($/hour)	Experience ($/hour)	Annual $	Total # Empl.	Mean ($/hour)	Entry ($/hour)	Median ($/hour)	Experience ($/hour)	Annual $
49-3023	Automotive Service Technicians & Mechanics	490	14.75	11.36	14.71	18.44	30,682	490	14.20	10.94	14.14	17.77	29,540
49-3031	Bus & Truck Mechanics & Diesel Engine Specialists	350	13.80	10.70	13.51	17.27	28,700	350	13.28	10.28	12.98	16.66	27,610
49-3042	Mobile Heavy Equipment Mechanics, Except Engines	390	15.14	11.83	13.97	16.85	31,499	390	14.75	11.50	13.61	16.43	30,690
49-3051	Motorboat Mechanics	50	14.60	10.96	13.77	17.88	30,363	50	14.06	10.55	13.26	17.23	29,240
49-3053	Outdoor Power Equipment & Other Small Engine Mechanics	*	10.79	8.05	9.76	14.36	22,434	*	10.39	7.75	9.40	13.84	21,600
49-3092	Recreational Vehicle Service Technician	*	12.18	9.81	12.14	14.83	25,342	N/A	N/A	N/A	N/A	N/A	N/A
49-3093	Tire Repairers & Changers	*	7.96	7.22	7.93	8.66	16,558	*	7.66	6.95	7.64	8.34	15,930
49-3099	All Other Vehicle & Mobile Equipment Mechanics, Installers, & Repairmen	*	8.40	7.57	8.12	8.68	17,467	*	8.09	7.29	7.82	8.36	16,820
49-9012	Control & Valve Installers & Repairmen, Except Mechanical Door	40	17.75	11.67	16.40	24.55	36,916	40	17.09	11.25	15.80	23.64	35,550
49-9021	Heating, Air Conditioning, & Refrigeration Mechanics & Installers	120	12.88	11.02	12.65	14.39	26,793	120	12.40	10.61	12.18	13.86	25,800
49-9041	Industrial Machinery Mechanics	180	17.00	14.34	15.97	17.60	35,372	180	16.37	13.81	15.38	16.95	34,060
49-9042	Maintenance & Repair Workers, General	640	10.69	7.74	9.67	12.19	22,233	640	10.70	7.85	9.75	12.29	22,250
49-9043	Maintenance Workers, Machinery	*	14.03	9.34	12.70	19.74	29,189	*	14.14	9.92	13.62	20.16	29,420
49-9044	Millwrights	100	16.43	9.68	14.84	20.95	34,181	100	15.83	9.32	14.29	20.17	32,920
49-9052	Telecommunications Line Installers & Repairmen	70	17.89	12.07	19.11	23.15	37,216	*	17.23	11.63	18.40	22.29	35,840
49-9069	Precision Instrument & Equipment Repairmen, All Other	*	16.93	13.81	17.46	19.93	35,215	N/A	N/A	N/A	N/A	N/A	N/A
49-9096	Riggers	*	10.57	8.90	9.94	11.03	21,987	*	10.15	8.59	9.52	10.44	21,120
49-9098	Helpers--Installation, Maintenance, & Repair Workers	220	8.88	7.21	8.48	10.17	18,471	190	8.55	6.94	8.15	9.79	17,780
49-9099	Installation, Maintenance, & Repair Workers, All Other	170	14.27	12.24	13.96	16.32	29,671	170	13.74	11.79	13.45	15.71	28,570

A-13

Table A-1

Regional Labor Market Area and Houma Metropolitan Statistical Area— 1999 Wage Comparison

SOC-Code	Occupational Title	RLMA 3						Houma MSA					
		Total # Empl.	Mean ($/hour)	Entry ($/hour)	Median ($/hour)	Experience ($/hour)	Annual $	Total # Empl.	Mean ($/hour)	Entry ($/hour)	Median ($/hour)	Experience ($/hour)	Annual $
Production Occupations													
51-1011	First-Line Supervisors/ Managers of Production & Operating Workers	460	21.76	14.54	19.29	29.41	45,263	400	21.97	14.76	20.19	29.49	45,690
51-2041	Structural Metal Fabricators & Fitters	*	14.10	12.25	14.42	16.20	29,331	*	13.71	12.05	13.97	15.61	28,520
51-2092	Team Assemblers	130	11.76	10.35	12.04	13.37	24,475	130	11.42	10.05	11.69	12.98	23,760
51-2099	Assemblers & Fabricators, All Other	*	13.73	12.22	14.44	15.98	28,551	*	13.33	11.86	14.02	15.51	27,720
51-3011	Bakers	110	7.13	5.88	6.42	8.06	14,841	110	6.84	5.78	6.18	7.76	14,230
51-3021	Butchers & Meat Cutters	200	10.02	6.50	9.99	13.03	20,854	200	9.66	6.26	9.63	12.56	20,080
51-3022	Meat, Poultry, & Fish Cutters & Trimmers	80	6.87	5.75	6.19	7.87	14,301	80	6.62	5.76	6.05	7.64	13,780
51-4033	Grinding, Polishing & Buffing Machine Tool Setter, Operator, Metal & Plastic	*	12.56	11.45	12.55	13.64	26,121	30	12.19	11.12	12.18	13.24	25,360
51-4034	Lathe & Turning Machine Tool Setter, Operator, Metal & Plastic	200	15.80	11.30	13.74	21.41	32,859	200	15.34	10.97	13.34	20.79	31,900
51-4041	Machinists	520	14.43	12.08	14.53	16.44	29,998	520	13.73	11.61	13.96	15.78	28,550
51-4121	Welders, Cutters, Solderers, & Brazers	1,690	14.65	12.68	14.72	16.36	30,475	1,650	14.17	12.24	14.23	15.89	29,470
51-6011	Laundry & Dry-Cleaning Workers	160	5.93	5.72	6.13	6.55	12,344	160	5.76	5.55	5.96	6.36	11,980
51-6021	Pressers, Textile, Garment, & Related Material	*	6.03	5.73	6.12	6.56	12,545	*	5.84	5.64	5.96	6.37	12,140
51-8031	Water & Liquid Waste Treatment Plant & System Operator	130	11.06	8.67	10.85	12.38	23,015	130	10.21	8.19	10.31	11.80	21,230
51-8093	Petroleum Pump System Operator, Refinery Operator, & Gaugers	810	17.87	15.20	16.99	20.05	37,167	*	17.26	14.70	16.40	19.36	35,890
51-9061	Inspectors, Testers, Sorters, Samplers, and Weighers	140	16.40	12.31	15.55	21.61	34,110	130	15.78	12.02	15.13	20.82	32,820
51-9122	Painters, Transportation Equipment	110	13.34	10.74	12.42	15.10	27,745	110	12.95	10.43	12.06	14.65	26,940
51-9198	Helpers--Production Workers	*	7.38	6.01	6.64	8.41	15,367	*	7.25	5.81	6.46	8.22	15,090
51-9199	Production Workers, All Other	*	12.28	6.30	12.03	18.61	25,530	*	12.02	6.09	12.38	18.04	25,000

Table A-1

Regional Labor Market Area and Houma Metropolitan Statistical Area—1999 Wage Comparison

SOC-Code	Occupational Title	RLMA 3						Houma MSA					
		Total # Empl.	Mean ($/hour)	Entry ($/hour)	Median ($/hour)	Experience ($/hour)	Annual $	Total # Empl.	Mean ($/hour)	Entry ($/hour)	Median ($/hour)	Experience ($/hour)	Annual $
	Transportation and Material Moving Occupations												
53-1021	First-Line Supervisors/Managers of Helpers, Laborers, & Material Movers, Hand	60	13.63	9.48	12.28	17.40	28,353	50	12.84	8.84	11.79	15.76	26,720
53-1031	First-Line Supervisors/Managers of Transportation & Material-Moving Machine & Vehicle	80	18.42	15.94	18.47	20.59	38,306	80	17.76	15.38	17.81	19.86	36,950
53-3021	Bus Drivers, Transit & Intercity	60	8.17	6.44	8.37	9.85	16,989	60	7.87	6.22	8.07	9.50	16,360
53-3022	Bus Drivers, School	*	8.54	6.26	7.80	9.85	17,768	*	8.05	5.99	7.22	8.66	16,740
53-3031	Driver/Sales Workers	**	11.26	9.71	10.95	13.10	23,433	*	10.86	9.36	10.56	12.63	22,600
53-3032	Truck Drivers, Heavy & Tractor-Trailer	760	9.71	7.89	8.78	10.79	20,184	760	9.36	7.61	8.47	10.41	19,470
53-3033	Truck Drivers, Light or Delivery Services	530	10.21	7.46	8.59	10.95	21,246	520	9.90	7.18	8.29	10.63	20,590
53-3041	Taxi Drivers & Chauffeurs	110	6.71	5.85	6.39	7.63	13,945	80	6.49	5.77	6.24	7.48	13,500
53-3099	Motor Vehicle Operator, All Other	*	10.79	6.71	10.41	14.61	22,458	*	10.41	6.47	10.04	14.09	21,660
53-4031	Railroad Conductors & Yardmasters	*	6.87	6.17	7.00	7.90	14,307	N/A	N/A	N/A	N/A	N/A	N/A
53-5011	Sailors & Marine Oilers	1,380	10.80	8.48	10.83	12.81	22,469	1,380	10.42	8.18	10.44	12.35	21,670
53-5021	Captains, Mates, & Pilots of Water Vessels	1,590	22.49	18.34	22.16	25.94	46,785	1,590	21.65	17.67	21.34	24.97	45,030
53-5022	Motorboat Operators	*	17.67	13.72	15.86	18.91	36,762	*	17.05	13.23	15.30	18.24	35,460
53-5099	All Other Water Transportation Workers	*	11.68	10.32	12.02	13.09	24,288	*	11.26	9.95	11.59	12.62	23,420
53-7021	Crane & Tower Operators	110	14.65	12.83	14.50	16.18	30,474	110	14.28	12.43	14.22	15.73	29,700
53-7051	Industrial Truck & Tractor Operators	210	9.52	7.97	9.34	11.11	19,798	170	9.17	7.69	8.91	10.64	19,070
53-7061	Cleaners of Vehicles & Equipment	310	7.01	5.96	6.53	7.52	14,587	310	6.72	5.78	6.27	7.23	13,980
53-7062	Laborers & Freight, Stock, & Material Movers, Hand	1,220	8.32	7.25	8.20	9.53	17,312	1,200	8.02	7.00	7.90	9.18	16,690
53-7064	Packers & Packagers, Hand	430	6.49	5.91	6.38	6.92	13,505	430	6.23	5.71	6.13	6.65	12,960
53-7072	Pump Operators, Except Wellhead Pumpers	120	16.12	8.65	19.11	23.32	33,545	120	15.55	8.34	18.44	22.49	32,350

SOC Code – Standard occupational classification.

* Suppressed - Relative standard error for employment greater than 50 percent.

** Hourly wages for occupation where workers typically work fewer than 2,080 hours per year not available.

Table A-2

Houma Metropolitan Statistical Area—1998, Occupational Employment Statistics (OES) Survey
(Bureau of Labor Statistics, Department of Labor, website: http://stats.bls.gov/oeshome.htm)

Occupation Code	Occupation Title	Total Employment	Median Wage/Hour($)	Mean Wage/Hour($)	Annual Wage($)
10000	Managerial and Administrative Occupations				
13000	Staff and Administrative Specialty Managerial Occupations				
13002	Financial Managers	260	20.05	22.90	47,630
13005	Personnel, Training, and Labor Relations Managers	90	22.29	23.18	48,220
13008	Purchasing Managers	120	16.03	18.79	39,080
13011	Marketing, Advertising, and Public Relations Managers	220	31.84	31.03	64,540
13014	Administrative Services Managers	170	13.91	18.12	37,700
13017	Engineering, Mathematical, and Natural Sciences Managers	110	28.97	28.04	58,330
15000	Line and Middle Management Industry Specific Managerial Occupations				
15005	Education Administrators	150	24.48	26.51	55,140
15008	Medicine and Health Services Managers	200	22.57	22.02	45,810
15011	Property and Real Estate Managers and Administrators	90	10.36	10.05	20,910
15014	Industrial Production Managers	80	22.38	25.40	52,830
15017	Construction Managers	80	19.47	22.05	45,860
15021	Mining, Quarrying, and Oil and Gas Well Drilling Managers	40	32.36	29.73	61,840
15023	Communications, Transportation, and Utilities Operations Managers	110	25.85	25.89	53,860
15026	Food Service and Lodging Managers	130	14.12	26.79	55,720
19000	Other Managerial and Administrative Occupations				
19002	Public Administration Chief Executives, Legislators, and General Administrators	60	17.70	16.08	33,440
19005	General Managers and Top Executives	2,250	20.87	24.17	50,280
19999	All Other Managers and Administrators	400	20.92	21.70	45,130
20000	Professional, Paraprofessional, and Technical Occupations				
21000	Management Support Occupations				
21108	Loan Officers and Counselors	100	12.46	14.51	30,190
21114	Accountants and Auditors	390	15.38	17.51	36,420
21199	All Other Financial Specialists	40	12.84	14.69	30,560
21305	Purchasing Agents and Buyers, Farm Products	(*)	11.29	9.07	18,870

Table A-2

Houma Metropolitan Statistical Area—1998, Occupational Employment Statistics (OES) Survey
(Bureau of Labor Statistics, Department of Labor, website: http://stats.bls.gov/oeshome.htm)

Occupation Code	Occupation Title	Total Employment	Median Wage/Hour($)	Mean Wage/Hour($)	Annual Wage($)
21308	Purchasing Agents, Except Wholesale, Retail, and Farm Products	110	14.58	15.01	31,230
21511	Personnel, Training, and Labor Relations Specialists	60	16.01	16.31	33,920
21902	Cost Estimators	60	18.93	19.84	41,280
21999	All Other Management Support Workers	(*)	14.07	14.89	30,980
22000	Engineers and Related Occupations				
22121	Civil Engineers, Including Traffic	30	22.38	24.71	51,390
22135	Mechanical Engineers	50	25.04	24.73	51,440
22138	Marine Engineers	40	12.27	12.38	25,760
22199	All Other Engineers	230	18.75	19.26	40,060
22311	Surveyors and Mapping Scientists	140	9.10	11.29	23,470
22502	Civil Engineering Technicians and Technologists	50	12.82	15.34	31,900
22505	Electrical and Electronic Engineering Technicians and Technologists	100	13.16	14.71	30,590
22514	Drafters	170	12.66	13.64	28,360
22521	Surveying and Mapping Technicians	100	13.12	14.18	29,500
24000	Natural Scientists and Related Occupations				
24105	Chemists, Except Biochemists	(*)	14.66	18.70	38,900
24511	Petroleum Technicians and Technologists	30	20.85	21.84	45,430
25000	Computer, Mathematical, Operations Research, and Related Occupations				
25102	Systems Analysts, Electronic Data Processing	30	17.71	18.43	38,330
25104	Computer Support Specialists	50	15.42	16.70	34,740
25105	Computer Programmers	70	17.67	17.61	36,620
27000	Social Scientists and Other Social, Recreational, and Religious Occupations				
27302	Social Workers, Medical and Psychiatric	60	14.08	14.48	30,110
27307	Residential Counselors	50	6.10	7.79	16,210
27308	Human Services Workers	190	8.16	8.43	17,520
28000					Law and Related Occupations
28108	Lawyers	300	27.57	29.72	61,810
28305	Paralegal Personnel	30	11.55	11.97	24,890

Table A-2

Houma Metropolitan Statistical Area—1998, Occupational Employment Statistics (OES) Survey
(Bureau of Labor Statistics, Department of Labor, website: http://stats.bls.gov/oeshome.htm)

Occupation Code	Occupation Title	Total Employment	Median Wage/Hour($)	Mean Wage/Hour($)	Annual Wage($)
31000	Teachers, Educators, Librarians, and Related Occupations				
31114	Nursing Instructors, Postsecondary	(*)	*	*	38,150
31303	Teachers, Preschool	70	6.09	9.28	19,310
31314	Teachers and Instructors, Vocational Education and Training	250	8.87	12.25	25,480
31321	Instructors and Coaches, Sports and Physical Training	80	6.38	9.80	20,370
31399	All Other Teachers and Instructors	(*)	*	*	35,750
31502	Librarians, Professional	90	20.93	21.35	44,410
31514	Vocational and Educational Counselors	80	22.86	23.32	48,500
31517	Instructional Coordinators	40	20.51	21.80	45,350
32000	Health Practitioners, Technologists, Technicians, and Related Health Occupations				
32102	Physicians and Surgeons	180	#	55.15	114,710
32105	Dentists	60	28.26	30.95	64,380
32302	Respiratory Therapists	90	14.11	14.15	29,440
32308	Physical Therapists	60	36.30	36.15	75,190
32314	Speech-Language Pathologists and Audiologists	60	18.93	20.94	43,550
32502	Registered Nurses	1,200	17.91	18.40	38,280
32505	Licensed Practical Nurses	590	10.46	11.59	24,100
32508	Emergency Medical Technicians	70	9.36	10.15	21,110
32517	Pharmacists	120	24.36	25.37	52,780
32519	Pharmacy Technicians and Aides	60	7.37	7.37	15,330
32523	Dietetic Technicians	(*)	7.38	8.21	17,080
32902	Medical and Clinical Laboratory Technologists	100	16.54	16.70	34,740
32905	Medical and Clinical Laboratory Technicians	70	11.21	12.09	25,140
32908	Dental Hygienists	40	12.60	12.96	26,970
32911	Medical Records Technicians	40	8.05	8.13	16,900
32919	Radiologic Technologists	80	12.91	13.62	28,320
32928	Surgical Technologists and Technicians	30	9.60	9.89	20,570
32999	All Other Health Professionals, Paraprofessionals, and Technicians	250	11.56	16.01	33,300

Table A-2

Houma Metropolitan Statistical Area—1998, Occupational Employment Statistics (OES) Survey
(Bureau of Labor Statistics, Department of Labor, website: http://stats.bls.gov/oeshome.htm)

Occupation Code	Occupation Title	Total Employment	Median Wage/Hour($)	Mean Wage/Hour($)	Annual Wage($)
34000	Writers, Artists, Entertainers, Athletes, and Related Occupations				
34023	Photographers	30	6.18	7.06	14,680
34044	Merchandise Displayers and Window Trimmers	30	8.37	8.02	16,680
39000	Other Professional, Paraprofessional, and Technical Occupations				
39999	All Other Professional, Paraprofessional, and Technical Workers	200	14.19	15.41	32,050
40000	Sales and Related Occupations				
41000	First Line Supervisors and Manager/Supervisors - Sales Workers				
41002	First-Line Supervisors and Managers/Supervisors - Sales and Related Workers	980	11.18	13.40	27,880
43000	Sales Occupations, Services				
43002	Sales Agents and Placers, Insurance	150	16.31	22.57	46,940
43017	Sales Agents, Selected Business Services	110	16.19	19.26	40,060
49000	Merchandise, Products, and Other Sales and Sales Related Occupations				
49002	Sales Engineers	30	24.66	25.21	52,440
49005	Sales Representatives, Scientific and Related Products and Services, Except Retail	150	16.71	17.47	36,350
49008	Sales Representatives, Except Retail and Scientific and Related Products and Services	570	17.66	19.55	40,660
49011	Salespersons, Retail	1,890	6.51	8.53	17,740
49014	Salespersons, Parts	200	9.75	10.11	21,020
49017	Counter and Rental Clerks	250	6.56	7.84	16,300
49021	Stock Clerks, Sales Floor	1,020	6.33	6.95	14,460
49023	Cashiers	2,290	6.06	6.27	13,040
49999	All Other Sales and Related Workers	310	7.71	11.99	24,930
50000	Clerical and Administrative Support Occupations				
51000	First Line Supervisors and Manager/Supervisors - Clerical Workers				
51002	First-Line Supervisors and Managers/Supervisors - Clerical and Administrative Support Workers	780	11.55	13.62	28,320
53000	Industry Specific Clerical and Administrative Support Occupations				

Table A-2

Houma Metropolitan Statistical Area—1998, Occupational Employment Statistics (OES) Survey
(Bureau of Labor Statistics, Department of Labor, website: http://stats.bls.gov/oeshome.htm)

Occupation Code	Occupation Title	Total Employment	Median Wage/Hour($)	Mean Wage/Hour($)	Annual Wage($)
53102	Tellers	400	6.29	6.46	13,430
53105	New Accounts Clerks	100	7.77	7.86	16,360
53121	Loan and Credit Clerks	50	8.05	8.10	16,840
53123	Adjustment Clerks	110	7.28	8.36	17,390
53311	Insurance Claims Clerks	30	8.29	9.09	18,900
53314	Insurance Policy Processing Clerks	50	9.45	9.27	19,270
53508	Bill and Account Collectors	80	8.93	9.67	20,120
53808	Hotel Desk Clerks	50	6.79	7.06	14,690
53905	Teacher Aides and Educational Assistants, Clerical	590	9.32	8.69	18,080
55000	Secretarial and General Office Occupations				
55102	Legal Secretaries	170	10.28	10.45	21,730
55105	Medical Secretaries	130	8.93	8.95	18,620
55108	Secretaries, Except Legal and Medical	1,510	8.22	8.65	18,000
55302	Stenographers and/or Court Reporters	30	9.60	10.13	21,080
55305	Receptionists and Information Clerks	620	7.43	7.57	15,740
55307	Typists, Including Word Processing	110	7.82	8.13	16,910
55314	Personnel Clerks, Except Payroll and Timekeeping	70	10.02	10.21	21,240
55321	File Clerks	70	6.33	6.57	13,670
55323	Order Clerks, Materials, Merchandise, and Service	110	7.82	8.38	17,430
55332	Interviewing Clerks, Except Personnel and Social Welfare	50	7.67	7.86	16,340
55335	Customer Service Representatives, Utilities	80	11.19	12.38	25,750
55338	Bookkeeping, Accounting, and Auditing Clerks	940	9.07	9.42	19,600
55341	Payroll and Timekeeping Clerks	90	9.64	10.31	21,450
55344	Billing, Cost, and Rate Clerks	230	8.99	9.92	20,620
55347	General Office Clerks	1,880	7.41	7.95	16,530
56000	Electronic Data Processing and Other Office Machine Occupations				
56002	Billing, Posting, and Calculating Machine Operators	30	9.25	8.99	18,690
56011	Computer Operators, Except Peripheral Equipment	30	8.30	9.24	19,210

Table A-2

Houma Metropolitan Statistical Area—1998, Occupational Employment Statistics (OES) Survey
(Bureau of Labor Statistics, Department of Labor, website: http://stats.bls.gov/oeshome.htm)

Occupation Code	Occupation Title	Total Employment	Median Wage/Hour($)	Mean Wage/Hour($)	Annual Wage($)
56017	Data Entry Keyers, Except Composing	80	7.34	7.49	15,580
57000	Communications, Mail, and Message Distributing Occupations				
57102	Switchboard Operators	90	7.12	7.26	15,090
58000	Material Recording, Scheduling, Dispatching, and Distributing Occupations				
58002	Dispatchers, Police, Fire, and Ambulance	40	8.16	8.58	17,850
58005	Dispatchers, Except Police, Fire, and Ambulance	240	12.67	13.27	27,600
58008	Production, Planning, and Expediting Clerks	70	11.21	12.65	26,310
58014	Meter Readers, Utilities	30	10.31	10.09	20,990
58023	Stock Clerks - Stockroom, Warehouse or Storage Yard	600	7.60	8.27	17,190
58026	Order Fillers, Wholesale and Retail Sales	30	11.43	14.43	30,020
58028	Shipping, Receiving, and Traffic Clerks	370	8.75	11.13	23,150
58099	All Other Material Recording, Scheduling, and Distributing Workers	60	10.28	11.42	23,750
59000	Other Clerical and Administrative Support Occupations				
59999	All Other Clerical and Administrative Support Workers	320	8.73	9.09	18,910
60000	Service Occupations				
61000	First-Line Supervisors and Managers/Supervisors - Service Occupations				
61008	Housekeeping Supervisors	50	8.55	10.57	21,990
61099	All Other Supervisors and Managers/Supervisors - Service Workers	400	8.48	10.58	22,010
63000	Protective Service Occupations				
63014	Police Patrol Officers	90	10.06	10.27	21,370
63047	Guards and Watch Guards	150	6.58	7.29	15,170
63099	All Other Protective Service Workers	70	10.56	10.13	21,070
65000	Food and Beverage Preparation and Service Occupations				
65002	Hosts and Hostesses, Restaurant, Lounge, or Coffee Shop	70	5.79	5.71	11,880
65005	Bartenders	120	6.63	6.77	14,090
65008	Waiters and Waitresses	770	5.75	5.57	11,570
65014	Dining Room and Cafeteria Attendants and Bartender Helpers	50	5.79	5.62	11,690
65017	Counter Attendants - Lunchroom, Coffee Shop, or Cafeteria	(*)	6.15	6.35	13,210

A-21

Table A-2

Houma Metropolitan Statistical Area—1998, Occupational Employment Statistics (OES) Survey
(Bureau of Labor Statistics, Department of Labor, website: http://stats.bls.gov/oeshome.htm)

Occupation Code	Occupation Title	Total Employment	Median Wage/Hour($)	Mean Wage/Hour($)	Annual Wage($)
65021	Bakers, Bread and Pastry	160	5.92	6.63	13,790
65023	Butchers and Meat Cutters	150	8.65	9.13	18,990
65026	Cooks, Restaurant	250	5.96	6.41	13,330
65028	Cooks, Institution or Cafeteria	560	8.85	8.95	18,620
65032	Cooks, Fast Food	490	5.73	5.58	11,600
65035	Cooks, Short Order	(*)	5.87	5.67	11,800
65038	Food Preparation Workers	880	5.90	6.51	13,550
65041	Combined Food Preparation and Service Workers	890	5.70	5.80	12,060
65099	All Other Food Service Workers	440	7.38	8.05	16,740
66000	Health Service and Related Occupations				
66002	Dental Assistants	120	7.68	8.31	17,290
66005	Medical Assistants	110	8.96	9.07	18,870
66008	Nursing Aides, Orderlies, and Attendants	790	6.06	6.43	13,360
66011	Home Health Aides	610	6.20	6.74	14,020
66099	All Other Health Service Workers	100	7.03	7.40	15,390
67000	Cleaning and Building Service Occupations				
67002	Maids and Housekeeping Cleaners	520	6.58	6.59	13,710
67005	Janitors and Cleaners, Except Maids and Housekeeping Cleaners	1,090	6.11	6.47	13,450
67099	All Other Cleaning and Building Service Workers	130	6.46	7.87	16,360
68000	Personal Service Occupations				
68005	Hairdressers, Hairstylists, and Cosmetologists	100	5.74	5.77	12,000
68014	Amusement and Recreation Attendants	90	6.20	6.93	14,420
68038	Child Care Workers	170	5.75	5.80	12,060
69000	Other Service Occupations				
69999	All Other Service Workers	130	6.04	7.00	14,560
70000	Agricultural, Forestry, Fishing, and Related Occupations				
79000	Other Agricultural, Forestry, Fishing, and Related Occupations				
79011	Graders and Sorters, Agricultural Products	40	5.75	5.80	12,070

Table A-2

Houma Metropolitan Statistical Area—1998, Occupational Employment Statistics (OES) Survey
(Bureau of Labor Statistics, Department of Labor, website: http://stats.bls.gov/oeshome.htm)

Occupation Code	Occupation Title	Total Employment	Median Wage/Hour($)	Mean Wage/Hour($)	Annual Wage($)
79041	Laborers, Landscaping and Groundskeeping	360	6.73	7.03	14,610
79806	Veterinary Assistants	30	6.02	6.01	12,510
80000	Production, Construction, Operating, Maintenance, and Material Handling Occupations				
81000	First-Line Supervisors and Managers/Supervisors - Production, Construction, Maintenance, and Related Workers				
81002	First-Line Supervisors and Managers/Supervisors - Mechanics, Installers, and Repairers	280	15.98	18.11	37,670
81005	First-Line Supervisors and Managers/Supervisors - Construction Trades and Extractive Workers	420	26.09	24.69	51,360
81008	First-Line Supervisors and Managers/Supervisors - Production and Operating Workers	200	18.24	20.00	41,600
81011	First-Line Supervisors and Managers/Supervisors - Transportation and Material-Moving Machine and Vehicle Operators	220	16.45	17.78	36,990
81017	First-Line Supervisors and Managers/Supervisors - Helpers, Laborers, and Material Movers, Hand	150	14.22	16.33	33,960
81099	All Other First-Line Supervisors and Managers/Supervisors - Production, Construction, Maintenance, and Related Workers	390	19.36	20.06	41,730
83000	Inspectors and Related Occupations				
83002	Precision Inspectors, Testers, and Graders	70	14.56	15.45	32,140
83005	Production Inspectors, Testers, Graders, Sorters, Samplers, and Weighers	110	11.48	12.12	25,210
85000	Mechanics, Installers, and Repairers				
85110	Machinery Maintenance Mechanics	480	14.72	16.51	34,330
85116	Machinery Maintenance Mechanics, Marine Equipment	150	12.82	13.60	28,300
85128	Machinery Maintenance Workers	50	9.45	10.38	21,600
85132	Maintenance Repairers, General Utility	1,040	8.96	9.52	19,790
85302	Automotive Mechanics	440	11.84	12.99	27,020
85305	Automotive Body and Related Repairers	60	12.80	13.52	28,120
85311	Bus and Truck Mechanics and Diesel Engine Specialists	180	12.08	12.66	26,330
85314	Mobile Heavy Equipment Mechanics, Except Engines	170	12.10	12.91	26,850

Table A-2

Houma Metropolitan Statistical Area—1998, Occupational Employment Statistics (OES) Survey
(Bureau of Labor Statistics, Department of Labor, website: http://stats.bls.gov/oeshome.htm)

Occupation Code	Occupation Title	Total Employment	Median Wage/Hour($)	Mean Wage/Hour($)	Annual Wage($)
85702	Telephone and Cable Television Line Installers and Repairers	100	14.18	14.76	30,700
85717	Electronics Repairers, Commercial and Industrial Equipment	50	14.38	13.79	28,680
85902	Heating, Air Conditioning, and Refrigeration Mechanics and Installers	120	11.60	11.56	24,050
85935	Riggers	180	9.31	10.33	21,480
85953	Tire Repairers and Changers	50	5.84	6.01	12,500
85999	All Other Mechanics, Installers, and Repairers	450	11.50	12.08	25,130
87000	Construction Trades and Extractive Occupations				
87102	Carpenters	430	12.26	12.68	26,360
87105	Ceiling Tile Installers and Acoustical Carpenters	(*)	11.82	12.08	25,130
87202	Electricians	410	14.59	14.73	30,640
87311	Concrete and Terrazzo Finishers	30	8.17	8.84	18,390
87402	Painters and Paperhangers, Construction and Maintenance	340	10.87	11.23	23,360
87502	Plumbers, Pipefitters, and Steamfitters	310	14.26	14.21	29,570
87508	Pipelayers	60	7.88	8.88	18,470
87917	Service Unit Operators	220	11.16	13.32	27,710
87999	All Other Construction and Extractive Workers, Except Helpers	30	10.08	10.26	21,350
89000	Precision Production Occupations				
89108	Machinists	580	13.95	13.98	29,080
89121	Shipfitters	380	13.53	13.17	27,390
89132	Sheet Metal Workers	30	9.43	9.70	20,170
89999	All Other Precision Workers	230	10.41	10.54	21,920
91000	Machine Setters, Set-Up Operators, Operators, and Tenders				
91502	Numerical Control Machine Tool Operators and Tenders, Metal and Plastic	100	12.07	12.15	25,280
92726	Laundry and Dry-Cleaning Machine Operators and Tenders, Except Pressing	100	6.62	6.86	14,260
92951	Coating, Painting, and Spraying Machine Setters and Set-Up Operators	80	11.00	11.41	23,730
92974	Packaging and Filling Machine Operators and Tenders	80	7.70	8.07	16,790

Table A-2

Houma Metropolitan Statistical Area—1998, Occupational Employment Statistics (OES) Survey
(Bureau of Labor Statistics, Department of Labor, website: http://stats.bls.gov/oeshome.htm)

Occupation Code	Occupation Title	Total Employment	Median Wage/Hour($)	Mean Wage/Hour($)	Annual Wage($)
92998	All Other Machine Operators and Tenders	1,250	15.97	16.52	34,370
93000	Hand Occupations, Including Assemblers and Fabricators				
93914	Welders and Cutters	2,550	13.69	13.70	28,500
93956	Assemblers and Fabricators, Except Machine, Electrical, Electronic, and Precision	410	11.58	12.05	25,070
93999	All Other Hand Workers	1,250	12.31	11.85	24,640
95000	Plant and System Occupations				
95002	Water and Liquid Waste Treatment Plant and System Operators	120	9.31	9.39	19,530
95017	Gaugers	(*)	16.28	16.73	34,790
95099	All Other Plant and System Operators	260	14.82	15.70	32,650
97000	Transportation and Material-Moving Machine and Vehicle Operators				
97102	Truck Drivers, Heavy or Tractor-Trailer	940	10.37	11.42	23,760
97105	Truck Drivers, Light, Include Delivery and Route Workers	810	7.27	9.30	19,350
97117	Driver/Sales Workers	110	11.10	10.82	22,510
97502	Captains, Water Vessel	1,340	22.21	23.49	48,860
97505	Mates, Ship, Boat, and Barge	370	18.35	18.64	38,770
97514	Able Seamen	470	12.01	11.93	24,800
97517	Ordinary Seamen and Marine Oilers	930	10.09	9.92	20,630
97805	Service Station Attendants	(*)	10.29	9.31	19,370
97899	All Other Transportation and Related Workers	180	15.24	16.14	33,570
97923	Excavating and Loading Machine Operators	60	10.67	10.29	21,390
97938	Grader, Bulldozer, and Scraper Operators	100	11.18	11.66	24,250
97944	Crane and Tower Operators	320	13.66	13.25	27,560
97947	Industrial Truck and Tractor Operators	190	8.50	8.98	18,670
97989	All Other Material-Moving Equipment Operators	100	9.55	9.71	20,200
98000	Helpers, Laborers, and Material Movers, Hand				
98102	Helpers, Mechanics and Repairers	500	7.56	7.91	16,440
98312	Helpers, Carpenters and Related Workers	90	7.88	8.64	17,980

Table A-2

Houma Metropolitan Statistical Area—1998, Occupational Employment Statistics (OES) Survey
(Bureau of Labor Statistics, Department of Labor, website: http://stats.bls.gov/oeshome htm)

Occupation Code	Occupation Title	Total Employment	Median Wage/Hour($)	Mean Wage/Hour($)	Annual Wage($)
98313	Helpers, Electricians and Power-Line Transmission Installers	30	8.26	8.45	17,580
98315	Helpers, Plumbers, Pipefitters, and Steamfitters	160	8.93	9.14	19,020
98319	Helpers, All Other Construction Trades Workers	130	8.48	8.74	18,180
98502	Machine Feeders and Offbearers	(*)	7.48	8.15	16,950
98799	All Other Freight, Stock, and Material Movers, Hand	340	7.14	7.68	15,980
98902	Hand Packers and Packagers	320	5.94	6.06	12,600
98905	Vehicle Washers and Equipment Cleaners	210	6.07	6.25	13,000
98999	All Other Helpers, Laborers, and Material Movers, Hand	2,000	7.81	8.24	17,140

Occupation Code - a unique, five-digit numerical identifier for each OES occupation.
Occupation Title - a descriptive title that corresponds to the OES code.
Total Employment - the estimated total occupational employment; rounded to nearest 10 (excludes self-employed).
Median Wage/Hour - estimated median hourly wage; the 50% percentile wage.
Mean Wage/Hour - estimated mean hourly wage; an occupation's total wages divided by its employment (the average wage).
Annual Wage - estimated mean annual wage; the estimated mean hourly wage of an occupation multiplied by 2,080 hours.

Table A-3

Houma Metropolitan Area—Lafourche and Terrebonne Parishes
(Data are from the1990 Census special tabulation of occupation by industry.
These counts are for all industries.)

Number in Experienced Labor Force	Census Occupation Code	Occupation Title
36	3	Legislators
8	4	Chief Executives and General Administrators, Public Administration
149	5	Administrators and Officials, Public Administration
45	6	Administrators, Protective Service
369	7	Financial Managers
151	8	Personnel and Labor Relations Managers
36	9	Purchasing Managers
204	13	Managers, Marketing, Advertising, and Public Relations
449	14	Administrators, Education and Related Fields
77	15	Managers, Medicine and Health
19	16	Postmasters and Mail Superintendents
726	17	Managers, Food Serving and Lodging Establishments
184	18	Managers, Properties and Real Estate
41	19	Funeral Directors
233	21	Managers, Service Organizations, n.e.c.
2,545	22	Managers and Administrators, n.e.c.
523	23	Accountants and Auditors
17	24	Underwriters
241	25	Other Financial Officers
51	26	Management Analysts
208	27	Personnel, Training, and Labor Relations Specialists
113	29	Buyers, Wholesale and Retail Trade (except farm products)
191	33	Purchasing Agents and Buyers
71	35	Construction Inspectors
84	36	Inspectors and Compliance Officers (except construction)
68	37	Management Related Occupations, n.e.c.
16	43	Architects
6	45	Metallurgical and Materials Engineers
9	46	Mining Engineers
209	47	Petroleum Engineers
15	48	Chemical Engineers
126	53	Civil Engineers
12	54	Agricultural Engineers
43	55	Electrical and Electronic Engineers
45	56	Industrial Engineers
27	57	Mechanical Engineers
120	58	Marine and Naval Architects
49	59	Engineers, n.e.c.
17	63	Surveyors and Mapping Scientists
31	64	Computer Systems Analysts and Scientists

Table A-3

Houma Metropolitan Area—Lafourche and Terrebonne Parishes
(Data are from the1990 Census special tabulation of occupation by industry.
These counts are for all industries.)

Number in Experienced Labor Force	Census Occupation Code	Occupation Title
20	65	Operations and Systems Researchers and Analysts
12	67	Statisticians
20	73	Chemists, Except Biochemists
15	75	Geologists and Geodesists
28	77	Agricultural and Food Scientists
33	78	Biological and Life Scientists
193	84	Physicians
121	85	Dentists
13	86	Veterinarians
18	87	Optometrists
32	89	Health Diagnosing Practitioners, n.e.c.
883	95	Registered Nurses
90	96	Pharmacists
59	97	Dietitians
45	98	Respiratory Therapists
31	103	Physical Therapists
52	104	Speech Therapists
51	105	Therapists, n.e.c.
13	106	Physicians' Assistants
10	118	Psychology Teachers
7	127	Engineering Teachers
7	134	Health Specialties Teachers
15	135	Business, Commerce, and Marketing Teachers
9	137	Art, Drama, and Music Teachers
8	143	English Teachers
286	154	Postsecondary Teachers, Subject Not Specified
104	155	Teachers, Prekindergarten and Kindergarten
3,265	156	Teachers, Elementary School
429	157	Teachers, Secondary School
27	158	Teachers, Special Education
344	159	Teachers, n.e.c.
109	163	Counselors, Educational and Vocational
98	164	Librarians
9	165	Archivists and Curators
16	166	Economists
21	167	Psychologists
411	174	Social Workers
50	175	Recreation Workers
164	176	Clergy
44	177	Religious Workers, n.e.c.

Table A-3

Houma Metropolitan Area—Lafourche and Terrebonne Parishes
(Data are from the 1990 Census special tabulation of occupation by industry.
These counts are for all industries.)

Number in Experienced Labor Force	Census Occupation Code	Occupation Title
215	178	Lawyers
9	179	Judges
18	183	Authors
208	185	Designers
38	186	Musicians and Composers
43	187	Actors and Directors
20	188	Painters, Sculptors, Craft-Artists, and Artist Printmakers
30	189	Photographers
32	193	Dancers
17	194	Artists, Performers, and Related Workers, n.e.c.
50	195	Editors and Reporters
64	197	Public Relations Specialists
29	198	Announcers
157	199	Athletes
239	203	Clinical Laboratory Technologists and Technicians
29	204	Dental Hygienists
20	205	Health Record Technologists and Technicians
110	206	Radiologic Technicians
323	207	Licensed Practical Nurses
239	208	Health Technologists and Technicians, n.e.c.
168	213	Electrical and Electronic Technicians
5	215	Mechanical Engineering Technicians
151	216	Engineering Technicians, n.e.c.
170	217	Drafting Occupations
56	218	Surveying and Mapping Technicians
50	223	Biological Technicians
110	224	Chemical Technicians
89	225	Science Technicians, n.e.c.
96	226	Airplane Pilots and Navigators
19	227	Air Traffic Controllers
53	228	Broadcast Equipment Operators
93	229	Computer Programmers
125	234	Legal Assistants
277	235	Technicians, n.e.c.
2,666	243	Supervisors and Proprietors, Sales Occupations
471	253	Insurance Sales Occupations
210	254	Real Estate Sales Occupations
73	255	Securities and Financial Services Sales Occupations
60	256	Advertising and Related Sales Occupations
178	257	Sales Occupations, Other Business Services

Table A-3

Houma Metropolitan Area—Lafourche and Terrebonne Parishes
(Data are from the1990 Census special tabulation of occupation by industry.
These counts are for all industries.)

Number in Experienced Labor Force	Census Occupation Code	Occupation Title
13	258	Sales Engineers
1,002	259	Sales Representatives, Mining, Manufacturing, and Wholesale
170	263	Sales Workers, Motor Vehicles and Boats
273	264	Sales Workers, Apparel
102	265	Sales Workers, Shoes
119	266	Sales Workers, Furniture and Home Furnishings
106	267	Sales Workers, Radio, TV, Hi-Fi, and Appliances
116	268	Sales Workers, Hardware and Building Supplies
78	269	Sales Workers, Parts
1,561	274	Sales Workers, Other Commodities
144	275	Sales Counter Clerks
4,047	276	Cashiers
194	277	Street and Door-To-Door Sales Workers
107	278	News Vendors
15	283	Demonstrators, Promoters and Models, Sales
12	285	Sales Support Occupations, n.e.c.
221	303	Supervisors, General Office
24	305	Supervisors, Financial Records Processing
59	307	Supervisors, Distribution, Scheduling, and Adjusting Clerks
270	308	Computer Operators
2,974	313	Secretaries
55	314	Stenographers
363	315	Typists
155	316	Interviewers
47	317	Hotel Clerks
31	318	Transportation Ticket and Reservation Agents
603	319	Receptionists
113	323	Information Clerks, n.e.c.
8	325	Classified-Ad Clerks
99	327	Order Clerks
45	328	Personnel Clerks (except payroll and timekeeping)
55	329	Library Clerks
147	335	File Clerks
45	336	Records Clerks
1,400	337	Bookkeepers, Accounting and Auditing Clerks
56	338	Payroll and Timekeeping Clerks
61	339	Billing Clerks
52	343	Cost and Rate Clerks
7	344	Billing, Posting, and Calculating Machine Operators
156	348	Telephone Operators

Table A-3

Houma Metropolitan Area—Lafourche and Terrebonne Parishes
(Data are from the1990 Census special tabulation of occupation by industry.
These counts are for all industries.)

Number in Experienced Labor Force	Census Occupation Code	Occupation Title
12	353	Communications Equipment Operators, n.e.c.
126	354	Postal Clerks (except mail carriers)
134	355	Mail Carriers, Postal Service
58	356	Mail Clerks (excluding postal service)
118	357	Messengers
235	359	Dispatchers
101	363	Production Coordinators
187	364	Traffic, Shipping and Receiving Clerks
521	365	Stock and Inventory Clerks
72	366	Meter Readers
61	368	Weighers, Measurers, and Checkers -- Samplers
105	373	Expediters
7	374	Material Recording, Scheduling and Distributing Clerks, n.e.c.
75	375	Insurance Adjusters, Examiners, and Investigators
210	376	Investigators and Adjusters, Except Insurance
55	377	Eligibility Clerks, Social Welfare
151	378	Bill and Account Collectors
876	379	General Office Clerks
585	383	Bank Tellers
168	385	Data-Entry Keyers
33	386	Statistical Clerks
187	387	Teachers' Aides
347	389	Administrative Support Occupations, n.e.c.
6	404	Cooks, Private Household
34	405	Housekeepers and Butlers
172	406	Child Care Workers, Private Household
342	407	Private Household Cleaners and Servants
35	414	Supervisors, Police and Detectives
10	415	Supervisors, Guards
5	416	Fire Inspection and Fire Prevention Occupations
81	417	Firefighting Occupations
292	418	Police and Detectives, Public Service
185	423	Sheriffs, Bailiffs, and Other Law Enforcement Officers
67	424	Correctional Institution Officers
7	425	Crossing Guards
373	426	Guards and Police (excluding public service)
67	427	Protective Service Occupations
182	433	Supervisors, Food Preparation and Service Occupations
399	434	Bartenders
1,025	435	Waiters and Waitresses

Table A-3

Houma Metropolitan Area—Lafourche and Terrebonne Parishes
(Data are from the1990 Census special tabulation of occupation by industry.
These counts are for all industries.)

Number in Experienced Labor Force	Census Occupation Code	Occupation Title
2,207	436	Cooks
112	438	Food Counter, Fountain and Related Occupations
319	439	Kitchen Workers, Food Preparation
211	443	Waiters'/Waitresses' Assistants
757	444	Miscellaneous Food Preparation Occupations
120	445	Dental Assistants
198	446	Health Aids, Except Nursing
1,595	447	Nursing Aides, Orderlies and Attendants
86	448	Supervisors, Cleaning and Building Service Workers
593	449	Maids and Housemen
1,847	453	Janitors and Cleaners
70	455	Pest Control Occupations
41	456	Supervisors, Personal Service Occupations
105	457	Barbers
782	458	Hairdressers and Cosmetologists
89	459	Attendants, Amusement and Recreation Facilities
20	461	Guides
6	463	Public Transportation Attendants
36	465	Welfare Service Aides
211	466	Family Child Care Providers
300	467	Early Childhood Teacher's Assistants
227	468	Child Care Workers, n.e.c.
155	469	Personal Service Occupations, n.e.c.
154	473	Farmers, Except Horticultural
9	474	Horticultural Specialty Farmers
130	475	Managers, Farms, Except Horticultural
13	476	Managers, Horticultural Specialty Farms
9	477	Supervisors, Farm Workers
326	479	Farm Workers
31	485	Supervisors, Related Agricultural Occupations
516	486	Groundskeepers and Gardeners (except farm)
23	487	Animal Caretakers (except farm)
85	488	Graders and Sorters, Agricultural Products
10	494	Supervisors, Forestry and Logging Workers
26	496	Timber Cutting and Logging Occupations
236	497	Captains and Other Officers, Fishing Vessels
1,939	498	Fishers
32	499	Hunters and Trappers
312	503	Supervisors, Mechanics and Repairers
673	505	Automobile Mechanics (except apprentices)

Table A-3

Houma Metropolitan Area—Lafourche and Terrebonne Parishes
(Data are from the1990 Census special tabulation of occupation by industry.
These counts are for all industries.)

Number in Experienced Labor Force	Census Occupation Code	Occupation Title
413	507	Bus, Truck, and Stationary Engine Mechanics
34	508	Aircraft Engine Mechanics
245	509	Small Engine Repairers
137	514	Automobile Body and Related Repairers
18	515	Aircraft Mechanics, Excluding Engine
249	516	Heavy Equipment Mechanics
25	517	Farm Equipment Mechanics
314	518	Industrial Machinery Repairers
35	519	Machinery Maintenance Occupations
194	523	Electronic Repairers, Communications and Industrial Equipment
44	525	Data Processing Equipment Repairers
62	526	Household Appliance and Power Tool Repairers
53	527	Telephone Line Installers and Repairers
158	529	Telephone Installers and Repairers
50	533	Miscellaneous Electrical and Electronic Equipment Repairers
86	534	Heating, Air Conditioning, and Refrigeration Mechanics
18	535	Camera, Watch, and Musical Instrument Repairers
12	536	Locksmiths and Safe Repairers
14	538	Office Machine Repairers
81	539	Mechanical Controls and Valve Repairers
7	543	Elevator Installers and Repairers
295	547	Specified Mechanics and Repairers, n.e.c.
379	549	Not Specified Mechanics and Repairers
15	554	Supervisors, Carpenters and Related Work
17	555	Supervisors, Electricians and Power Transmission Installers
51	556	Supervisors, Painters, Paperhangers, and Plasterers
6	557	Supervisors, Plumbers, Pipefitters, and Steamfitters
434	558	Supervisors, Construction, n.e.c.
92	563	Brickmasons and Stonemasons (except apprentices)
15	565	Tile Setters, Hard and Soft
70	566	Carpet Installers
1,009	567	Carpenters (except apprentices)
25	569	Carpenter Apprentices
55	573	Drywall Installers
675	575	Electricians (except apprentices)
7	576	Electrician Apprentices
79	577	Electrical Power Installers and Repairers
566	579	Painters, Construction and Maintenance
8	583	Paperhangers
534	585	Plumbers, Pipefitters, and Steamfitters (except apprentices)

Table A-3

Houma Metropolitan Area—Lafourche and Terrebonne Parishes
(Data are from the1990 Census special tabulation of occupation by industry.
These counts are for all industries.)

Number in Experienced Labor Force	Census Occupation Code	Occupation Title
112	588	Concrete and Terrazzo Finishers
26	589	Glaziers
364	593	Insulation Workers
12	594	Paving, Surfacing, and Tamping Equipment Operators
89	595	Roofers
9	596	Sheetmetal Duct Installers
39	597	Structural Metal Workers
20	598	Drillers, Earth
423	599	Construction Trades, n.e.c.
907	613	Supervisors, Extractive Occupations
1,149	614	Drillers, Oil Well
96	615	Explosives Workers
192	616	Mining Machine Operators
448	617	Mining Occupations, n.e.c.
801	628	Supervisors, Production Occupations
30	634	Tool and Die Makers (except apprentices)
18	636	Precision Assemblers, Metal
493	637	Machinists (except apprentices)
8	639	Machinist Apprentices
73	643	Boilermakers
27	645	Patternmakers and Model Makers, Metal
333	646	Lay-Out Workers
15	647	Precious Stones and Metals Workers
8	649	Engravers, Metal
79	653	Sheet Metal Workers (except apprentices)
77	666	Dressmakers
10	667	Tailors
34	668	Upholsterers
6	669	Shoe Repairers
21	674	Miscellaneous Precision Apparel and Fabric Workers
35	677	Optical Goods Workers
38	678	Dental Laboratory and Medical Appliance Technicians
11	679	Bookbinders
38	684	Miscellaneous Precision Workers, n.e.c.
309	686	Butchers and Meat Cutters
110	687	Bakers
53	688	Food Batchmakers
16	689	Inspectors, Testers, and Graders
6	693	Adjusters and Calibrators
48	694	Water and Sewage Treatment Plant Operators

Table A-3

Houma Metropolitan Area—Lafourche and Terrebonne Parishes
(Data are from the 1990 Census special tabulation of occupation by industry.
These counts are for all industries.)

Number in Experienced Labor Force	Census Occupation Code	Occupation Title
46	695	Power Plant Operators
188	696	Stationary Engineers
232	699	Miscellaneous Plant and System Operators
11	704	Lathe and Turning Machine Operators
7	706	Punching and Stamping Press Machine Operators
24	707	Rolling Machine Operators
19	708	Drilling and Boring Machine Operators
15	717	Fabricating Machine Operators, n.e.c.
9	719	Molding and Casting Machine Operators
15	723	Metal Plating Machine Operators
137	725	Miscellaneous Metal and Plastic Processing Machine Operators
8	727	Sawing Machine Operators
4	728	Shaping and Joining Machine Operators
17	733	Miscellaneous Woodworking Machine Operators
44	734	Printing Press Operators
15	736	Typesetters and Compositors
51	744	Textile Sewing Machine Operators
132	747	Pressing Machine Operators
154	748	Laundering and Dry Cleaning Machine Operators
147	754	Packaging and Filling Machine Operators
14	755	Extruding and Forming Machine Operators
61	756	Mixing and Blending Machine Operators
41	757	Separating, Filtering, and Clarifying Machine Operators
48	759	Painting and Paint Spraying Machine Operators
26	766	Furnace, Kiln, and Oven Operators, Except Food
6	768	Crushing and Grinding Machine Operators
79	769	Slicing and Cutting Machine Operators
61	774	Photographic Process Machine Operators
350	777	Miscellaneous and Not Specified Machine Operators, n.e.c.
340	779	Machine Operators, Not Specified
2,810	783	Welders and Cutters
191	785	Assemblers
302	786	Hand Cutting and Trimming Occupations
8	787	Hand Molding, Casting, and Forming Occupations
29	789	Hand Painting, Coating, and Decorating Occupations
6	793	Hand Engraving and Printing Occupations
252	796	Production Inspectors, Checkers, and Examiners
76	797	Production Testers
11	798	Production Samplers and Weighers
81	799	Graders and Sorters (except agricultural)

Table A-3

Houma Metropolitan Area—Lafourche and Terrebonne Parishes
(Data are from the1990 Census special tabulation of occupation by industry.
These counts are for all industries.)

Number in Experienced Labor Force	Census Occupation Code	Occupation Title
57	803	Supervisors, Motor Vehicle Operators
2,422	804	Truck Drivers
163	806	Driver-Sales Workers
416	808	Bus Drivers
58	809	Taxicab Drivers and Chauffeurs
6	814	Motor Transportation Occupations, n.e.c.
87	824	Locomotive Operating Occupations
9	825	Railroad Brake, Signal, and Switch Operators
2,088	828	Ship Captains and Mates (except fishing boats)
1,229	829	Sailors and Deckhands
30	833	Marine Engineers
159	834	Bridge, Lock and Lighthouse Tenders
18	843	Supervisors, Material Moving Equipment Operators
124	844	Operating Engineers
21	845	Longshore Equipment Operators
155	848	Hoist and Winch Operators
360	849	Crane and Tower Operators
136	853	Excavating and Loading Machine Operators
42	855	Grader, Dozer, and Scraper Operators
172	856	Industrial Truck and Tractor Equipment Operators
300	859	Miscellaneous Material Moving Equipment Operators
5	864	Supervisors, Handlers, Equipment Cleaners, and Laborers, n.e.c.
15	865	Helpers, Mechanics and Repairers
203	866	Helpers, Construction Trades
16	867	Helpers, Surveyor
37	868	Helpers, Extractive Occupations
895	869	Construction Laborers
122	874	Production Helpers
83	875	Garbage Collectors
15	876	Stevedores
1,120	877	Stock Handlers and Baggers
7	878	Machine Feeders and Offbearers
310	883	Freight, Stock, and Material Handlers, n.e.c.
293	885	Garage and Service Station Related Occupations
168	887	Vehicle Washers and Equipment Cleaners
511	888	Hand Packers and Packagers
1,626	889	Laborers (except construction)

n.e.c. – not else classified.

Table A-4

Houma Metropolitan Area—Lafourche and Terrebonne Parishes
(Data are from the 1990 Census special tabulation of occupation by industry. These counts are for
SIC=353, Construction and Related Machinery, and SIC=373, Ship and Boat Building and Repairing.)

Number in Experienced Labor Force	Census Occupation Code	Occupation Title
10	7	Financial Managers
11	13	Managers, Marketing, Advertising, and Public Relations
152	22	Managers and Administrators, n.e.c.
9	25	Other Financial Officers
4	27	Personnel, Training, and Labor Relations Specialists
38	33	Purchasing Agents and Buyers
8	36	Inspectors and Compliance Officers (except construction)
7	56	Industrial Engineers
5	57	Mechanical Engineers
54	58	Marine and Naval Architects
16	59	Engineers, n.e.c.
7	64	Computer Systems Analysts and Scientists
18	213	Electrical and Electronic Technicians
15	217	Drafting Occupations
8	226	Airplane Pilots and Navigators
6	229	Computer Programmers
8	235	Technicians, n.e.c.
6	243	Supervisors and Proprietors, Sales Occupations
20	259	Sales Representatives, Mining, Manufacturing, and Wholesale
31	308	Computer Operators
19	313	Secretaries
8	319	Receptionists
47	337	Bookkeepers, Accounting and Auditing Clerks
8	338	Payroll and Timekeeping Clerks
11	363	Production Coordinators
74	365	Stock and Inventory Clerks
6	376	Investigators and Adjusters (except insurance)
15	379	General Office Clerks
18	389	Administrative Support Occupations, n.e.c.
7	417	Firefighting Occupations
10	426	Guards and Police, Excluding Public Service
4	436	Cooks
44	453	Janitors and Cleaners
7	469	Personal Service Occupations, n.e.c.
16	507	Bus, Truck, and Stationary Engine Mechanics
32	509	Small Engine Repairers
15	516	Heavy Equipment Mechanics
58	518	Industrial Machinery Repairers
8	519	Machinery Maintenance Occupations
8	534	Heating, Air Conditioning, and Refrigeration Mechanics

Table A-4

Houma Metropolitan Area—Lafourche and Terrebonne Parishes
(Data are from the 1990 Census special tabulation of occupation by industry. These counts are for
SIC=353, Construction and Related Machinery, and SIC=373, Ship and Boat Building and Repairing.)

Number in Experienced Labor Force	Census Occupation Code	Occupation Title
6	539	Mechanical Controls and Valve Repairers
37	547	Specified Mechanics and Repairers, n.e.c.
10	549	Not Specified Mechanics and Repairers
5	555	Supervisors, Electricians and Power Transmission Installers
29	556	Supervisors, Painters, Paperhangers, and Plasterers
6	557	Supervisors, Plumbers, Pipefitters, and Steamfitters
143	567	Carpenters (except apprentices)
103	575	Electricians (except apprentices)
73	579	Painters, Construction and Maintenance
77	585	Plumbers, Pipefitters, and Steamfitters (except apprentices)
14	593	Insulation Workers
7	599	Construction Trades, n.e.c.
8	613	Supervisors, Extractive Occupations
8	615	Explosives Workers
7	617	Mining Occupations, n.e.c.
309	628	Supervisors, Production Occupations
7	634	Tool and Die Makers (except apprentices)
114	637	Machinists (except apprentices)
8	639	Machinist Apprentices
9	645	Patternmakers and Model Makers, Metal
312	646	Lay-Out Workers
24	653	Sheet Metal Workers (except apprentices)
5	696	Stationary Engineers
7	706	Punching and Stamping Press Machine Operators
9	719	Molding and Casting Machine Operators
110	725	Miscellaneous Metal and Plastic Processing Machine Operators
14	744	Textile Sewing Machine Operators
7	747	Pressing Machine Operators
15	759	Painting and Paint Spraying Machine Operators
8	774	Photographic Process Machine Operators
108	777	Miscellaneous and Not Specified Machine Operators, n.e.c.
49	779	Machine Operators, Not Specified
849	783	Welders and Cutters
17	785	Assemblers
6	789	Hand Painting, Coating, and Decorating Occupations
21	796	Production Inspectors, Checkers, and Examiners
8	797	Production Testers
69	804	Truck Drivers
51	828	Ship Captains and Mates (except fishing boats)
16	829	Sailors and Deckhands

Houma Metropolitan Area—Lafourche and Terrebonne Parishes
(Data are from the 1990 Census special tabulation of occupation by industry. These counts are for
SIC=353, Construction and Related Machinery, and SIC=373, Ship and Boat Building and Repairing.)

Number in Experienced Labor Force	Census Occupation Code	Occupation Title
1	849	Crane and Tower Operators
24	856	Industrial Truck and Tractor Equipment Operators
6	859	Miscellaneous Material Moving Equipment Operators
5	865	Helpers, Mechanics and Repairers
42	866	Helpers, Construction Trades
18	869	Construction Laborers
37	874	Production Helpers
7	876	Stevedores
8	883	Freight, Stock, and Material Handlers, n.e.c.
11	887	Vehicle Washers and Equipment Cleaners
139	889	Laborers (except construction)

n.e.c. – not else classified.

Table A-5

Regional Labor Market Area 3—Assumption, Lafourche, and Terrebonne Parishes
Occupational Employment Statistics
(Louisiana Department of Labor)

Occupation Code	Occupational Title	1998 Employment	Projected 2008 Employment	Projected Total Growth	Area 3 Average Wage ($)	State Average Wage ($)
13002	Financial Managers	340	400	60	22.06	23.85
13005	Personnel Managers	110	140	30	23.28	21.83
13008	Purchasing Managers	100	120	20	18.88	18.13
13011	Marketing & Public Relations Managers	180	220	40	30.88	24.15
13014	Administrative Services Managers	210	250	40	18.76	19.9
13017	Engineering, Math & Science Managers	190	250	60	28.54	30.46
15002	Postmasters & Mail Superintendents	10	10	0	23.49	22.74
15005	Education Administrators	330	390	60	27.32	25.55
15008	Health Services Managers	180	240	60	21.88	23.89
15011	Property & Real Estate Managers	70	90	20	10.05	11.96
15014	Industrial Production Managers	100	120	20	25.31	28.45
15017	Construction Managers	120	160	40	24.32	21.83
15021	Mining & Oil & Gas Drilling Managers	90	100	10	29.74	36.5
15023	Transportation & Public Utility Managers	160	190	30	25.89	22.4
15026	Food Service & Lodging Managers	300	370	70	26.5	15.5
15031	Nursery & Greenhouse Managers	*	*	*	N/A	N/A
15032	Lawn Service Managers	30	30	0	N/A	9.97
19002	Government Chief Executives & Legislators	60	70	10	13.69	11.6
19005	General Managers & Top Executives	2,330	2,850	520	24.29	25.08
19999	All Other Managers & Administrative	1,330	1,510	180	22.33	21.22
21102	Underwriters	40	30	-10	N/A	16.14
21105	Credit Analysts	10	10	0	N/A	14.26
21108	Loan Officers & Counselors	110	130	20	14.52	16.39
21111	Tax Preparers	20	20	0	N/A	9.63
21114	Accountants & Auditors	530	580	50	17.38	17.01
21117	Budget Analysts	30	30	0	22.02	22.14
21199	All Other Financial Specialists	90	100	10	17.48	16.01

A-40

Table A-5

Regional Labor Market Area 3—Assumption, Lafourche, and Terrebonne Parishes
Occupational Employment Statistics
(Louisiana Department of Labor)

Occupation Code	Occupational Title	1998 Employment	Projected 2008 Employment	Projected Total Growth	Area 3 Average Wage ($)	State Average Wage ($)
21302	Buyers Wholesale & Retail Trade	50	60	10	11.28	14.1
21305	Buyers Farm Products	20	20	0	N/A	11.78
21308	Purchasing Agents	140	180	40	15.39	16.97
21502	Claims Takers Unemployment Benefits	10	0	-10	N/A	16.25
21505	Special Agents Insurance	10	20	10	14.11	14.75
21508	Employment Interviewers	30	30	0	N/A	11.47
21511	Personnel Specialists	170	210	40	13.41	16.65
21902	Cost Estimators	90	120	30	20.61	19.98
21905	Management Analysts	60	70	10	N/A	21.06
21908	Construction & Building Inspectors	20	20	0	18.92	17.87
21911	Enforcement Inspectors (except construction)	90	110	20	19.38	17.14
21914	Tax Examiners & Collectors	40	60	20	N/A	14.97
21917	Assessors	10	20	10	N/A	18.93
21921	Claims Examiners Property/Casualty Insurance	10	10	0	N/A	16.85
21999	All Other Management Support Workers	460	560	100	14.47	15.05
22105	Metallurgists & Ceramics & Materials Engineers	*	*	*	N/A	23.6
22108	Mining Engineers (including safety)	10	20	10	N/A	23.41
22111	Petroleum Engineers	190	210	20	22.16	32.5
22114	Chemical Engineers	20	20	0	N/A	31.11
22117	Nuclear Engineers	10	10	0	N/A	N/A
22121	Civil Engineers	90	100	10	N/A	27.61
22123	Agricultural Engineers	*	*	*	N/A	24.07
22126	Electrical & Electronic Engineers	60	80	20	25.57	26.53
22127	Computer Engineers	30	60	30	N/A	22.35
22128	Industrial Engineers (except safety)	70	70	0	26.2	25.68
22132	Safety Engineers (except mining)	30	40	10	20.51	22.27
22135	Mechanical Engineers	80	100	20	25.42	24.37

Table A-5

Regional Labor Market Area 3—Assumption, Lafourche, and Terrebonne Parishes
Occupational Employment Statistics
(Louisiana Department of Labor)

Occupation Code	Occupational Title	1998 Employment	Projected 2008 Employment	Projected Total Growth	Area 3 Average Wage ($)	State Average Wage ($)
22138	Marine Engineers	30	30	0	13.3	26.39
22199	All Other Engineers	250	300	50	20.8	25.19
22302	Architects (except landscape & marine)	20	20	0	N/A	21.93
22308	Landscape Architects	10	10	0	N/A	13.25
22311	Surveyors & Mapping Scientists	30	30	0	11.52	16.52
22502	Civil Engineering Technicians	60	80	20	15.34	13.79
22505	Electrical & Electronic Engineering Technicians	150	200	50	14.76	16.87
22508	Industrial Engineering Technicians	10	10	0	N/A	17.77
22511	Mechanical Engineering Technicians	40	50	10	20.28	21.05
22514	Drafters	300	330	30	14.08	15.91
22517	Estimators & Drafters Utilities	*	*	*	N/A	20.09
22521	Surveying & Mapping Technicians	80	100	20	11.45	12.95
22599	All Other Engineering Technician	200	230	30	17.95	17.88
24105	Chemists (except biochemists)	20	30	10	N/A	23.94
24108	Meteorologists & Space Scientists	*	*	*	N/A	23.84
24111	Geologists, Geophysicists & Oceanographers	190	150	-40	N/A	30.01
24199	All Other Physical Scientists	50	50	0	N/A	24.85
24302	Foresters & Conservation Scientists	10	10	0	N/A	20.11
24305	Agricultural & Food Scientists	10	10	0	N/A	19.23
24308	Biological Scientists	20	20	0	N/A	19.17
24311	Medical Scientists	*	*	*	N/A	N/A
24399	All Other Life Scientists	10	10	0	N/A	20.11
24502	Biological, Agricultural & Food Technicians	10	10	0	N/A	15.61
24505	Chemical Technicians (except health)	20	20	0	9.17	19.11
24511	Petroleum Technicians	170	170	0	21.84	18.87
24599	All Other Science Technicians	60	70	10	11.04	15.27
25102	Systems Analysts	150	260	110	18.44	22.08

Table A-5

Regional Labor Market Area 3—Assumption, Lafourche, and Terrebonne Parishes
Occupational Employment Statistics
(Louisiana Department of Labor)

Occupation Code	Occupational Title	1998 Employment	Projected 2008 Employment	Projected Total Growth	Area 3 Average Wage ($)	State Average Wage ($)
25103	Data Base Administrators	20	20	0	16.89	20.73
25104	Computer Support Specialists	110	180	70	16.71	16.2
25105	Computer Programmers	160	200	40	17.57	21.02
25108	Computer Programmer Aides	20	20	0	12.33	14.45
25111	Numerical Tool/Process Control Programmers	10	10	0	13.27	17.27
25199	All Other Computer Scientists	10	30	20	11.62	20.68
25302	Operations/Systems Analysts (except computer)	10	10	0	N/A	19.34
25310	Mathematical Scientists	*	*	*	N/A	N/A
25315	Financial Analysts (statistical)	*	*	*	N/A	23.95
25319	Mathematicians & Math Scientists	*	*	*	13.93	N/A
27102	Economists & Market Research Analysts	10	10	0	N/A	22.31
27105	Urban & Regional Planners	20	30	10	N/A	17.12
27108	Psychologists	50	60	10	17.47	19.35
27199	All Other Social Scientists	10	10	0	16.05	15.43
27302	Social Workers (medical & psychiatric)	90	120	30	14.48	15.8
27305	Social Workers (except medical & psychiatric)	170	240	70	N/A	14.48
27307	Residential Counselors	60	90	30	7.88	7.44
27308	Human Services Workers	100	150	50	8.43	9.42
27311	Recreation Workers	70	90	20	N/A	7.6
27502	Clergy	*	*	*	N/A	15.02
27505	Religious Activities & Education Directors	*	*	*	N/A	16.87
28102	Judges & Magistrates	20	30	10	N/A	14.44
28105	Administrative Law Judges	20	20	0	11.64	N/A
28108	Lawyers	310	340	30	26.59	32.74
28302	Law Clerks	40	40	0	N/A	12.22
28305	Paralegals	50	80	30	N/A	13.92
28308	Title Searchers	*	*	*	N/A	13.54

Table A-5

Regional Labor Market Area 3—Assumption, Lafourche, and Terrebonne Parishes
Occupational Employment Statistics
(Louisiana Department of Labor)

Occupation Code	Occupational Title	1998 Employment	Projected 2008 Employment	Projected Total Growth	Area 3 Average Wage ($)	State Average Wage ($)
28311	Title Examiners & Abstractors	*	*	*	N/A	14.05
28399	All Other Legal Assistants	30	40	10	N/A	12.59
31111	Lecturers	*	*	*	N/A	N/A
31114	Nursing Instructors	30	30	0	N/A	**
31117	Graduate Assistants (teaching)	100	130	30	N/A	N/A
31202	Life Sciences Teachers, College	10	10	0	N/A	**
31204	Chemistry Teachers, College	*	*	*	N/A	**
31206	Physics Teachers, College	*	*	*	N/A	**
31209	All Other Physics Science Teachers, Postsecondary	*	*	*	N/A	**
31211	Health Diagnostics Teachers, Postsecondary	40	60	20	N/A	N/A
31212	Health Specialties Teachers, College	10	10	0	N/A	N/A
31213	Communications Teachers, Post Secondary	10	10	0	N/A	N/A
31214	English Language & Literature Teachers, Postsecondary	20	20	0	N/A	**
31215	Foreign Language & Literature Teachers, Postsecondary	*	*	*	N/A	**
31218	Art, Drama & Music Teachers, College	20	30	10	N/A	**
31222	Engineering Teachers, College	40	60	20	N/A	N/A
31224	Mathematical Sciences Teachers, College	10	20	10	N/A	**
31226	Computer Science Teachers, College	30	40	10	N/A	**
31231	Anthropology & Sociology Teachers, Postsecondary	*	*	*	N/A	**
31233	Economics Teachers, Postsecondary	*	*	*	N/A	**
31234	Geography Teachers, Postsecondary	*	*	*	N/A	N/A
31235	History Teachers, Postsecondary	*	*	*	N/A	**
31236	Political Science Teachers, Postsecondary	*	*	*	N/A	**
31237	Psychology Teachers, Postsecondary	10	10	0	N/A	**
31242	Business Teachers, Postsecondary	10	20	10	N/A	**
31244	Law Teachers, Postsecondary	*	*	*	N/A	N/A
31246	Criminal Justice & Law Enforce Teachers, Postsecondary	*	*	*	N/A	**

Table A-5

Regional Labor Market Area 3—Assumption, Lafourche, and Terrebonne Parishes
Occupational Employment Statistics
(Louisiana Department of Labor)

Occupation Code	Occupational Title	1998 Employment	Projected 2008 Employment	Projected Total Growth	Area 3 Average Wage ($)	State Average Wage ($)
31247	Social Work Teachers, Postsecondary	10	10	0	N/A	**
31252	Education Teachers, Postsecondary	10	20	10	N/A	**
31254	Philosophy and Religion Teachers, Postsecondary	*	*	*	N/A	**
31256	Library Science Teachers, Postsecondary	*	*	*	N/A	N/A
31258	Parks, Recreation, Leisure, & Fitness Studies Teachers	*	*	*	N/A	N/A
31262	Home Economic Teachers, Postsecondary	*	*	*	N/A	N/A
31299	All Other Postsecondary Teachers	290	370	80	**	**
31303	Teachers, Preschool	110	140	30	10.06	8.35
31304	Teachers, Kindergarten	150	170	20	**	**
31305	Teachers, Elementary School	1,330	1,550	220	**	**
31308	Teachers, Secondary School	740	940	200	N/A	**
31311	Teachers, Special Education	430	600	170	**	**
31314	Teachers, Vocational Education & Training	330	370	40	14.3	13.45
31317	Instructors, Nonvocational Education	50	60	10	N/A	11.04
31321	Instructors & Coaches-Sports, Physical Training	80	100	20	9.79	13.08
31399	All Other Teachers, Instructors	300	340	40	**	**
31502	Librarians	100	110	10	21.39	17.97
31505	Library Technical Assistants	40	50	10	N/A	9.28
31508	Audio Visual Specialists	*	*	*	N/A	14.15
31511	Curators, Archivists & Museum Technicians	*	*	*	N/A	10.97
31514	Counselors (vocational & educational)	150	190	40	23.64	18.09
31517	Education Program Specialists	60	70	10	22.75	14.38
31521	Teacher Aides (paraprofessional)	210	290	80	N/A	6.19
32102	Physicians & Surgeons	280	330	50	55.15	44.69
32105	Dentists	50	50	0	30.95	47.52
32108	Optometrists	20	20	0	N/A	28.67
32111	Podiatrists	*	*	*	N/A	41.55

Table A-5

Regional Labor Market Area 3—Assumption, Lafourche, and Terrebonne Parishes
Occupational Employment Statistics
(Louisiana Department of Labor)

Occupation Code	Occupational Title	1998 Employment	Projected 2008 Employment	Projected Total Growth	Area 3 Average Wage ($)	State Average Wage ($)
32113	Chiropractors	20	30	10	N/A	N/A
32114	Veterinarians	10	20	10	22.3	26.42
32199	All Other Health Practitioners	10	10	0	33.82	28.99
32302	Respiratory Therapists	60	90	30	14.25	16.41
32305	Occupational Therapists	40	50	10	28.56	26.23
32308	Physical Therapists	60	80	20	36.14	30.34
32311	Corrective & Manual Arts Therapists	*	*	*	N/A	17.86
32314	Speech Pathologists & Audiologists	70	100	30	21.15	19.63
32317	Recreational Therapists	20	20	0	N/A	13.03
32399	All Other Therapists	20	20	0	14.94	16.75
32502	Registered Nurses	1,230	1,450	220	18.46	20.19
32505	Licensed Practical Nurses	650	750	100	11.7	11.68
32508	Emergency Medical Technicians	50	80	30	10.15	9.99
32511	Physician Assistants	40	50	10	N/A	15.82
32514	Opticians (dispensing)	50	60	10	9.03	12.48
32517	Pharmacists	120	120	0	26.08	26.08
32518	Pharmacy Technicians	70	80	10	7.43	8
32521	Dietitians	30	30	0	15.75	16
32523	Dietetic Technicians	20	30	10	N/A	8.89
32902	Medical Laboratory Technologists	110	120	10	16.69	17.82
32905	Medical Laboratory Technicians	100	110	10	12.41	11.73
32908	Dental Hygienists	60	90	30	12.96	19.39
32911	Medical Records Technicians	40	60	20	8.33	10.04
32913	Radiation Therapists	20	20	0	N/A	18.46
32914	Nuclear Medicine Technologists	10	10	0	20.34	19.31
32919	Radiologic Technologists	100	110	10	13.71	14.6
32923	Electroencephalograph Technologists	*	*	*	N/A	13.13

A-46

Table A-5

Regional Labor Market Area 3—Assumption, Lafourche, and Terrebonne Parishes
Occupational Employment Statistics
(Louisiana Department of Labor)

Occupation Code	Occupational Title	1998 Employment	Projected 2008 Employment	Projected Total Growth	Area 3 Average Wage ($)	State Average Wage ($)
32925	Cardiology Technologists	20	20	0	N/A	15.08
32926	Electrocardiograph Technicians	10	10	0	8.32	8.98
32928	Surgical Technologists	40	50	10	9.89	11.57
32931	Psychiatric Technicians	60	60	0	N/A	8.16
32951	Veterinary Technicians	10	10	0	N/A	8.06
32999	All Other Health Professional, Paraprofessional, Technician	430	570	140	14.75	14.15
34002	Writers & Editors	50	80	30	15.24	13.33
34005	Technical Writers & Editors	10	10	0	N/A	17.05
34008	Public Relations Specialists	40	40	0	17.02	15.15
34011	Reporters	30	30	0	N/A	13.68
34014	TV & Radio News Broadcasters	*	*	*	N/A	22.64
34017	Announcers-Radio & TV	30	30	0	N/A	8.77
34023	Photographers	50	60	10	N/A	9.59
34026	Camera Operators-TV & Motion Pictures	10	10	0	N/A	10.64
34028	Broadcast Technicians	20	20	0	N/A	10.05
34032	Film Editors	*	*	*	N/A	18.74
34035	Artists & Commercial Artists	60	80	20	N/A	12.52
34038	Designers (except interior designers)	150	210	60	9.49	19.79
34041	Interior Designers	30	30	0	7.01	10.39
34044	Merchandise Displayers & Window Trimmers	20	20	0	7.95	8.8
34051	Musicians (instrumental)	10	10	0	N/A	N/A
34053	Dancers & Choreographers	*	*	*	N/A	7.61
34056	Producers, Directors, Actors & Entertainers	20	30	10	**	N/A
34058	Athletes, Coaches, Umpires & Related Workers	10	20	10	N/A	N/A
39002	Airplane Dispatchers & Air Traffic Controllers	*	*	*	N/A	26.42
39005	Traffic Technicians	*	*	*	N/A	14.54
39008	Radio Operators	10	10	0	N/A	8.02

Table A-5

Regional Labor Market Area 3—Assumption, Lafourche, and Terrebonne Parishes
Occupational Employment Statistics
(Louisiana Department of Labor)

Occupation Code	Occupational Title	1998 Employment	Projected 2008 Employment	Projected Total Growth	Area 3 Average Wage ($)	State Average Wage ($)
39011	Funeral Directors & Morticians	10	10	0	N/A	14.04
39014	Embalmers	10	10	0	13.94	13.07
39999	All Other Professional, Paraprofessional, Technician	310	370	60	12.65	16.93
41002	Supervisors-Sales	1,530	1,730	200	13.45	14.84
43002	Insurance Sales Agents	120	140	20	22.7	18.64
43005	Real Estate Brokers	10	10	0	N/A	37.77
43008	Real Estate Sales Agents	60	70	10	N/A	14.26
43011	Real Estate Appraisers	10	10	0	N/A	19.43
43014	Securities Sales Representatives	30	40	10	N/A	27.56
43017	Business Services Sales Representatives	160	220	60	18.63	17.18
43021	Travel Agents	70	70	0	N/A	10.94
43023	Advertising Sales Representatives	50	70	20	13.36	16.11
43099	All Other Service Sales Occupations	50	80	30	14.19	14.85
49002	Sales Engineers	80	100	20	25.21	23.66
49005	Sales Representatives-Scientific Product, Services	300	360	60	17.53	20.6
49008	Sales Representatives (except scientific, retail)	650	800	150	19.52	17.41
49011	Retail Salespersons	2,340	2,740	400	8.48	8.51
49014	Parts Salespersons	230	260	30	10.09	11.37
49017	Counter & Rental Clerks	230	300	70	7.84	7.53
49021	Stock Clerks-Sales Floor	1,030	1,020	-10	6.94	6.89
49023	Cashiers	2,710	3,020	310	6.25	6.44
49026	Telemarketers, Vendors, Door-to-Door Sales Workers	190	270	80	13.62	9.73
49034	Demonstrators and Promoters	30	30	0	N/A	8.33
49075	Gaming Change Person	20	20	0	N/A	N/A
49076	Casino Cage Cashiers	10	10	0	N/A	N/A
49077	Currency Counting Clerk	10	10	0	N/A	N/A
49999	All Other Sales & Related Workers	310	370	60	11.89	10.85

Table A-5

Regional Labor Market Area 3—Assumption, Lafourche, and Terrebonne Parishes
Occupational Employment Statistics
(Louisiana Department of Labor)

Occupation Code	Occupational Title	1998 Employment	Projected 2008 Employment	Projected Total Growth	Area 3 Average Wage ($)	State Average Wage ($)
51002	Supervisors-Clerical Workers	820	1,010	190	13.43	14.09
53102	Tellers	340	320	-20	6.48	7.66
53105	New Accounts Clerks-Banking	60	70	10	N/A	8.96
53108	Transit Clerks-Banking	*	*	*	N/A	8.25
53111	Loan Interviewers	10	10	0	N/A	11.87
53114	Credit Authorizers	*	*	*	N/A	10.34
53117	Credit Checkers	10	10	0	N/A	9.25
53121	Loan & Credit Clerks	70	70	0	8.1	9.72
53123	Adjustment Clerks-Merchandise & Billing	160	210	50	8.29	9.48
53126	Statement Clerks-Banking	*	*	*	N/A	9.44
53128	Brokerage Clerks	*	*	*	N/A	12.55
53302	Insurance Adjusters, Examiners & Investigators	60	80	20	N/A	18.83
53305	Insurance Appraisers-Auto Damage	*	*	*	N/A	20.26
53308	Insurance Examining Clerks-Banking	10	10	0	N/A	8.89
53311	Insurance Claims Clerks	50	60	10	9.09	10.41
53314	Insurance Policy Processing Clerks	50	60	10	9.14	10.17
53502	Welfare Eligibility Workers	70	70	0	N/A	13.32
53505	Investigators (clerical)	*	*	*	N/A	10.6
53508	Bill & Account Collectors	120	150	30	9.67	9.93
53702	Court Clerks	100	140	40	10.75	11.21
53705	Municipal Clerks	40	60	20	7.23	10.26
53708	License Clerks	30	30	0	N/A	8.79
53802	Travel Clerks	*	*	*	N/A	7.85
53805	Reservation & Transportation Ticket Agents	50	50	0	N/A	11.56
53808	Hotel Desk Clerks	50	60	10	7.06	6.87
53902	Library Assistants & Bookmobile Drivers	50	70	20	7.67	7.35
53905	Teacher Aides (clerical)	400	560	160	8.71	7.04

Regional Labor Market Area 3—Assumption, Lafourche, and Terrebonne Parishes
Occupational Employment Statistics
(Louisiana Department of Labor)

Occupation Code	Occupational Title	1998 Employment	Projected 2008 Employment	Projected Total Growth	Area 3 Average Wage ($)	State Average Wage ($)
53908	Advertising Clerks	*	*	*	N/A	9.35
53911	Proofreaders	10	10	0	N/A	8.4
53914	Real Estate Clerks	*	*	*	N/A	10.71
55102	Legal Secretaries	140	140	0	N/A	12.35
55105	Medical Secretaries	90	100	10	8.95	8.85
55108	Secretaries (except legal & medical)	1,480	1,550	70	8.67	9.79
55302	Stenos, Court Reporters & Transcriptionists	120	140	20	10.38	11.63
55305	Receptionists & Information Clerks	590	720	130	7.49	7.82
55307	Typists (including word processing)	210	180	-30	8.14	8.56
55314	Personnel Clerks (except payroll)	50	50	0	10.39	10.86
55317	Correspondence Clerks	10	10	0	N/A	10.33
55321	File Clerks	110	120	10	6.65	7.18
55323	Order Clerks	120	130	10	8.28	9.77
55326	Purchasing Clerks	20	20	0	8.17	10.53
55328	Statistical Clerks	10	10	0	N/A	9.3
55332	Interviewing Clerks	60	70	10	7.9	8.05
55335	Customer Service Representatives-Utilities	60	80	20	11.6	11.72
55338	Bookkeeping & Accounting Clerks	1,060	1,070	10	9.37	10.12
55341	Payroll Clerks	100	110	10	10.39	11.05
55344	Billing, Cost & Rate Clerks	170	200	30	9.86	9.87
55347	General Office Clerks	2,110	2,570	460	8.02	8.67
56002	Billing/Posting/Calculating Machine Operators	50	50	0	8.91	8.98
56005	Duplicating Machine Operators	20	30	10	6.86	8.46
56008	Mail Machine Operators	10	20	10	N/A	7.48
56011	Computer Operators (except peripheral equipment)	90	70	-20	9.47	11.07
56014	Peripheral Computer Equipment Operators	10	10	0	N/A	8.99
56017	Data Entry Keyers (except printing)	140	160	20	7.57	8.61

Table A-5

Regional Labor Market Area 3—Assumption, Lafourche, and Terrebonne Parishes
Occupational Employment Statistics
(Louisiana Department of Labor)

Occupation Code	Occupational Title	1998 Employment	Projected 2008 Employment	Projected Total Growth	Area 3 Average Wage ($)	State Average Wage ($)
56021	Data Entry Keyers (printing)	*	*	*	N/A	10.07
56099	All Other Office Machine Operators	20	20	0	7.44	9.9
57102	Switchboard Operators	140	130	-10	7.39	7.19
57108	Central Office Operators	10	10	0	N/A	N/A
57111	Telegraph & Teletype Operators	*	*	*	N/A	12.25
57199	All Other Communication Operator	10	10	0	13.11	16.07
57302	Mail Clerks, Except Mail Machine, Postal Service	40	50	10	N/A	8.08
57305	Mail Carriers	70	70	0	N/A	16.27
57308	Postal Service Clerks	10	10	0	N/A	16.14
57311	Messengers	60	70	10	7.4	7.63
58002	Dispatchers-Police, Fire & Ambulance	50	60	10	8.58	8.44
58005	Dispatchers (except police, fire & ambulance)	270	340	70	13.3	13.32
58008	Production & Expediting Clerks	150	180	30	12.71	13.63
58011	Transportation Agents	10	10	0	N/A	10.68
58014	Meter Readers-Utilities	40	50	10	10.1	9.28
58017	Weighers, Measurers & Checkers (clerical)	20	20	0	9.1	9.68
58021	Marking Clerks	*	*	*	N/A	7.45
58023	Stock Clerks-Stockroom, Warehouse, Storage Yard	650	780	130	8.3	8.65
58026	Order Fillers-Wholesale & Retail Sales	80	90	10	14.42	8.29
58028	Shipping, Receiving & Traffic Clerks	390	440	50	11.22	11.48
58099	All Other Material Workers	50	60	10	11.36	11.42
59999	All Other Clerical & Admin Support	400	490	90	10.09	9.7
61002	Supervisors-Fire Fighting	30	40	10	N/A	14.75
61005	Supervisors-Police & Detectives	40	50	10	10.34	15.96
61008	Supervisors-Cleaning & Building Services	50	50	0	10.57	9.26
61075	Boxtender, Dice	*	*	*	N/A	N/A
61080	Gaming Supervisors	20	20	0	N/A	N/A

Table A-5

Regional Labor Market Area 3—Assumption, Lafourche, and Terrebonne Parishes
Occupational Employment Statistics
(Louisiana Department of Labor)

Occupation Code	Occupational Title	1998 Employment	Projected 2008 Employment	Projected Total Growth	Area 3 Average Wage ($)	State Average Wage ($)
61099	All Other Service Supervisors	450	570	120	10.32	11.17
62021	Cooks-Private Household	*	*	*	N/A	N/A
62031	Housekeepers & Butlers-Private Household	*	*	*	N/A	N/A
62041	Child Care Workers-Private Household	50	40	-10	N/A	N/A
62051	Cleaners & Servants-Private Household	90	120	30	N/A	N/A
63002	Fire Inspectors	10	20	10	N/A	18.3
63005	Forest Fire Inspectors & Prevention Specialists	30	30	0	N/A	14.65
63008	Fire Fighters	110	150	40	N/A	10.5
63011	Police Detectives	50	70	20	N/A	12.72
63014	Police Patrol Officers	320	510	190	10.27	10.09
63017	Correction Officers & Jailers	370	580	210	N/A	9.56
63021	Parking Enforcement Officers	10	10	0	N/A	N/A
63023	Bailiffs	10	20	10	N/A	8.01
63028	Criminal Investigators-Public Service	*	*	*	N/A	27
63032	Sheriffs & Deputy Sheriffs	90	140	50	N/A	10.03
63035	Private Detectives & Investigators	20	30	10	8.05	11.75
63038	Railroad & Transit Police	*	*	*	N/A	15.65
63041	Fish & Game Wardens	10	10	0	N/A	N/A
63044	Crossing Guards	30	40	10	N/A	6.47
63047	Security Guards	500	650	150	7.25	7.54
63099	All Other Protective Service Workers	80	100	20	10.08	8.85
65002	Hosts & Hostesses-Restaurants & Lounges	110	130	20	5.71	6.48
65005	Bartenders	220	230	10	6.38	6.59
65008	Waiters & Waitresses	870	1,100	230	5.56	6
65011	Food Servers (outside)	30	40	10	N/A	6.16
65014	Dining Room, Cafeteria & Bartender Helpers	160	170	10	5.62	5.95
65017	Counter Attendants-Coffee Shop or Cafeteria	200	220	20	6.7	6.52

Table A-5

Regional Labor Market Area 3—Assumption, Lafourche, and Terrebonne Parishes
Occupational Employment Statistics
(Louisiana Department of Labor)

Occupation Code	Occupational Title	1998 Employment	Projected 2008 Employment	Projected Total Growth	Area 3 Average Wage ($)	State Average Wage ($)
65021	Bakers-Bakery Shops & Restaurants	150	170	20	6.63	7.41
65023	Meat Cutters	190	170	-20	9.07	8.84
65026	Cooks-Restaurants	350	450	100	6.43	7.15
65028	Cooks-Institution or Cafeteria	320	340	20	8.95	6.79
65032	Cooks-Fast Food	590	760	170	5.57	5.75
65035	Cooks-Short Order	190	240	50	N/A	6.36
65038	Food Preparation Workers	710	810	100	6.51	6.21
65041	Fast Food Workers	810	990	180	5.8	5.92
65099	All Other Food Service Workers	460	480	20	7.31	6.85
66002	Dental Assistants	110	150	40	8.31	8.3
66005	Medical Assistants	140	210	70	9.07	8.23
66008	Nursing Aides	910	1,110	200	6.43	6.3
66011	Home Health Aides	210	340	130	6.76	8.09
66014	Psychiatric Aides	60	70	10	N/A	7.41
66017	Physical Therapy Assistants & Aides	40	50	10	8.16	10.98
66021	Occupational Therapy Assistants & Aides	10	10	0	N/A	12.42
66023	Ambulance Drivers & Attendants	10	10	0	N/A	7.17
66026	Pharmacy Assistants	30	30	0	N/A	N/A
66099	All Other Health Service Workers	120	150	30	7.27	7.93
67002	Maids & Room Cleaners	470	530	60	6.58	6.2
67005	Janitors	1,260	1,410	150	6.66	6.84
67008	Pest Controllers & Assistants	60	80	20	N/A	9.96
67099	All Other Clean, Building Service	160	180	20	8.48	7.12
68002	Barbers	*	*	*	N/A	9.14
68005	Cosmetologists	150	180	30	5.77	8.33
68008	Manicurists	10	10	0	N/A	6.55
68011	Shampooers	10	10	0	N/A	6.17

Table A-5

Regional Labor Market Area 3—Assumption, Lafourche, and Terrebonne Parishes
Occupational Employment Statistics
(Louisiana Department of Labor)

Occupation Code	Occupational Title	1998 Employment	Projected 2008 Employment	Projected Total Growth	Area 3 Average Wage ($)	State Average Wage ($)
68014	Amusement & Recreation Attendants	60	70	10	6.93	6.51
68017	Guides	20	20	0	N/A	7.12
68021	Ushers & Ticket Takers	30	40	10	N/A	6.48
68023	Baggage Porters & Bellhops	30	40	10	N/A	6.65
68026	Flight Attendants	10	10	0	N/A	N/A
68028	Transportation Attendants (except flight)	10	10	0	N/A	N/A
68032	Locker & Dressing Room Attendants	*	*	*	N/A	6.69
68035	Personal & Home Care Aides	120	180	60	7.35	6.29
68038	Child Care Workers	390	520	130	5.8	6.13
68041	Funeral Attendants	10	10	0	N/A	6.82
68074	Craps (dice) Dealers	20	20	0	N/A	N/A
68075	Blackjack Dealers	40	40	0	N/A	N/A
68080	All Other Dealers	20	20	0	N/A	N/A
68081	Slot Carousel Workers	*	*	*	N/A	N/A
69999	All Other Service Workers	310	340	30	7	7.09
71005	Farm Managers & Operators	40	40	0	N/A	N/A
72002	Supervisors-Ag Services, Forestry & Fishing	30	30	0	N/A	13.01
73008	Log Handling Equipment Operators	*	*	*	N/A	11.74
73011	Logging Tractor Operators	*	*	*	N/A	9.44
77002	Captains/Other Officers, Fishing	30	40	10	N/A	N/A
77008	Fishers	110	130	20	N/A	N/A
79002	Forest & Conservation Workers	10	10	0	N/A	11.67
79011	Agricultural Graders & Sorters	10	10	0	5.8	7.61
79017	Animal Caretakers (except farm)	20	20	0	N/A	8
79021	Farm Equipment Operators	30	20	-10	N/A	7
79033	Pruners	10	10	0	N/A	9.8
79036	Sprayers/Applicators-Trees & Lawns	*	*	*	N/A	8.57

Table A-5

Regional Labor Market Area 3—Assumption, Lafourche, and Terrebonne Parishes
Occupational Employment Statistics
(Louisiana Department of Labor)

Occupation Code	Occupational Title	1998 Employment	Projected 2008 Employment	Projected Total Growth	Area 3 Average Wage ($)	State Average Wage ($)
79041	Laborers, Landscape/Groundkeep	420	550	130	7.03	7.68
79801	Farm Workers	490	480	-10	N/A	N/A
79806	Veterinary Assistants	20	30	10	6.01	7.05
79856	Farm Workers, Food & Fiber Crops	20	20	0	N/A	6.51
79858	Farm Workers, Farm & Ranch Animals	*	*	*	N/A	5.76
79999	All Other Agriculture, Forest, Fish	140	150	10	8.9	9.01
81002	Supervisors-Mechanics, Installers & Repairers	310	380	70	18.05	19.7
81005	Supervisors-Construction & Extractive Workers	790	1,040	250	24.38	18.76
81008	Supervisors-Production & Operating Workers	310	380	70	19.71	20.63
81011	Supervisors-Transportation/Material Moving Equipment Operators	170	200	30	17.92	19.24
81017	Supervisors-Helpers, Laborers, Material Handler	170	210	40	16.34	15.33
81099	All Other First Line Supervisors, Prod. Construction Maintenance	400	500	100	20.32	18.99
83002	Precision Inspectors, Testers & Graders	90	100	10	15.27	16.26
83005	Production Inspectors, Testers & Graders	150	170	20	12.7	14.29
83008	Transportation Inspectors	20	20	0	N/A	15.25
83099	All Other Inspectors, Testers	90	110	20	13.78	13.72
85110	Industrial Machinery Mechanics	380	460	80	16.33	15.45
85116	Marine Equipment Mechanics	100	130	30	13.6	14.54
85118	Machinery Mechanics-Water or Power Plant	40	40	0	N/A	18.82
85119	All Other Machinery Maint. Mechanics	40	50	10	12.79	19.94
85123	Millwrights	60	90	30	N/A	14.59
85128	Machinery Maintenance Workers	100	130	30	10.53	13.81
85132	Maintenance Repairers (general)	820	930	110	9.42	10.65
85302	Auto Mechanics	580	750	170	12.75	13.2
85305	Auto Body Repairers	130	160	30	13.52	12.53
85308	Motorcycle Repairers	10	10	0	N/A	10.31
85311	Bus, Truck & Diesel Engine Mechanics	150	190	40	12.67	13.48

Table A-5

Regional Labor Market Area 3—Assumption, Lafourche, and Terrebonne Parishes
Occupational Employment Statistics
(Louisiana Department of Labor)

Occupation Code	Occupational Title	1998 Employment	Projected 2008 Employment	Projected Total Growth	Area 3 Average Wage ($)	State Average Wage ($)
85314	Mobile Heavy Equip Mechanics (except engines)	120	160	40	12.74	13.64
85321	Farm Equipment Mechanics	30	30	0	N/A	10.56
85323	Aircraft Mechanics	30	30	0	N/A	14.93
85326	Aircraft Engine Specialists	*	*	*	N/A	15.49
85328	Small Engine Specialists	20	20	0	N/A	10.03
85502	Central Telephone Office/Pbx Installers, Repairers	10	10	0	19.05	20.17
85505	Frame Wirers-Central Telephone Office	*	*	*	N/A	20.07
85508	Telegraph & Teletype Installers & Repairers	*	*	*	N/A	N/A
85514	Radio Mechanics	*	*	*	N/A	14.61
85599	All Other Communications Equip Mechanics	30	40	10	10.67	13.83
85702	Telephone & Cable TV Line Installers, Repairers	70	100	30	14.76	14.68
85705	Data Processing Equipment Repairers	10	20	10	N/A	14.41
85708	Electronic Home Entertainment Equipment Repairers	20	20	0	N/A	11.2
85711	Electric Home Appliance/Power Tool Repairers	20	30	10	9.8	10.97
85714	Electric Motor & Transformer Repairers	40	30	-10	N/A	13.18
85717	Electronics Repairers-Commercial/Indust Equip	30	30	0	13.79	17.43
85721	Powerhouse, Substation & Relay Electricians	*	*	*	N/A	18.33
85723	Electrical Power Line Installers & Repairers	60	80	20	N/A	16.08
85726	Telephone Installers & Repairers	20	10	-10	N/A	17.84
85728	Electrical Repairers-Transportation Equipment	60	100	40	N/A	14.77
85799	All Other Electric, Electronic Mechanics	50	70	20	18.32	13.26
85902	Heating, A/C & Refrigeration Mechanics	190	250	60	11.56	12.59
85905	Precision Instrument Repairers	30	40	10	17.55	19.8
85908	Electromedical Equipment Repairers	10	10	0	N/A	13.47
85911	Electric Meter Installers & Repairers	10	10	0	N/A	17.08
85914	Camera & Photographic Equipment Repairers	20	20	0	N/A	6.98
85917	Watchmakers	*	*	*	N/A	N/A

Table A-5

Regional Labor Market Area 3—Assumption, Lafourche, and Terrebonne Parishes
Occupational Employment Statistics
(Louisiana Department of Labor)

Occupation Code	Occupational Title	1998 Employment	Projected 2008 Employment	Projected Total Growth	Area 3 Average Wage ($)	State Average Wage ($)
85921	Musical Instrument Repairers & Tuners	*	*	*	N/A	9.89
85923	Locksmiths & Safe Repairers	10	10	0	N/A	11.56
85926	Office Machine Repairers	20	30	10	N/A	11.29
85928	Mechanical Control Installers & Repairers	10	10	0	N/A	16.95
85932	Elevator Installers & Repairers	*	*	*	N/A	N/A
85935	Riggers	220	320	100	10.27	12.94
85938	Mobile Home/Prefab Building Install/Repairers	20	30	10	9.3	9.9
85944	Gas Appliance Repairers	10	10	0	N/A	15.31
85947	Coin & Vending Machine Servicers & Repairers	10	10	0	N/A	10.87
85953	Tire Repairers & Changers	70	80	10	6.5	7.36
85956	Menders-Garments & Linens	*	*	*	N/A	7.01
85975	Slot & Amusement Machine Repairers	*	*	*	N/A	N/A
85999	All Other Mechanics, Installers & Repairers	470	610	140	12.97	13.59
87102	Carpenters	520	640	120	12.62	12.81
87105	Ceiling Tile Installers	10	20	10	N/A	12.88
87108	Drywall Installers	110	140	30	N/A	12.84
87111	Tapers	*	*	*	N/A	15.77
87114	Lathers	*	*	*	N/A	14.69
87202	Electricians	590	770	180	14.57	15.21
87302	Brickmasons	60	90	30	N/A	13.13
87305	Stonemasons	*	*	*	N/A	N/A
87308	Hard Tile Setters	10	20	10	N/A	9.23
87311	Concrete & Terrazzo Finishers	50	70	20	9.19	11.66
87314	Reinforcing Metal Workers	10	20	10	N/A	16.98
87317	Plasterers & Stucco Masons	10	20	10	N/A	12.35
87402	Painters & Paperhangers Construction	720	910	190	11.17	11.01
87502	Plumbers & Pipefitters	710	890	180	14.22	15.25

Table A-5

Regional Labor Market Area 3—Assumption, Lafourche, and Terrebonne Parishes
Occupational Employment Statistics
(Louisiana Department of Labor)

Occupation Code	Occupational Title	1998 Employment	Projected 2008 Employment	Projected Total Growth	Area 3 Average Wage ($)	State Average Wage ($)
87505	Pipelaying Fitters	20	20	0	N/A	20.56
87508	Pipelayers	20	30	10	8.88	9.74
87511	Septic Tank & Sewer Pipe Servicers	10	10	0	N/A	8.77
87602	Carpet Installers	30	30	0	12.42	10.93
87605	Floor Layers (except carpet, wood & hard tile)	*	*	*	N/A	11.57
87608	Floor Sanding Machine Operators	*	*	*	N/A	N/A
87705	Pile Driver Operators	10	10	0	N/A	14.42
87708	Paving & Surfacing Equipment Operators	30	50	20	N/A	9.81
87711	Highway Maintenance Workers	60	80	20	9.73	9.59
87714	Rail Track Laying Equipment Operators	*	*	*	N/A	N/A
87802	Insulation Workers	220	290	70	N/A	12.55
87803	Hazardous Materials Removal Workers	30	40	10	N/A	12.76
87805	Sheet Metal Duct Installers	10	20	10	N/A	11.72
87808	Roofers	50	70	20	N/A	10.72
87811	Glaziers	40	50	10	N/A	10.12
87814	Structural Metal Workers	30	40	10	12.37	12.73
87817	Fence Erectors	*	*	*	N/A	7.34
87899	All Other Construction Workers	130	180	50	9.18	11.91
87902	Earth Drillers (except oil & gas)	10	10	0	N/A	13.55
87905	Blasters & Explosives Workers	10	10	0	N/A	13.67
87911	Rotary Drill Operators, Oil & Gas	210	300	90	N/A	18.19
87914	Derrick Operators, Oil & Gas	220	310	90	N/A	17.79
87917	Service Unit Operators, Oil & Gas	210	310	100	13.32	12.54
87921	Roustabouts	590	670	80	N/A	9.73
87989	All Other Extractive Workers (except helpers)	260	390	130	13.64	14.11
87999	All Other Construction & Extractive Workers	70	100	30	10.18	10.07
89102	Tool & Die Makers	10	10	0	N/A	18.99

Table A-5

Regional Labor Market Area 3—Assumption, Lafourche, and Terrebonne Parishes
Occupational Employment Statistics
(Louisiana Department of Labor)

Occupation Code	Occupational Title	1998 Employment	Projected 2008 Employment	Projected Total Growth	Area 3 Average Wage ($)	State Average Wage ($)
89108	Machinists	680	900	220	13.97	14.61
89111	Tool Grinders, Filers & Sharpeners	10	10	0	N/A	14.09
89117	Precision Layout Workers, Metal	10	10	0	N/A	14.23
89121	Shipfitters	230	300	70	13.17	12.38
89123	Jewelers & Silversmiths	10	10	0	13.51	11.28
89132	Sheet Metal Workers	160	200	40	9.7	11.86
89135	Boilermakers	110	150	40	N/A	17.89
89199	All Other Precision Metal Workers	40	50	10	12.12	14.12
89302	Pattern & Model Makers, Wood	*	*	*	N/A	12
89308	Wood Machinists	*	*	*	N/A	8.55
89311	Cabinetmakers & Bench Carpenters	60	80	20	N/A	9.83
89314	Furniture Finishers	10	10	0	N/A	9.1
89399	All Other Precision Woodworkers	*	*	*	N/A	9.58
89505	Custom Tailors & Sewers	30	30	0	6.39	7.31
89508	Upholsterers	10	10	0	N/A	10.91
89511	Precision Shoe & Leather Workers	*	*	*	N/A	7.78
89514	Spotters-Dry Cleaning	*	*	*	N/A	6.65
89517	Pressers-Delicate Fabrics	10	10	0	N/A	6.18
89702	Hand Compositors & Typesetters	10	0	-10	N/A	9.75
89705	Job Printers	*	*	*	N/A	11.59
89707	Electronic Pagination System Operators	*	*	*	N/A	11.64
89713	Camera Operators	*	*	*	N/A	10.22
89717	Strippers-Printing	*	*	*	N/A	12.71
89718	Platemakers	*	*	*	N/A	10.44
89719	All Other Lithographic & Photoengraving Workers	*	*	*	N/A	N/A
89721	Bookbinders	*	*	*	N/A	9.46
89799	All Other Precision Printing Workers	*	*	*	N/A	10.4

Table A-5

Regional Labor Market Area 3—Assumption, Lafourche, and Terrebonne Parishes
Occupational Employment Statistics
(Louisiana Department of Labor)

Occupation Code	Occupational Title	1998 Employment	Projected 2008 Employment	Projected Total Growth	Area 3 Average Wage ($)	State Average Wage ($)
89805	Bakers, Manufacturing	40	20	-20	N/A	9.61
89808	Food Batchmakers	20	10	-10	N/A	9.09
89902	Foundry Mold & Core Makers (precision)	*	*	*	N/A	11.38
89905	Molders & Shapers (except jewelry & foundry)	*	*	*	N/A	N/A
89911	Detail Design Decorators (precision)	10	10	0	N/A	7.77
89914	Photographic Process Workers (precision)	10	10	0	N/A	7.64
89917	Optical Goods Workers (precision)	*	*	*	N/A	10.11
89921	Dental Laboratory Technicians (precision)	10	10	0	N/A	11.48
89923	Medical Appliance Makers	*	*	*	N/A	17.95
89999	All Other Precision Workers	100	120	20	N/A	11.15
91102	Sawing Machine Setters, Metal/Plastic	10	10	0	9.61	9.67
91105	Lathe & Turning Machine Setters, Metal/Plastic	20	30	10	N/A	11.82
91108	Drilling & Boring Machine Setters, Metal/Plastic	10	10	0	10.58	10.42
91111	Milling & Planing Machine Setters, Metal/Plastic	20	30	10	15.2	14.61
91114	Grinding/Buffing Machine Setters, Metal/Plastic	10	10	0	N/A	8.73
91117	Machine Tool Cutting Operators, Metal/Plastic	20	20	0	N/A	9.74
91302	Punching Machine Setters, Metal/Plastic	10	10	0	N/A	12.18
91305	Press & Brake Machine Setters, Metal/Plastic	20	20	0	N/A	9.39
91308	Shear & Slitter Machine Setters, Metal/Plastic	10	10	0	N/A	7.2
91311	Extruding Machine Setters, Metal/Plastic	*	*	*	N/A	10.66
91314	Rolling Machine Setters, Metal/Plastic	*	*	*	N/A	N/A
91317	Forging Machine Setters, Metal/Plastic	20	20	0	N/A	N/A
91321	Machine Forming Operators, Metal/Plastic	40	40	0	13.12	9.73
91502	Numerical Control Machine Tool Operators, Metal/Plastic	40	70	30	12.15	12.3
91505	Combination Machine Tool Setters, Metal/Plastic	10	10	0	N/A	10.97
91508	Combination Machine Tool Operators, Metal/Plastic	20	30	10	N/A	15.05
91702	Welding Machine Setters	10	10	0	N/A	10.08

Table A-5

Regional Labor Market Area 3—Assumption, Lafourche, and Terrebonne Parishes
Occupational Employment Statistics
(Louisiana Department of Labor)

Occupation Code	Occupational Title	1998 Employment	Projected 2008 Employment	Projected Total Growth	Area 3 Average Wage ($)	State Average Wage ($)
91705	Welding Machine Operators	120	160	40	N/A	13.52
91714	Metal Fabricators-Structural Metal Products	50	70	20	N/A	12.76
91902	Plastic Molding Machine Setters	*	*	*	N/A	12.83
91905	Plastic Molding Machine Operators	*	*	*	N/A	N/A
91908	Metal Molding & Casting Machine Setters	40	50	10	N/A	11.28
91911	Metal Molding & Casting Machine Operators	10	10	0	N/A	N/A
91917	Electrolytic Plating Machine Setters, Metal/Plastic	10	20	10	N/A	8.3
91921	Electrolytic Plating Machine Operators, Metal/Plastic	*	*	*	N/A	10.98
91923	Nonelectrolytic Plating Machine Setters, Metal/Plastic	*	*	*	N/A	N/A
91926	Nonelectrolytic Plating Machine Operators, Metal/Plastic	*	*	*	N/A	N/A
91932	Heat Treating Machine Operators, Metal/Plastic	*	*	*	N/A	N/A
91935	Furnace Operators & Tenders	*	*	*	N/A	10.46
92197	All Other Metal & Plastic Machine Setters/Operators	*	*	*	20.88	11.54
92198	All Other Metal/Plastic Operators/Tenders	20	30	10	14.92	9.41
92308	Sawing Machine Operators & Tenders	*	*	*	N/A	9.49
92512	Offset Lithographic Press Setters	*	*	*	N/A	11.34
92515	Letterpress Setters	*	*	*	N/A	13.06
92519	All Other Printing Press Setters/Operators	*	*	*	N/A	9.93
92524	Screen Printing Machine Setters	10	10	0	N/A	8.14
92525	Bindery Machine Setters	*	*	*	N/A	10.99
92541	Typesetting & Composing Machine Operators	*	*	*	N/A	11.4
92543	Printing Press Operators	30	40	10	10.05	11.42
92545	Photoengraving & Lithographic Machine Operators	*	*	*	N/A	12.05
92546	Bindery Machine Operators	10	20	10	N/A	9.29
92549	All Other Printing, Binding, Related	*	*	*	N/A	8.7
92717	Sewing Machine Operators-Garment	10	10	0	N/A	6.6
92721	Sewing Machine Operators-Non-Garment	20	20	0	N/A	7.45

Table A-5

Regional Labor Market Area 3—Assumption, Lafourche, and Terrebonne Parishes
Occupational Employment Statistics
(Louisiana Department of Labor)

Occupation Code	Occupational Title	1998 Employment	Projected 2008 Employment	Projected Total Growth	Area 3 Average Wage ($)	State Average Wage ($)
92726	Laundry & Dry-cleaning Machine Operators	80	90	10	6.86	6.53
92728	Pressing Machine Operators-Textiles/Garments	20	30	10	N/A	6.38
92905	Motion Picture Projectionists	*	*	*	N/A	6.45
92908	Photographic Processing Machine Operators	20	20	0	N/A	9.45
92914	Paper Goods Machine Setters	10	10	0	N/A	14.32
92917	Cooking Machine Operators-Food/Tobacco	10	10	0	N/A	8.12
92921	Roasting/Drying Machine Operators-Food/Tobacco	10	10	0	N/A	10.96
92923	Furnace, Kiln, Oven & Kettle Operators	10	10	0	14.2	16.73
92926	Boiler Operators & Tenders (low pressure)	10	10	0	9.84	12.26
92935	Chemical Equipment Controllers & Operators	*	*	*	N/A	20.49
92938	Chemical Equipment Tenders	*	*	*	N/A	21.5
92941	Cutting & Slicing Machine Setters	*	*	*	N/A	10.64
92944	Cutting & Slicing Machine Operators	*	*	*	N/A	9.99
92947	Painters-Transportation Equipment	40	50	10	N/A	13.28
92951	Coating & Painting Machine Setters	40	60	20	11.41	11.55
92953	Coating & Painting Machine Operators	80	110	30	12.72	10.11
92958	Cleaning/Pickling Equipment Operators	30	40	10	N/A	11.33
92962	Separating & Filtering Machine Operators	50	40	-10	N/A	20.97
92965	Crushing/Grinding/Mixing Machine Operators	30	20	-10	N/A	19.53
92971	Extruding & Forming Machine Operators	20	20	0	N/A	13.93
92974	Packaging & Filling Machine Operators	120	100	-20	8.07	10.58
92997	All Other Machine Setters/Operators	60	60	0	12.06	14.53
92998	All Other Machine Operators	610	790	180	15.57	12.74
93102	Aircraft Structure Assemblers (precision)	*	*	*	N/A	N/A
93105	Machine Builders/Precision Machine Assemblers	20	30	10	N/A	13.49
93108	Structural Metal Fitters (precision)	210	230	20	N/A	13.32
93111	Electromechanical Equipment Assemblers (precision)	10	10	0	N/A	10.54

Table A-5

Regional Labor Market Area 3—Assumption, Lafourche, and Terrebonne Parishes
Occupational Employment Statistics
(Louisiana Department of Labor)

Occupation Code	Occupational Title	1998 Employment	Projected 2008 Employment	Projected Total Growth	Area 3 Average Wage ($)	State Average Wage ($)
93114	Electrical & Electronic Assemblers (precision)	20	20	0	N/A	10.67
93197	All Other Precision Assemblers	10	10	0	13.02	10.89
93902	Machine Assemblers	30	40	10	N/A	10.01
93905	Electrical & Electronic Assemblers	*	*	*	N/A	11.08
93911	Glaziers-Manufacturing	10	20	10	N/A	9.96
93914	Welders & Cutters	2,150	2,770	620	$13.72	$14.06
93917	Solderers & Brazers	10	20	10	N/A	9.42
93921	Pressers (hand)	*	*	*	N/A	6.46
93923	Sewers (hand)	*	*	*	N/A	7.36
93935	Cannery Workers	90	40	-50	N/A	6.93
93938	Meat, Poultry & Fish Cutters (hand)	40	20	-20	N/A	7.53
93944	Molders & Casters (hand)	*	*	*	N/A	8.06
93947	Painting, Coating & Decorating Workers (hand)	30	50	20	N/A	9.15
93953	Grinding & Polishing Workers (Hand)	40	50	10	8.26	8.6
93956	Assemblers (except machine/electronic/precision)	420	540	120	12.05	10.48
93999	All Other Hand Workers	650	850	200	11	12.28
95002	Water & Waste Treatment Plant Operators	80	100	20	9.64	10.63
95005	Gas Plant Operators	20	20	0	N/A	20.03
95008	Chemical Plant & System Operators	20	30	10	N/A	22.07
95011	Petroleum Pump System Operators	30	40	10	N/A	22.21
95014	Petroleum Refinery & Control Panel Operators	70	90	20	N/A	18.73
95017	Gaugers	230	290	60	16.72	17.83
95021	Power Plant Operators (except auxiliary equipment)	20	20	0	N/A	20.77
95023	Auxiliary Equipment Operators-Power	10	10	0	N/A	N/A
95026	Power Reactor Operators	*	*	*	N/A	N/A
95028	Power Distributors & Dispatchers	10	10	0	N/A	17.5
95032	Stationary Engineers	20	10	-10	N/A	13.71

Table A-5

Regional Labor Market Area 3—Assumption, Lafourche, and Terrebonne Parishes
Occupational Employment Statistics
(Louisiana Department of Labor)

Occupation Code	Occupational Title	1998 Employment	Projected 2008 Employment	Projected Total Growth	Area 3 Average Wage ($)	State Average Wage ($)
95099	All Other Plant & System Operators	310	370	60	16.05	13.63
97102	Truck Drivers-Heavy or Tractor-Trailer	1,050	1,280	230	11.41	12.07
97105	Truck Drivers-Light (including delivery)	890	1,090	200	9.24	9.16
97108	Bus Drivers (except school)	60	80	20	N/A	10.14
97111	School Bus Drivers	380	440	60	15.06	8.87
97114	Taxi Drivers & Chauffeurs	60	80	20	N/A	7.74
97117	Driver/Sales Workers	140	150	10	10.82	9.95
97199	All Other Motor Vehicle Operators	30	30	0	7.63	8.66
97502	Captains-Water Vessel	1,060	1,160	100	23.5	19.97
97505	Mates-Ship, Boat & Barge	470	530	60	18.91	13.47
97508	Pilots-Ship	130	140	10	N/A	17.58
97511	Motorboat Operators	20	20	0	N/A	11.93
97514	Able Seamen	310	340	30	11.93	10.9
97517	Ordinary Seamen & Marine Oilers	730	810	80	9.92	8.93
97521	Ship Engineers	210	230	20	N/A	14.47
97702	Aircraft Pilots & Flight Engineers	30	30	0	**	N/A
97802	Bridge, Lock & Lighthouse Tenders	10	10	0	N/A	10.77
97805	Service Station Attendants	60	70	10	N/A	7.61
97808	Parking Lot Attendants	20	20	0	N/A	6.52
97899	All Other Transportation Workers	220	280	60	12.09	15.04
97902	Longshore Equipment Operators	140	160	20	N/A	19.36
97908	Oil Pumpers (except wellhead)	30	30	0	N/A	16.8
97911	Wellhead Pumpers	70	60	-10	N/A	16.36
97914	Main-Line Station Engineers-Oil & Gas	10	20	10	N/A	N/A
97917	Gas Pumping Station Operators	*	*	*	N/A	20.62
97921	Gas Compressor Operators	10	10	0	21.48	18.83
97923	Excavating & Loading Machine Operators	30	50	20	10.15	11.47

Table A-5

Regional Labor Market Area 3—Assumption, Lafourche, and Terrebonne Parishes
Occupational Employment Statistics
(Louisiana Department of Labor)

Occupation Code	Occupational Title	1998 Employment	Projected 2008 Employment	Projected Total Growth	Area 3 Average Wage ($)	State Average Wage ($)
97926	Dragline Operators	*	*	*	N/A	13.56
97928	Dredge Operators	10	10	0	N/A	14.98
97938	Grader, Bulldozer & Scraper Operators	90	130	40	11.68	11.53
97941	Hoist & Winch Operators	50	70	20	N/A	14.88
97944	Crane & Tower Operators	220	300	80	13.21	14.35
97947	Industrial Truck & Tractor Operators	230	270	40	9.05	10.79
97951	Conveyor Operators & Tenders	10	10	0	8.73	10.14
97953	Pump Operators	30	30	0	12.56	19.18
97956	Operating Engineers	50	70	20	11.8	14.15
97989	All Other Material Equipment Moving Operators	130	150	20	12.92	10.68
97999	All Other Material Moving Equipment Operators	60	80	20	15.41	11.79
98102	Mechanic & Repairer Helpers	340	450	110	7.91	8.69
98311	Brick & Stonemason & Hard Tile Setter Helpers	20	20	0	N/A	8.4
98312	Carpenter Helpers	100	130	30	8.64	8.95
98313	Electrician Helpers	100	120	20	8.45	8.46
98314	Painter, Paperhanger & Plasterer Helpers	40	50	10	N/A	8.17
98315	Plumber & Pipefitter Helpers	90	120	30	9.13	9.54
98316	Roofer Helpers	20	20	0	N/A	7.87
98319	Helpers, All Other Construction	220	370	150	N/A	8.52
98323	Extractive Worker Helpers	10	10	0	N/A	9.08
98502	Machine Feeders & Offbearers	50	40	-10	8.31	8.93
98702	Stevedores (except equipment operators)	370	350	-20	N/A	16.14
98705	Refuse & Recyclable Materials Collectors	40	40	0	N/A	9.15
98799	Freight, Stock & Material Handlers	310	340	30	7.67	8.53
98902	Hand Packers & Packagers	360	400	40	6.05	6.5
98905	Vehicle Washers & Equipment Cleaners	150	200	50	6.26	6.83
98999	All Other Helpers, Laborers, & Material Movers	1,920	2,480	560	8.24	8.34

Table A-5

Regional Labor Market Area 3—Assumption, Lafourche, and Terrebonne Parishes
Occupational Employment Statistics
(Louisiana Department of Labor)

Occupation Code	Occupational Title	1998 Employment	Projected 2008 Employment	Projected Total Growth	Area 3 Average Wage ($)	State Average Wage ($)

Annual Total Growth = demand in the occupation as a function of replacement demand (retirements + turnover) + net growth.

N/A—Not Available.

* 1998 employment under 10 suppressed.

** Hourly wages for occupations where workers typically work fewer than 2,080 hours per year not available.

Table A-6

Louisiana Department of Labor Region 3—Lafourche, Terrebonne, and Assumption Parishes
(Data are from the 1990 Census Special Tabulation of Occupation by Industry.
These counts are for all industries.)

Number in Experienced Labor Force	Census Occupation Code	Occupation Title
36	3	Legislators
11	4	Chief Executives and General Administrators, Public Administration
183	5	Administrators and Officials, Public Administration
67	6	Administrators, Protective Service
393	7	Financial Managers
165	8	Personnel and Labor Relations Managers
36	9	Purchasing Managers
217	13	Managers, Marketing, Advertising, and Public Relations
498	14	Administrators, Education and Related Fields
83	15	Managers, Medicine and Health
32	16	Postmasters and Mail Superintendents
805	17	Managers, Food Serving and Lodging Establishments
200	18	Managers, Properties and Real Estate
47	19	Funeral Directors
239	21	Managers, Service Organizations, n.e.c.
2,701	22	Managers and Administrators, n.e.c.
553	23	Accountants and Auditors
23	24	Underwriters
268	25	Other Financial Officers
63	26	Management Analysts
223	27	Personnel, Training, and Labor Relations Specialists
115	29	Buyers, Wholesale and Retail Trade (except farm products)
203	33	Purchasing Agents and Buyers
90	35	Construction Inspectors
84	36	Inspectors and Compliance Officers (except construction)
74	37	Management Related Occupations, n.e.c.
16	43	Architects
6	45	Metallurgical and Materials Engineers
9	46	Mining Engineers
209	47	Petroleum Engineers
21	48	Chemical Engineers
142	53	Civil Engineers
12	54	Agricultural Engineers
58	55	Electrical and Electronic Engineers
45	56	Industrial Engineers
40	57	Mechanical Engineers
126	58	Marine and Naval Architects
58	59	Engineers, n.e.c.
17	63	Surveyors and Mapping Scientists
38	64	Computer Systems Analysts and Scientists

Table A-6

Louisiana Department of Labor Region 3—Lafourche, Terrebonne, and Assumption Parishes
(Data are from the 1990 Census Special Tabulation of Occupation by Industry.
These counts are for all industries.)

Number in Experienced Labor Force	Census Occupation Code	Occupation Title
20	65	Operations and Systems Researchers and Analysts
12	67	Statisticians
35	73	Chemists (except biochemists)
15	75	Geologists and Geodesists
28	77	Agricultural and Food Scientists
33	78	Biological and Life Scientists
204	84	Physicians
121	85	Dentists
13	86	Veterinarians
18	87	Optometrists
32	89	Health Diagnosing Practitioners, n.e.c.
931	95	Registered Nurses
92	96	Pharmacists
72	97	Dietitians
47	98	Respiratory Therapists
31	103	Physical Therapists
52	104	Speech Therapists
51	105	Therapists, n.e.c.
13	106	Physicians' Assistants
10	118	Psychology Teachers
7	127	Engineering Teachers
7	134	Health Specialties Teachers
15	135	Business, Commerce, and Marketing Teachers
9	137	Art, Drama, and Music Teachers
8	143	English Teachers
296	154	Postsecondary Teachers, Subject Not Specified
118	155	Teachers, Prekindergarten and Kindergarten
3,649	156	Teachers, Elementary School
454	157	Teachers, Secondary School
27	158	Teachers, Special Education
365	159	Teachers, n.e.c.
120	163	Counselors, Educational and Vocational
105	164	Librarians
9	165	Archivists and Curators
16	166	Economists
21	167	Psychologists
433	174	Social Workers
50	175	Recreation Workers
182	176	Clergy
52	177	Religious Workers, n.e.c.

Table A-6

Louisiana Department of Labor Region 3—Lafourche, Terrebonne, and Assumption Parishes
(Data are from the 1990 Census Special Tabulation of Occupation by Industry.
These counts are for all industries.)

Number in Experienced Labor Force	Census Occupation Code	Occupation Title
240	178	Lawyers
9	179	Judges
18	183	Authors
216	185	Designers
56	186	Musicians and Composers
54	187	Actors and Directors
25	188	Painters, Sculptors, Craft-Artists, and Artist Printmakers
37	189	Photographers
32	193	Dancers
24	194	Artists, Performers, and Related Workers, n.e.c.
71	195	Editors and Reporters
73	197	Public Relations Specialists
29	198	Announcers
163	199	Athletes
256	203	Clinical Laboratory Technologists and Technicians
29	204	Dental Hygienists
26	205	Health Record Technologists and Technicians
134	206	Radiologic Technicians
351	207	Licensed Practical Nurses
244	208	Health Technologists and Technicians, n.e.c.
194	213	Electrical and Electronic Technicians
5	215	Mechanical Engineering Technicians
170	216	Engineering Technicians, n.e.c.
175	217	Drafting Occupations
56	218	Surveying and Mapping Technicians
71	223	Biological Technicians
144	224	Chemical Technicians
115	225	Science Technicians, n.e.c.
100	226	Airplane Pilots and Navigators
19	227	Air Traffic Controllers
53	228	Broadcast Equipment Operators
107	229	Computer Programmers
131	234	Legal Assistants
288	235	Technicians, n.e.c.
2,854	243	Supervisors and Proprietors, Sales Occupations
551	253	Insurance Sales Occupations
217	254	Real Estate Sales Occupations
73	255	Securities and Financial Services Sales Occupations
70	256	Advertising and Related Sales Occupations
191	257	Sales Occupations, Other Business Services

Table A-6

Louisiana Department of Labor Region 3—Lafourche, Terrebonne, and Assumption Parishes
(Data are from the 1990 Census Special Tabulation of Occupation by Industry.
These counts are for all industries.)

Number in Experienced Labor Force	Census Occupation Code	Occupation Title
13	258	Sales Engineers
1,029	259	Sales Representatives, Mining, Manufacturing, and Wholesale
214	263	Sales Workers, Motor ☐ehicles and Boats
279	264	Sales Workers, Apparel
107	265	Sales Workers, Shoes
124	266	Sales Workers, Furniture and Home Furnishings
113	267	Sales Workers, Radio, T☐, Hi-Fi, and Appliances
130	268	Sales Workers, Hardware, and Building Supplies
89	269	Sales Workers, Parts
1,669	274	Sales Workers, Other Commodities
147	275	Sales Counter Clerks
4,538	276	Cashiers
207	277	Street and Door-To-Door Sales Workers
118	278	News ☐endors
15	283	Demonstrators, Promoters and Models, Sales
12	285	Sales Support Occupations, n.e.c.
252	303	Supervisors, ☐eneral Office
5	304	Supervisors, Computer Equipment Operators
24	305	Supervisors, Financial Records Processing
59	307	Supervisors, Distribution, Scheduling, and Ad☐usting Clerks
313	308	Computer Operators
3,365	313	Secretaries
65	314	Stenographers
410	315	Typists
155	316	Interviewers
50	317	Hotel Clerks
33	318	Transportation Ticket and Reservation Agents
640	319	Receptionists
119	323	Information Clerks, n.e.c.
8	325	Classified-Ad Clerks
99	327	Order Clerks
45	328	Personnel Clerks (except payroll and timekeeping)
79	329	Library Clerks
170	335	File Clerks
53	336	Records Clerks
1,553	337	Bookkeepers, Accounting, and Auditing Clerks
79	338	Payroll and Timekeeping Clerks
66	339	Billing Clerks
52	343	Cost and Rate Clerks
18	344	Billing, Posting, and Calculating Machine Operators

Table A-6

Louisiana Department of Labor Region 3—Lafourche, Terrebonne, and Assumption Parishes
(Data are from the 1990 Census Special Tabulation of Occupation by Industry.
These counts are for all industries.)

Number in Experienced Labor Force	Census Occupation Code	Occupation Title
163	348	Telephone Operators
12	353	Communications Equipment Operators, n.e.c.
144	354	Postal Clerks (excluding mail carriers)
169	355	Mail Carriers, Postal Service
65	356	Mail Clerks (excluding postal service)
124	357	Messengers
235	359	Dispatchers
127	363	Production Coordinators
200	364	Traffic, Shipping and Receiving Clerks
587	365	Stock and Inventory Clerks
75	366	Meter Readers
77	368	Weighers, Measurers, and Checkers -- Samplers
105	373	Expediters
13	374	Material Recording, Scheduling and Distributing Clerks, n.e.c.
87	375	Insurance Adjusters, Examiners, and Investigators
212	376	Investigators and Adjusters (except insurance)
55	377	Eligibility Clerks, Social Welfare
151	378	Bill and Account Collectors
957	379	General Office Clerks
665	383	Bank Tellers
172	385	Data-Entry Keyers
33	386	Statistical Clerks
232	387	Teachers Aides
367	389	Administrative Support Occupations, n.e.c.
11	403	Launderers and Ironers
7	404	Cooks, Private Household
34	405	Housekeepers and Butlers
185	406	Child Care Workers, Private Household
397	407	Private Household Cleaners and Servants
35	414	Supervisors, Police and Detectives
22	415	Supervisors, Guards
5	416	Fire Inspection and Fire Prevention Occupations
81	417	Firefighting Occupations
309	418	Police and Detectives, Public Service
196	423	Sheriffs, Bailiffs, and Other Law Enforcement Officers
69	424	Correctional Institution Officers
7	425	Crossing Guards
424	426	Guards and Police (excluding public service)
74	427	Protective Service Occupations
192	433	Supervisors, Food Preparation and Service Occupations

Table A-6

Louisiana Department of Labor Region 3—Lafourche, Terrebonne, and Assumption Parishes
(Data are from the 1990 Census Special Tabulation of Occupation by Industry.
These counts are for all industries.)

Number in Experienced Labor Force	Census Occupation Code	Occupation Title
424	434	Bartenders
1,190	435	Waiters and Waitresses
2,497	436	Cooks
136	438	Food Counter, Fountain, and Related Occupations
329	439	☐itchen Workers, Food Preparation
221	443	Waiters☐Waitresses☐Assistants
804	444	Miscellaneous Food Preparation Occupations
138	445	Dental Assistants
211	446	Health Aids (except nursing)
1,889	447	Nursing Aides, Orderlies, and Attendants
86	448	Supervisors, Cleaning and Building Service Workers
628	449	Maids and Housemen
2,141	453	Janitors and Cleaners
70	455	Pest Control Occupations
64	456	Supervisors, Personal Service Occupations
106	457	Barbers
863	458	Hairdressers and Cosmetologists
89	459	Attendants, Amusement and Recreation Facilities
20	461	☐uides
6	463	Public Transportation Attendants
45	465	Welfare Service Aides
231	466	Family Child Care Providers
322	467	Early Childhood Teacher☐ Assistants
269	468	Child Care Workers, n.e.c.
165	469	Personal Service Occupations, n.e.c.
220	473	Farmers (except horticultural)
9	474	Horticultural Specialty Farmers
265	475	Managers, Farms (except horticultural)
13	476	Managers, Horticultural Specialty Farms
20	477	Supervisors, Farm Workers
631	479	Farm Workers
31	485	Supervisors, Related Agricultural Occupations
609	486	☐roundskeepers and ☐ardeners (except farm)
25	487	Animal Caretakers (except farm)
85	488	☐raders and Sorters, Agricultural Products
10	494	Supervisors, Forestry and Logging Workers
37	496	Timber Cutting and Logging Occupations
238	497	Captains and Other Officers, Fishing ☐essels
1,996	498	Fishers
32	499	Hunters and Trappers

Table A-6

Louisiana Department of Labor Region 3—Lafourche, Terrebonne, and Assumption Parishes
(Data are from the 1990 Census Special Tabulation of Occupation by Industry.
These counts are for all industries.)

Number in Experienced Labor Force	Census Occupation Code	Occupation Title
330	503	Supervisors, Mechanics and Repairers
749	505	Automobile Mechanics (except apprentices)
441	507	Bus, Truck, and Stationary Engine Mechanics
34	508	Aircraft Engine Mechanics
261	509	Small Engine Repairers
154	514	Automobile Body and Related Repairers
18	515	Aircraft Mechanics (excluding engine)
263	516	Heavy Equipment Mechanics
55	517	Farm Equipment Mechanics
352	518	Industrial Machinery Repairers
42	519	Machinery Maintenance Occupations
217	523	Electronic Repairers, Communications and Industrial Equipment
44	525	Data Processing Equipment Repairers
68	526	Household Appliance and Power Tool Repairers
55	527	Telephone Line Installers and Repairers
158	529	Telephone Installers and Repairers
59	533	Miscellaneous Electrical and Electronic Equipment Repairers
92	534	Heating, Air Conditioning, and Refrigeration Mechanics
18	535	Camera, Watch, and Musical Instrument Repairers
12	536	Locksmiths and Safe Repairers
14	538	Office Machine Repairers
88	539	Mechanical Controls and □alve Repairers
7	543	Elevator Installers and Repairers
42	544	Millwrights
371	547	Specified Mechanics and Repairers, n.e.c.
429	549	Not Specified Mechanics and Repairers
29	554	Supervisors, Carpenters and Related Work
22	555	Supervisors, Electricians and Power Transmission Installers
61	556	Supervisors, Painters, Paperhangers, and Plasterers
6	557	Supervisors, Plumbers, Pipefitters, and Steamfitters
499	558	Supervisors, Construction, n.e.c.
92	563	Brickmasons and Stonemasons (except apprentices)
15	565	Tile Setters, Hard and Soft
70	566	Carpet Installers
1,113	567	Carpenters (except apprentices)
25	569	Carpenter Apprentices
55	573	Drywall Installers
773	575	Electricians (except apprentices)
7	576	Electrician Apprentices
79	577	Electrical Power Installers and Repairers

Table A-6

Louisiana Department of Labor Region 3—Lafourche, Terrebonne, and Assumption Parishes
(Data are from the 1990 Census Special Tabulation of Occupation by Industry.
These counts are for all industries.)

Number in Experienced Labor Force	Census Occupation Code	Occupation Title
654	579	Painters, Construction and Maintenance
8	583	Paperhangers
850	585	Plumbers, Pipefitters, and Steamfitters (except apprentices)
15	587	Plumber, Pipefitter, and Steamfitter Apprentices
129	588	Concrete and Terra□o Finishers
26	589	□la□iers
375	593	Insulation Workers
12	594	Paving, Surfacing, and Tamping Equipment Operators
94	595	Roofers
18	596	Sheetmetal Duct Installers
53	597	Structural Metal Workers
20	598	Drillers, Earth
501	599	Construction Trades, n.e.c.
938	613	Supervisors, Extractive Occupations
1,184	614	Drillers, Oil Well
115	615	Explosives Workers
199	616	Mining Machine Operators
455	617	Mining Occupations, n.e.c.
883	628	Supervisors, Production Occupations
30	634	Tool and Die Makers (except apprentices)
18	636	Precision Assemblers, Metal
533	637	Machinists (except apprentices)
8	639	Machinist Apprentices
93	643	Boilermakers
27	645	Patternmakers and Model Makers, Metal
411	646	Lay-Out Workers
15	647	Precious Stones and Metals Workers
8	649	Engravers, Metal
102	653	Sheet Metal Workers (except apprentices)
5	659	Miscellaneous Precision Woodworkers
82	666	Dressmakers
10	667	Tailors
34	668	□pholsterers
6	669	Shoe Repairers
21	674	Miscellaneous Precision Apparel and Fabric Workers
35	677	Optical □oods Workers
38	678	Dental Laboratory and Medical Appliance Technicians
17	679	Bookbinders
38	684	Miscellaneous Precision Workers, n.e.c.
366	686	Butchers and Meat Cutters

Table A-6

Louisiana Department of Labor Region 3—Lafourche, Terrebonne, and Assumption Parishes
(Data are from the 1990 Census Special Tabulation of Occupation by Industry.
These counts are for all industries.)

Number in Experienced Labor Force	Census Occupation Code	Occupation Title
119	687	Bakers
60	688	Food Batchmakers
22	689	Inspectors, Testers, and Graders
6	693	Adjusters and Calibrators
56	694	Water and Sewage Treatment Plant Operators
46	695	Power Plant Operators
214	696	Stationary Engineers
310	699	Miscellaneous Plant and System Operators
17	704	Lathe and Turning Machine Operators
22	706	Punching and Stamping Press Machine Operators
36	707	Rolling Machine Operators
19	708	Drilling and Boring Machine Operators
3	709	Grinding, Abrading, Buffing, and Polishing Machine Operators
15	717	Fabricating Machine Operators, n.e.c.
9	719	Molding and Casting Machine Operators
15	723	Metal Plating Machine Operators
137	725	Miscellaneous Metal and Plastic Processing Machine Operators
8	727	Sawing Machine Operators
4	728	Shaping and Joining Machine Operators
17	733	Miscellaneous Woodworking Machine Operators
49	734	Printing Press Operators
15	736	Typesetters and Compositors
86	744	Textile Sewing Machine Operators
145	747	Pressing Machine Operators
154	748	Laundering and Dry Cleaning Machine Operators
2	753	Cementing and Gluing Machine Operators
168	754	Packaging and Filling Machine Operators
14	755	Extruding and Forming Machine Operators
67	756	Mixing and Blending Machine Operators
78	757	Separating, Filtering, and Clarifying Machine Operators
72	759	Painting and Paint Spraying Machine Operators
6	763	Roasting and Baking Machine Operators, Food
8	764	Washing, Cleaning, and Pickling Machine Operators
48	766	Furnace, Kiln, and Oven Operators (except food)
6	768	Crushing and Grinding Machine Operators
163	769	Slicing and Cutting Machine Operators
1	773	Motion Picture Projectionists
70	774	Photographic Process Machine Operators
478	777	Miscellaneous and Not Specified Machine Operators, n.e.c.
400	779	Machine Operators, Not Specified

Table A-6

Louisiana Department of Labor Region 3—Lafourche, Terrebonne, and Assumption Parishes
(Data are from the 1990 Census Special Tabulation of Occupation by Industry.
These counts are for all industries.)

Number in Experienced Labor Force	Census Occupation Code	Occupation Title
3,489	783	Welders and Cutters
233	785	Assemblers
317	786	Hand Cutting and Trimming Occupations
8	787	Hand Molding, Casting, and Forming Occupations
38	789	Hand Painting, Coating, and Decorating Occupations
6	793	Hand Engraving and Printing Occupations
276	796	Production Inspectors, Checkers, and Examiners
76	797	Production Testers
11	798	Production Samplers and Weighers
81	799	☐raders and Sorters (except agricultural)
57	803	Supervisors, Motor ☐ehicle Operators
2,716	804	Truck Drivers
163	806	Driver-Sales Workers
474	808	Bus Drivers
58	809	Taxicab Drivers and Chauffeurs
6	814	Motor Transportation Occupations, n.e.c.
87	824	Locomotive Operating Occupations
9	825	Railroad Brake, Signal, and Switch Operators
2,156	828	Ship Captains and Mates (except fishing boats)
1,317	829	Sailors and Deckhands
37	833	Marine Engineers
166	834	Bridge, Lock and Lighthouse Tenders
24	843	Supervisors, Material Moving Equipment Operators
173	844	Operating Engineers
29	845	Longshore Equipment Operators
189	848	Hoist and Winch Operators
439	849	Crane and Tower Operators
143	853	Excavating and Loading Machine Operators
54	855	☐rader, Do☐er, and Scraper Operators
220	856	Industrial Truck and Tractor Equipment Operators
354	859	Miscellaneous Material Moving Equipment Operators
5	864	Supervisors, Handlers, Equipment Cleaners, and Laborers, n.e.c.
22	865	Helpers, Mechanics and Repairers
239	866	Helpers, Construction Trades
16	867	Helpers, Surveyor
37	868	Helpers, Extractive Occupations
1,043	869	Construction Laborers
185	874	Production Helpers
86	875	☐arbage Collectors
15	876	Stevedores

Table A-6

Louisiana Department of Labor Region 3—Lafourche, Terrebonne, and Assumption Parishes
(Data are from the 1990 Census Special Tabulation of Occupation by Industry.
These counts are for all industries.)

Number in Experienced Labor Force	Census Occupation Code	Occupation Title
1,232	877	Stock Handlers and Baggers
15	878	Machine Feeders and Offbearers
344	883	Freight, Stock, and Material Handlers, n.e.c.
316	885	Garage and Service Station Related Occupations
184	887	Vehicle Washers and Equipment Cleaners
552	888	Hand Packers and Packagers
1798	889	Laborers (except construction)

n.e.c.—not else classified.

Table A-7

Louisiana Department of Labor Region 3—Lafourche, Terrebonne and Assumption Parishes
(Data are from the 1990 Census Special Tabulation of Occupation by Industry.
These counts are for SIC□353, Construction and Related Machinery, and
SIC□373, Ship and Boat Building and Repairing.)

Number in Experienced Labor Force	Census Occupation Code	Occupation Title
10	7	Financial Managers
11	13	Managers, Marketing, Advertising, and Public Relations
152	22	Managers and Administrators, n.e.c.
9	25	Other Financial Officers
4	27	Personnel, Training, and Labor Relations Specialists
38	33	Purchasing Agents and Buyers
8	36	Inspectors and Compliance Officers (except construction)
8	55	Electrical and Electronic Engineers
7	56	Industrial Engineers
5	57	Mechanical Engineers
54	58	Marine and Naval Architects
16	59	Engineers, n.e.c.
7	64	Computer Systems Analysts and Scientists
24	213	Electrical and Electronic Technicians
15	217	Drafting Occupations
8	226	Airplane Pilots and Navigators
6	229	Computer Programmers
8	235	Technicians, n.e.c.
6	243	Supervisors and Proprietors, Sales Occupations
20	259	Sales Representatives, Mining, Manufacturing, and Wholesale
31	308	Computer Operators
19	313	Secretaries
8	319	Receptionists
56	337	Bookkeepers, Accounting and Auditing Clerks
8	338	Payroll and Timekeeping Clerks
11	363	Production Coordinators
6	364	Traffic, Shipping and Receiving Clerks
74	365	Stock and Inventory Clerks
6	376	Investigators and Ad□usters (except insurance)
23	379	□eneral Office Clerks
18	389	Administrative Support Occupations, n.e.c.
7	417	Firefighting Occupations
10	426	□uards and Police (excluding public service)
4	436	Cooks
44	453	Janitors and Cleaners
7	469	Personal Service Occupations, n.e.c.
5	505	Automobile Mechanics (except apprentices)
16	507	Bus, Truck, and Stationary Engine Mechanics
32	509	Small Engine Repairers

Table A-7

Louisiana Department of Labor Region 3—Lafourche, Terrebonne and Assumption Parishes
(Data are from the 1990 Census Special Tabulation of Occupation by Industry.
These counts are for SIC□353, Construction and Related Machinery, and
SIC□373, Ship and Boat Building and Repairing.)

Number in Experienced Labor Force	Census Occupation Code	Occupation Title
15	516	Heavy Equipment Mechanics
10	517	Farm Equipment Mechanics
64	518	Industrial Machinery Repairers
8	519	Machinery Maintenance Occupations
8	534	Heating, Air Conditioning, and Refrigeration Mechanics
6	539	Mechanical Controls and □alve Repairers
40	547	Specified Mechanics and Repairers, n.e.c.
17	549	Not Specified Mechanics and Repairers
8	554	Supervisors, Carpenters and Related Work
5	555	Supervisors, Electricians and Power Transmission Installers
29	556	Supervisors, Painters, Paperhangers, and Plasterers
6	557	Supervisors, Plumbers, Pipefitters, and Steamfitters
158	567	Carpenters (except apprentices)
116	575	Electricians (except apprentices)
80	579	Painters, Construction and Maintenance
118	585	Plumbers, Pipefitters, and Steamfitters (except apprentices)
14	593	Insulation Workers
7	599	Construction Trades, n.e.c.
8	613	Supervisors, Extractive Occupations
8	615	Explosives Workers
7	617	Mining Occupations, n.e.c.
324	628	Supervisors, Production Occupations
7	634	Tool and Die Makers (except apprentices)
114	637	Machinists (except apprentices)
8	639	Machinist Apprentices
9	645	Patternmakers and Model Makers, Metal
390	646	Lay-Out Workers
29	653	Sheet Metal Workers (except apprentices)
5	696	Stationary Engineers
7	706	Punching and Stamping Press Machine Operators
5	707	Rolling Machine Operators
9	719	Molding and Casting Machine Operators
110	725	Miscellaneous Metal and Plastic Processing Machine Operators
14	744	Textile Sewing Machine Operators
7	747	Pressing Machine Operators
26	759	Painting and Paint Spraying Machine Operators
8	774	Photographic Process Machine Operators
119	777	Miscellaneous and Not Specified Machine Operators, n.e.c.
53	779	Machine Operators, Not Specified

Table A-7

Louisiana Department of Labor Region 3—Lafourche, Terrebonne and Assumption Parishes
(Data are from the 1990 Census Special Tabulation of Occupation by Industry.
These counts are for SIC☐353, Construction and Related Machinery, and
SIC☐373, Ship and Boat Building and Repairing.)

Number in Experienced Labor Force	Census Occupation Code	Occupation Title
1,013	783	Welders and Cutters
17	785	Assemblers
14	789	Hand Painting, Coating, and Decorating Occupations
21	796	Production Inspectors, Checkers, and Examiners
8	797	Production Testers
69	804	Truck Drivers
51	828	Ship Captains and Mates, Except Fishing Boats
16	829	Sailors and Deckhands
6	848	Hoist and Winch Operators
1	849	Crane and Tower Operators
24	856	Industrial Truck and Tractor Equipment Operators
20	859	Miscellaneous Material Moving Equipment Operators
5	865	Helpers, Mechanics and Repairers
42	866	Helpers, Construction Trades
18	869	Construction Laborers
73	874	Production Helpers
7	876	Stevedores
8	883	Freight, Stock, and Material Handlers, n.e.c.
11	887	☐ehicle Washers and Equipment Cleaners
153	889	Laborers (except construction)

n.e.c.—not else classified.

The Department of the Interior Mission

As the Nation's principal conservation agency, the Department of the Interior has responsibility for most of our nationally owned public lands and natural resources. This includes fostering sound use of our land and water resources; protecting our fish, wildlife, and biological diversity; preserving the environmental and cultural values of our national parks and historical places; and providing for the enjoyment of life through outdoor recreation. The Department assesses our energy and mineral resources and works to ensure that their development is in the best interests of all our people by encouraging stewardship and citizen participation in their care. The Department also has a major responsibility for American Indian reservation communities and for people who live in island territories under U.S. administration.

The Minerals Management Service Mission

As a bureau of the Department of the Interior, the Minerals Management Service's (MMS) primary responsibilities are to manage the mineral resources located on the Nation's Outer Continental Shelf (OCS), collect revenue from the Federal OCS and onshore Federal and Indian lands, and distribute those revenues.

Moreover, in working to meet its responsibilities, the **Offshore Minerals Management Program** administers the OCS competitive leasing program and oversees the safe and environmentally sound exploration and production of our Nation's offshore natural gas, oil and other mineral resources. The MMS **Minerals Revenue Management** meets its responsibilities by ensuring the efficient, timely and accurate collection and disbursement of revenue from mineral leasing and production due to Indian tribes and allottees, States and the U.S. Treasury.

The MMS strives to fulfill its responsibilities through the general guiding principles of: (1) being responsive to the public's concerns and interests by maintaining a dialogue with all potentially affected parties and (2) carrying out its programs with an emphasis on working to enhance the quality of life for all Americans by lending MMS assistance and expertise to economic development and environmental protection.

www.ingramcontent.com/pod-product-compliance
Lightning Source LLC
Chambersburg PA
CBHW051957280526
45793CB00005B/750